Theodore H. White

and Journalism as Illusion

Joyce Hoffmann
· · · · · · · · · ·

Theodore H. White
and Journalism as Illusion

University of Missouri Press

Columbia and London

· · · · · · · · · ·

Library of Congress Cataloging-in-Publication Data

Hoffmann, Joyce.
    Theodore H. White and journalism as illusion / Joyce Hoffmann.
        p.   cm.
    Based on the author's thesis (doctoral)—New York University.
    Includes bibliographical references and index.
    ISBN 0–8262–1010–4 (cloth : alk. paper)
    1. White, Theodore Harold, 1915–   .   2. Journalists—United States—
Biography.   3. Kennedy, John F. (John Fitzgerald), 1917–1963.   4. United
States—Politics and government—1961–1963—Historiography.   I. Title.
PN4874.W517H64   1995
070.92—dc20
    [B]   95-14794
                                                                      CIP

∞ This paper meets the requirements of the
American National Standard for Permanence of Paper
for Printed Library Materials, Z39.48, 1984.

Designer: Kristie Lee
Typesetter: BOOKCOMP
Printer and Binder: Thomson-Shore, Inc.
Typefaces: Giovanni and American Typewriter

. . . .

In memory of my parents

Betsy and Karl Hoffmann

Contents

. . . .

Acknowledgments

· · · · · · · · · ·

Among Theodore White's family members, friends, and associates, I am especially indebted to Nancy White Hector (Theodore White's first wife) whose enthusiasm for this project has been a continuing inspiration. She has also been extraordinarily generous with her time and her memories, as have her children, Heyden White Rostow and David Fairbank White. White's sister, Gladys, similarly gave her support and goodwill to this undertaking.

On the long list of personal friends whose advice, wisdom, and applause have sustained me, John Hall stands in first place. He has my everlasting gratitude for the countless hours he spent reading the various incarnations of this book, and I must thank his wife, Mary LaBeaume Hall, for happily enduring my repeated intrusions into their home. I am indebted as well to my sister, Janet Hobbs, for her encouragement and support, as I am to Walt Harrington, Betty Boyd Caroli, and Janis Ruden. And thanks to Daniel Gray for the quiet but unmistakable pride he takes in my accomplishments.

Among White's colleagues and friends who have shared their recollections, William Walton, Benjamin Bradlee, Marvin Kalb, Richard Clurman, Blair Clark, John Kenneth Galbraith, Penn Kimball, Muriel Blumenthal, Dr. and Mrs. Irving London, Arthur M. Schlesinger Jr., Al Ravenholt, and Milton Katz deserve special mention. I am equally grateful to the late John Hersey, with whom I corresponded before his death in 1993.

This book began as a doctoral dissertation in the American Studies program at New York University. As the head of my dissertation committee, Professor Paul Baker became both my critic and my cheerleader, knowing intuitively—as the best teachers do—just how to mix criticism with compliments. Other members of the NYU faculty who have my gratitude are Don White, Jay Rosen, Kenneth Silverman, Edwin Diamond, and Richard Cummingham.

I also owe an enormous thanks to the many librarians who have responded generously to my requests for help. I am particularly grateful to Caroline Preston, who catalogued the papers White bequeathed to Harvard University; Melanie Wisner and Denison Beach at Harvard University's Houghton Library; and Patrice Donoghue and James McCarthy at Harvard's

Pusey Library. William Johnson, chief archivist at the John F. Kennedy Library, has been most enthusiastic in his support of my research, an enthusiasm that library staffers June Payne and Maura Porter shared. And I owe a thank you to Nancy McAuliffe at Old Dominion University, Joan Hill, and Linda Wells for their assistance.

This project has also benefited from the financial support of New York University, a Goldsmith research grant from the Joan Shorenstein Barone Center for Press Politics and Public Policy at the John F. Kennedy School of Government, and the Theodore C. Sorenson research fellowship from the John F. Kennedy Library.

Thanks also to my tireless literary agent Robert Lescher, and to Beverly Jarrett, who saw the book possibilities in my doctoral dissertation long before they were apparent to me. It has been a special pleasure to work with John Brenner, whose unfailing patience and skillful editing I deeply appreciate.

In giving me permission to quote from Theodore White's books and private papers, the White family has asked me to say that they do not agree with my interpretation of his role as a journalist.

Theodore H. White

and Journalism as Illusion

Introduction

. . . .

. . . Theodore H. White

Journalism as Illusion

Theodore H. White was in a dentist's chair on the Upper East Side of Manhattan on a Friday morning in late November 1963, when he learned that Jacqueline Kennedy had telephoned to say she needed him. One week had passed since President John F. Kennedy's assassination in Dallas, and now his widow was beseeching the journalist, whom she considered an old friend, to come to Hyannisport. She had something she wanted *Life* magazine to say to America, and White, she insisted, had to bear her message. Because the Secret Service had brusquely refused her order to send a car for him—saying she was no longer the president's wife—and since a northeaster hitting Cape Cod made access by private plane impossible, White made the trip from New York City back to his native Massachusetts in a hired limousine. By the following morning, the journalist and the former first lady would create one of the twentieth century's most dubious but enduring illusions.

On the violent weekend just passed, Mrs. Kennedy's grace and dignity had made, in the words of Archibald MacLeish, "the darkest days the American people had known in a hundred years the deepest revelation of their inward strength." She had summoned White because she was angry, very angry. All week newspaper pundits had served up their instant appraisals of the brief and abruptly ended Kennedy administration. Arthur Krock's *New York Times* column had especially rankled her, as had the assessments of United Press International White House Correspondent Merriman Smith, and others. Krock's praise for Kennedy's "extraordinary attainments" had been tempered with a lament about the failure of "even advanced democracy and self-government to extirpate in mankind the resort to anarchy." The bullet that killed the president, Krock wrote, was forged in the conditions of intense political controversy and demonstrated that Americans still resorted to violence as an expression of their differences over how to deal with national and international problems. Walter Lippmann's "Today and Tomorrow" column just four days after the assassination had spoken of the forces of hatred and ungovernability and how "habit of intemperate speech and thought has become deeply ingrained. It is deepened by the strains of war and the frustrations of this revolutionary age."[1]

Mrs. Kennedy wanted White to rescue her husband's memory from these men. History should celebrate the Kennedy years as a time of hope and magic, she insisted. White sat mesmerized for more than two hours, listening to the rambling and disjointed monologue that darted between Dallas and the judgment day of history. Mrs. Kennedy said she regretted having wiped the caked blood from her face and hair aboard Air Force One; otherwise the famous photograph of Lyndon B. Johnson taking the presidential oath of office would have borne witness to the horror of the assassination. She sneered at the "bitter old men" who wrote history. Finally, she came to the thought that had become her obsession, a thought embodied in the lyrics of the Broadway musical—*Camelot*. Over and over again, she and the president had listened to the words sing out of their ten-year-old Victrola. And those words were what she wanted White to tell America: "Don't let it be forgot, that once there was a spot, for one brief shining moment . . ."[2]

Around midnight, White retreated to a maid's room with eleven pages of interview notes and wrote the first draft of his famous essay, mindful that *Life* was holding its presses at a cost of thirty thousand dollars an hour. When he finished, Mrs. Kennedy took a pencil to White's work, crossing out some of his words and adding her own in the margins. She hovered near the kitchen telephone—adamant that her Camelot portrayal remain the

1. Archibald MacLeish is quoted in William Manchester, *Death of a President*, 644. Arthur Krock's quotation is from his column "The Continuum," *New York Times*, November 24, 1963. Walter Lippmann's quotation is from his column, "Today and Tomorrow," November 26, 1963.
2. Theodore H. White, *In Search of History*, 523.

dominant theme—as he dictated the revised version to his editors. David Maness, on the other end of the telephone in New York, argued that perhaps the Camelot theme was overplayed. "Yes, isn't it lovely," answered White, trying to signal Maness that Mrs. Kennedy was within earshot. She could hear his objections but remained adamant—Camelot. So, with White's help, Jacqueline Kennedy enshrined that wistful vision of her husband's presidency on the national consciousness. Never mind that members of Kennedy's own White House staff later mocked her idea. "Jack Kennedy never spoke of Camelot," scoffed Arthur M. Schlesinger Jr. "That's not what the New Frontier was all about." Dean Rusk, Kennedy's secretary of state, was similarly derisive: "JFK would have kicked the idea of Camelot right out the window." And Roger Hilsman, an undersecretary of state during Kennedy's thousand-day presidency, scorned the thought in still stronger language: "If Jack Kennedy heard this stuff about Camelot, he would have vomited."[3]

Camelot was, of course, an illusion. And White knew it. He had written the story of the Kennedy presidency that night in just the way Mrs. Kennedy wanted it told because she believed "that history belonged to heroes; and heroes must not be forgotten." And White shared her sentiment that night. "I felt I should just lay a wreath on the grave of John Kennedy," White said years later, "that he not be forgot." Twenty-five years before, he had written stories from China that had portrayed Chiang Kai-shek as a similarly heroic character. That too turned out to be an illusion. In his autobiography, written fifteen years after that night in Hyannisport, White made a mild apology, conceding that the Camelot legend was "a misreading of history." While he acknowledged that there were no Galahads at the New Frontier round table, he continued to bestow laurels on Kennedy, crediting him with unleashing the forces of participatory democracy among Blacks, women, young people, and ethnic minorities. "He was a realistic dealer in men," White wrote of Kennedy a decade and a half after the assassination, "a master of games who

3. The notes of White's interview with Jacqueline Kennedy, known as the "Camelot Papers," which White donated to the John F. Kennedy Library in 1969, remained under restriction until May 19, 1995, one year after the death of Jacqueline Kennedy Onassis. The comment in White's phone conversation with David Maness is from a personal interview with Maness. The Kennedy staff's comments are gathered from a personal interview with Arthur M. Schlesinger Jr., March 23, 1990; and from Gerald S. Strober and Deborah Hart Strober, *Let Us Begin Anew: An Oral History of the Presidency of John F. Kennedy,* 423.

understood the importance of ideas. He assumed his responsibilities fully. He advanced the cause of America at home and abroad."[4]

White had once believed that history was an uncontrollable locomotive racing toward some predetermined destination. But after he witnessed history—in China, postwar Europe, and America—his thinking changed. History was not predestined. Individuals not only could but inevitably did redirect the locomotive and alter history. Not only did individual choices matter, they were the thread of history itself. For a brief time, White believed, John Kennedy maneuvered the locomotive.

A quarter of a century before his extraordinary night in the Kennedy compound, White had cut his professional teeth covering war and upheaval from Chungking, the wartime capital of Chiang Kai-shek's Nationalist government, between 1939 and 1945. After World War II, all of Europe became his beat. And when, in 1960, he turned his keen reportorial eye to the American presidency, White invented a new genre of political journalism with *The Making of the President 1960*. Despite his deep commitment to honor and justice—indeed, perhaps because of that very commitment— his journalism sometimes revealed less than the truth. Degrees of necessity, conviction, and kindness all compelled White to selectively arrange the facts and create news stories that occasionally were "winged with a hope and a passion that were entirely unreal."[5] Evident in White's work in those twenty-five years between Chungking and Camelot are a series of illusions that force us to examine both the notion of truth as a professional goal and the role moral reasoning should play in determining how truth is presented.

In his autobiography, *In Search of History*, White characterized himself as a storyteller. The stories he told were about the men, the events, and the ideas that shaped the history of twentieth-century America. He wrote about war and peace, about revolutions and assassination, about famines and scandals, and about the candidates who had aspired to become America's leader in the presidential election of 1960. Many of those stories helped to shape the popular consciousness about America and its place in the world.

Through all of this, White also gave us some of journalism's crowning achievements. He was, at times, a clear-eyed observer of the American political system and an original thinker who pioneered a style of campaign reporting that changed political journalism. Drawing on his educa-

4. Theodore White, personal interview, May 5, 1982; White, *In Search of History*, 523, 525.
5. Ibid., 205.

tion in the classics and the skills he had honed as a novelist, White took his reportorial skills into realms that most political journalists had left unexplored. A presidential election became, in his telling, an engagement of ambitions, a tale seasoned with drama, suspense, romance, and adventure. The 1960 campaign, as told by Theodore White, became a story of grand themes and large ideas—a literary journey of discovery that fused *Huckleberry Finn* with *Heart of Darkness*. In a sense, White gave America a new way of looking at itself.

Viewed from the perspective of the 1990s, it is clear that many of his stories created unrealistic images and expectations about China, postwar Europe, America's role as a superpower, and the men who became America's leaders and presidents. But illusions were part of America's journalistic tradition in the mid–twentieth century. In a variety of ways—both positive and negative—White is a representative figure in whom the professional practices of America's Establishment journalists are visible. White's style of journalism fit a model established by a generation of influential columnists and reporters who had functioned as a subsidiary of government during World War II and the postwar years. Walter Lippmann was the exemplar of this insider style; he often helped to formulate the very policies that he subsequently endorsed in his widely read column. Presidents, cabinet secretaries, and policy makers placed their faith in both his wisdom and his discretion. Other members of this closed circle of Washington elites who were linked by school ties and social connections included Arthur Krock of the *New York Times*, once a clubmate of Defense Secretary James Forrestal at Princeton University. Joseph Alsop had known the state department's Soviet expert, Charles Bohlen, at Harvard, where they were members of Porcellian. Whenever Secretary of State Dean Acheson lunched at the Metropolitan Club with James Reston, whose star was rising at the *New York Times* in the late 1940s, a front-page story about the State Department inevitably followed. John McCloy, assistant secretary of war and later high commissioner for Germany, was typical of many highly placed government officials who as a rule disliked dealing with the press but set aside that aversion for a select few. McCloy considered Alsop a friend, and he trusted Lippmann enough to show him army intelligence reports. And his Georgetown neighbor, Reston, wrote many stories in which McCloy was an unnamed source. Envisioning themselves as helpmates rather than adversaries of government, White and other journalists who enjoyed access in high places became adjuncts of the government's policy-making process.

Compassion often outranked professional protocol in White's system of values. He was, in the Yiddish vernacular of his immigrant grandparents, a "mensch" first and a journalist second—a quality that may well have resulted in as many commendable deeds as questionable ones. Whether it was professionally appropriate for a journalist to harangue a world leader, as White harangued Chiang Kai-shek about how his government's corrupt taxation policies were contributing to the death toll in a devastating famine in Honan Province, begs a dubious question. But White's sense of compassion also led him to commit what by today's standards would be considered journalistic sins. He knowingly misrepresented the political situation in China because he believed the survival of China and the defeat of fascism depended on it. He kept secrets in order to maintain access to his important sources. He allowed his subjects—John F. Kennedy and Robert S. McNamara among them—to read and change his work before it was published. In speaking about his old friend's vision of the reporter's role in a democratic society, former NBC news correspondent Marvin Kalb stated, "Teddy had all the correct instincts, but he lived by very few of them."[6]

From his years as a war correspondent in Chungking across two and a half decades to Camelot, one can see in White's work evidence of problems that continue to bedevil journalism: How does one balance the profession's conflicting and contradictory demands in the best service of one's readers? Where does one draw the line between compassion and professional responsibility? Can a journalist demonstrate loyalty to his country without compromising his professional integrity? When does "insider journalism" cross that invisible point at which it no longer serves the readers' interests? If "truth" is the goal, whose "truth" should be told? Although White was captivated by his proximity to powerful people and the compromises he made to ensure access seem glaring from the perspective of the 1990s, contemporary journalists continue to face the same quandaries and haven't necessarily demonstrated any greater ability to cope with them than White and many of his colleagues did in those troublesome cold war years. While journalism codes still tout objectivity as one of the profession's worthy aims, it remains persistently elusive. Journalists in the 1990s have exhibited no greater ability to keep an appropriate distance from their subjects, refrain from political involvement, and avoid conflicts of interest than their predecessors.

While the insiders of White's generation seemed too willing to ascribe only the noblest motives to the deeds of America's leaders, today's antithetical journalistic pose—the assumption that evil or at least immoral impulses

6. Marvin Kalb, personal interview, November 23, 1992.

drive those who wield power—may generate equal risks to democracy. White and his contemporaries were guided by a set of convictions grounded in their commitment to safeguarding their vision of the national interest. In contrast, their descendants in the contemporary media have no allegiance to ideology and appear to believe the depth of commitment to their profession is best measured by the belligerence of their attacks on those who wield power. We have, it seems, traded a journalism of illusion for a journalism of malice.

The significance of White's professional conduct and what makes it worthy of scrutiny lies not in how White may or may not have transgressed some ill-defined and ever-changing set of professional standards. White's career is important instead because it demonstrates the inherent contradictions in journalism's claim to its role as an independent observer and chronicler of events.

It would be impossible to disembody the work of any journalist from the individual who produced it. Personal values are reflected in the very selection and ordering of information in any article, essay, or book. In one sense, then, all journalism is interpretive and personal. Yet a commitment to professional canons is supposed to provide an appropriate degree of dispassion and detachment to prevent personal ideals from tainting one's reportage. White's interpretations, however, were invariably colored by some overarching philosophy that transcended his commitment to journalism— China's survival in the 1940s, the liberal consensus in the 1950s, the perceived (or perhaps misperceived) duty to one's country and one's president in the 1960s.

Theodore White was, above all, a man of his times. His character and values were shaped in Boston's Jewish ghetto and by the poverty his family endured during the Great Depression. Later, his generation was tested by a world war in which White made no secret of his partisanship with the Chinese in their struggle against Japan. America's victory in World War II would turn out to be a hollow triumph. "Waging peace" became every bit as fearsome as waging war. The threat of a nuclear Armageddon penetrated American culture. When the Soviet Union detonated its first atomic bomb in the early days of September 1949, there was a general agreement with Senator Arthur Vandenberg's gloomy observation: "This is now a different world."

In that different world, White and many of his contemporaries in the Establishment press joined the vast political consensus that transcended all but the most extreme fringes of the political right and left in the postwar decade. Political discord stopped at the water's edge in America. The Republicans and Democrats might quarrel over civil rights, labor unrest, and other domestic issues, but in the realm of foreign policy, the Left and the Right all but disappeared from America's political landscape. Across the political spectrum, Republicans and Democrats were in fundamental agreement that communism was evil; that Joseph Stalin, if left unguarded, would advance his reach around the globe; and that multiplying our nuclear firepower was essential for survival.

In 1992, six years after White's death, Harvard University opened the Theodore H. White Archive. Thousands of pages of correspondence, diaries, and manuscripts beginning with the impassioned jottings of a high school essayist and ending with drafts of an incomplete sequel to the first volume of his autobiography (which concluded in 1963) reveal in rich detail the conflicting forces that colored White's character and inevitably shaped his journalism.

Four critical periods emerge in that first quarter-century of White's career—his early years as a correspondent in China, his work as a consensus journalist in postwar Europe, his trend-setting approach to presidential politics in 1960, and finally his membership in the circle of friends whom Victor Navasky labeled "honorary Kennedys."[7]

In his reporting from Chungking, White with considerable misgivings applauded Chiang Kai-shek's Nationalist government and overlooked its obvious corruption and ineptitude. Subverting those truths would help defeat fascism, White believed, and would serve the best interests of both China and America. When he later tried to correct the flaws in the picture he had painted of China, first in his reporting for *Time* and later in his book *Thunder Out of China*, White discovered that misconceptions develop their own momentum, their own constituencies, and are not easily reversed.

During his years as a Paris-based correspondent after World War II, White adopted and promoted the ideology of the political Establishment in his reports on the reconstruction of Europe. The political consensus that had swept away so many ideological distinctions gave birth to a reportorial style that might be considered the journalism of consensus. His reports from Europe reflected the beliefs within this consensus: the nobility of American aims, the notion that economic stability would allow democracy to flourish, and the conviction that a united Europe could beat back the tyranny of communism. In its unquestioning acceptance of the cold war theology and

7. Victor Navasky, *Kennedy Justice*, 330.

in its apparent unwillingness to explore alternatives, White's work, as well as that of his contemporaries, helped to limit the range of debate on America's foreign policy options, the result of which helped to keep the nation locked into a costly arms race for four decades. As one of the selected insiders in whom American and European leaders confided, White was part of a group that had an important voice in defining the boundaries of legitimate political debate in America in the late 1940s and early 1950s.

Following his return from Europe in the mid–1950s, White became a national correspondent for *Collier's,* then one of the nation's leading maga-zines. Later he spent several years writing fiction, but in 1959 he set out to write a textbook about American politics, one that he hoped would introduce generations of students to the process of a democracy choosing its leader. And indeed, *The Making of the President 1960* did become a textbook, a classic that remains required reading for college students in history, journalism, and political science courses. White humanized the process of democracy and carried it into the realm of mythology. For White, an American presidential campaign was a story of democracy as epic. Would-be presidents were his major characters. In White's telling, an election was a magic moment when the people, in their collective wisdom, elected a leader who was somehow mystically transformed in the process. Because White was, above all, a patriot, he portrayed the American presidency as democracy's greatest prize, one that represented, he believed, "the most awesome transfer of power in the world."[8]

During the so-called Camelot years, White's style of insider journalism made him appear to be more of a helpmate than an adversary of the Kennedy administration. Had he relinquished his role as a guardian of the public interest for an unofficial partnership in the New Frontier? The glowing profiles he wrote of key cabinet members were part of a larger pattern that shaped American journalism in the Kennedy era—a pattern that helped to foster the flawed notion that Kennedy was surrounded by "the best and the brightest."

In depicting Kennedy—and later other American presidents—as larger-than-life figures grappling with larger-than-life issues, White most certainly helped to enlarge the expectations Americans came to have of their pres-idents. Because White's book altered the way print and broadcast jour-

8. Theodore H. White, memorandum to Penn Kimball, January 20, 1960, Theodore H. White Archive, Box 17, Folder 1, Harvard University Archive, Cambridge. The archive is hereafter cited as TWA and White is cited as THW.

nalists covered presidential elections, it definitively altered the shape of presidential politics in America. And having played a significant role in the creation of the celebrity politician in the early 1960s, White assumed the role of celebrity journalist. Thereafter, it seems, White began to lose both his edge and his effectiveness. He appeared too willing to bow to the whims and wishes of his powerful subjects. And yet, in a move that illustrates the inherent paradoxes of his personal and professional value systems, White later turned down a proposal by members of the Kennedy family that he write an "authorized" account of the Kennedy presidency because he insisted—as he would throughout his life—on control over his own work.

The irony embodied in White and his work is that although, in the words of Benjamin C. Bradlee, "he helped to set us [journalists] free,"[9] his own formula entrapped him. Theodore White blazed the trail in opening America's political process to greater scrutiny. But it was left to others to explore the wider realms of White's journalistic invention.

9. Benjamin C. Bradlee, personal interview, January 24, 1993.

Chapter One

· · · · · · · · · ·

· · · **The Birth of a Journalist**

The profession of journalism is one in which success
depends entirely on personality. One must inspire
confidence in other people and teach them to talk to
you and confide in you. —Theodore H. White, letter
to Mary and Gladys White, June 1, 1940

Journalism was to be a way station rather than a final destination in Theodore White's early career plans. The future he envisioned
when he graduated summa cum laude with Harvard's class of 1938 had
more to do with scholarship than with printer's ink. Tucked away in some
solitary academic refuge, he imagined he would write history, probably
Chinese history. However, John King Fairbank, Harvard's preeminent China
scholar who was both White's mentor and role model, pushed him toward
a different path, White recalled in his autobiography. Recognizing that an
unpolished young man reared in Boston's Jewish ghetto might not easily
fit into the rarefied world of Ivy League scholars, Fairbank encouraged his
protégé to try journalism. Fairbank was acquainted with Edgar Snow, the
American journalist who, in 1936, had spent four months in Yenan with
Mao Tse-tung and the Chinese Communist army units that had survived

the five-thousand-mile Long March. And in the young student, Fairbank thought he saw the appropriate "manners, lust and ego of someone who might be a journalist."[1]

To understand the manners, lust, and ego that White brought to his long and celebrated career in journalism is to understand the values and the motivations that a great many journalists carried to their profession in the mid–twentieth century. White brought to his career in journalism a deep-rooted sense of history, an immense patriotism, a belief that his interpretation of events could enrich the historic record, and a longing for acceptance. Journalism helped him to escape the poverty of his childhood. Journalism also garnered him respectability, fame, and wealth. And journalism allowed him to seek some measure of social justice.

White is best known in the lore of journalism as the courageous journalist who tirelessly fought Henry Luce, his stubborn, wrong-headed publisher who was one of Chiang Kai-shek's most ardent American admirers. As a result of their celebrated public quarrel, early in 1946 White reluctantly quit *Time*, the publication that had given him both his first job in journalism and a spiritual home. Although that legend has been repeated by an assortment of Luce biographers as evidence of Luce's unyielding and mulish personality, White's discord with his publisher characterizes only the latter years of his China sojourn. For more than three years after he arrived in China in the early days of 1939, White shared his boss's enthusiasm for the Nationalist regime and considered Chiang a hero and political genius for his success in uniting China's fractious warlords. In 1939, Chiang had been in power for thirteen years and China was fighting its Japanese invaders. There was little need for Luce to admonish White—as he had admonished Time Inc's senior executives in a confidential memo written in 1940—to promote the idea that the United States should give maximum support to China on the pages of *Time*, *Life*, and *Fortune*.[2] Well before Henry Luce defined his magazines' "journalistic duty" in China, White's reportage from Chungking celebrated the achievements of the Nationalist regime and glossed over its widespread corruption and incompetence. But while White sent glowing reports of the Kuomintang's rule from Chungking to his editors in New York, his letters and diaries reveal that he had recognized the rot in Chiang's government soon after he arrived in China but feared the consequences of disillusioning

1. White, *In Search of History*, 54.
2. Robert T. Elson, *The World of Time, Inc.*, 430.

Americans. Because he believed any revelation that might damage China's cause in its war against Japanese tyranny was "a disservice to democracy," as he wrote a friend in 1940, he pledged his allegiance to China.

When in his autobiography White looked back on his initiation as a journalist in Chungking, he wrote rather breezily that he considered himself "a sightseer," a traveler who collected impressions of places, personalities, and events in the Far East—the raw materials from which *Time*'s New York office would determine and explain what was historically significant.[3] His letters, however, reveal that serious questions about his role in China bedeviled White at the time. Should he serve American interests, Chinese interests, or his readers' interests? How simple it would have been had all the interests of these three publics been congruent. Obviously, though, they were not.

The choices that confronted White during those early years of his career seemed so unambiguous. On one side, the virtuous, stolid Chinese were waging a valiant fight against their brutal Japanese invaders. One side represented perfect virtue, the other represented consummate evil. Throughout his life, those same one-dimensional contrasts between light and darkness would shape White's view of the world—even long after events had blurred the issues into confounding shades of gray.

On May 6, 1915, Theodore Harold White was born in a house divided and into a world at war. His father, David White, was the son of a rabbi who had come to America from Pinsk in the late 1880s, fleeing both the prospect of conscription into Czar Alexander III's army and the confines of his family's strict Jewish orthodoxy. David White wanted neither to serve as the czar's foot soldier for twenty-five years, the required length of service for Jewish recruits, nor to worship the God of his fathers. In the doctrines of socialism David White had found an appealing substitute for his religion, and on a sign outside the R. H. White department store on Washington Street in Boston he had found a suitable replacement for Vladefsky, the surname of his forefathers. But David's wife, Mary Winkeller White, still followed some of the religious rituals her parents had brought from their shtetl in Minsk and that they still practiced with fervor in Dorchester, Boston's Jewish immigrant enclave, where the Whites and the Winkellers shared a two-story house at 74 Erie Street. They had bought the house in 1912 for two thousand dollars from a middle-class Protestant family that, like dozens of other such

3. White, *In Search of History*, 103.

families, had decided to flee the neighborhood rather than live alongside Boston's newest immigrants.

The discord between the doctrines of Karl Marx, which David White preached downstairs, and the teachings of the Talmud, which his in-laws so scrupulously followed upstairs, created a relentless family conflict, one that had a parallel beyond the walls of their shuttered, white clapboard home. Europe had been at war for nearly a year in 1915, and Todros, who was named for his paternal grandfather, was just one day old when a German submarine torpedoed the *Lusitania* near the Irish coast, killing 1,198 of the 1,959 passengers and crew members aboard.

Toddy (pronounced Tuhddy in Yiddish), as David and Mary White's eldest son was known among family and friends, was three years old when the doughboys came home from the Great War in Europe. Like so many of her Dorchester neighbors, Mary White was a fervent patriot, and she considered the soldiers heroes who deserved a grand welcome. So with her toddler and his older sister in tow, she trooped off to Mount Bowdoin Station where Boston's returning sons waved and threw candy to the children. Despite the many years of hardship and poverty she was to endure, all of her life Mary White rejoiced that she had been born in America. She called it "a grand and glorious country,"[4] a view her oldest son shared throughout his life.

For Mary White, however, life was far from grand and glorious. Her husband, who had gone to night school to learn English and later had attended Northeastern University, passed the Massachusetts bar exam in 1904. But causes interested David White much more than wealth. He marched with the women's suffragists in a demonstration in 1911 and cheered the demands women were making for fundamental rights. In the following decade, he protested the controversial conviction of Nicola Sacco and Bartolomeo Vanzetti, who were found guilty of murdering a shoe company paymaster in 1920. As the Commonwealth of Massachusetts prepared to execute the two anarchists in August 1927, David White had his son, then twelve, keep an all-night vigil so he "would never forget what capitalism did to workingmen."[5] Because David White invariably took on some of the city's poorest clients, when their children were growing up in the 1920s, the Whites never shared in the prosperity for which the decade is remembered in the popular imagination. The early 1920s marked the start of their economic decline. Mary

4. Mary W. White, letter to THW, November 26, 1938, TWA, Box 1, Folder 11.
5. White, *In Search of History,* 17.

White watched as the fortunes of others soared while hers sank. At night, after her children were in bed, she cried because there was no money. Those cries, which her children were not supposed to hear, reverberated in Toddy's memory and obscured his recollections of happier times the family shared. There were birthdays celebrated with family sing-alongs. With his sister thumping away at the keyboard of a secondhand piano and Toddy puffing into the mouth of his trumpet, the family sang patriotic songs and sentimental ballads. But in his recollections of his childhood, White remembered only the poverty. The early 1920s were bad, but the late 1920s—after the stock market crash—were worse. Before, there had been no money for shoes; after, there would be no money for food.

The xenophobic Boston of his childhood, White would remember years later, was the most anti-Semitic city in America. The aristocratic American historian Henry Adams may or may not have been speaking for his social class in Boston when he dismissed the entire Jewish race, saying, "The Jew makes me creep." Certainly the city's old Brahmins in their Beacon Hill mansions wanted as little to do with the Jews as with the Irish. Ironically, Boston's prosperous and well-assimilated German Jews—who had arrived in the mid–1800s—felt the same way about the new wave of Jewish immigrants. They viewed the eastern European refugees as uncouth and dangerously socialistic. A rabbi, Solomon Schindler, spearheaded an assault, telling his reformed congregation in Boston's Temple Israel that these newly arrived hordes were "a bane to the country and a curse to the Jews."[6]

Although White happily fled Dorchester's confines in his early twenties, the ghetto experience remained forever imprinted on him. His parents— particularly his mother—were determined that their children would conquer the invisible social and cultural barriers that made them outsiders in that city of old money and Puritan values. Mary White desperately wanted a better, more financially secure life for her children. She daydreamed them into jobs as teachers or government employees, imagining such positions as the pinnacle of success for her sons. Education, she was convinced, would secure two most cherished goals—security and acceptance. Education, she believed, was also the ticket to equality. But despite his abundant success, the struggle for acceptance encumbered White's life—he would never forget that he was born Jewish and poor. As the son and grandson of Jewish immigrants, it was left to White and his contemporaries to find a balance between the

6. Hillel Levine and Lawrence Harmon, *The Death of an American Jewish Community*, 32.

rigid, Old-World pieties of his grandparents and the inevitable accommodations that acceptance and worldly success would demand. Ultimately, White and the children he played with on Erie Street would have to redefine what it meant to be a Jew. But the poverty of White's Dorchester childhood left even deeper scars on White's soul.

When David White died in 1931, with America in the midst of the Great Depression, he left his wife and four children impoverished. Mary White, to her everlasting shame, had to ask for home relief—the dole. Toddy was able to finish his senior year at the prestigious Boston Public Latin School, but the family's penury required that he forgo college—despite his acceptance by Harvard—and find a job to supplement his mother's eleven-dollar weekly welfare allotment.

Instead of a daily commute to Harvard Square, White spent ten hours a day hawking newspapers on Boston's streetcars. Like some animated tabloid, he shouted the headlines, occasionally in Latin when he spied one of his more fortunate high school classmates commuting to college. He was, to his great dismay, not a student, but a peddler, just as his father had been after he arrived in America in the early 1890s. Quickly he learned that history, in the form of great events—such as Franklin Roosevelt's declaration of a Bank Holiday—sold more papers than tabloid tales of pickled babies in a barrel. Thus, history and money became entwined in the strange equation of his life. Thanks to his cleverness and cunning, he prospered as a newsboy. Even in the lowly business of hawking newspapers, he proved himself able to charm those in power. He also learned how to manipulate the system to his own advantage. He learned the ruse of collecting discarded papers and returning them with his unsold copies, and later he converted a number of his streetcar customers into home delivery customers; these schemes added several dollars to his weekly income. There was a Darwinian quality about this period of his life: as one of the fittest he not only survived, but also triumphed. But the job became a dispiriting, dead-end grind, a straitjacket that confined his intellect and ambition.

In despair, he reapplied to Harvard, and this time his acceptance came with the promise of a $220 stipend. Through the largesse of Harry Burroughs, a one-time newsboy who had become a rich Boston lawyer, White's dreary job provided him with the remaining $180 he needed to attend Harvard. Joined by a board of ten men, Burroughs himself interviewed each scholarship applicant. One judge glanced at White's frail physique and told his colleagues this boy didn't have the stamina to get through college. Burroughs disagreed. "Look at the light in his eye, he'll make good,"

Burroughs insisted. White's joy was unrestrained. "I'll be at Harvard next year," he wrote to a friend in the summer of 1934. "I and John Roosevelt and August Belmont and John Penrose Saltonstall will all study side by side in the cloistered halls of Fair Harvard! American Democracy! Newsboy and President's son!"[7]

White became a commuter student, a self-described "meatball" in the Harvard pecking order of the class of 1938.[8] Compared with those he characterized as Harvard's "white men" (the prep-school-educated sons of America's aristocracy) and "gray men" (those solidly middle-class public high school valedictorians from across America), the meatballs (scholarship students who commuted to the historic Yard on Boston's streetcars) were counted at the bottom. The white men, whose names were Kermit Roosevelt, Joseph P. Kennedy Jr., John P. Saltonstall, and Marshall Field, were Harvard's patricians—men who belonged to Porcellian and other exclusive clubs. Typical of the gray men—leaders of the school's prestigious extracurricular activities—in the Class of 1938 was Caspar Weinberger, who was president of the Harvard *Crimson* in his senior year and later secretary of defense in the Reagan administration, and Wiley Mayne, who later became a congressman from Sioux City, Iowa. The meatballs, by contrast, carried their lunch to campus in brown bags and shared each other's company in the spartan confines of Dudley Hall, then the commuter students' paltry counterpart to the comforts of Harvard's seven newly created houses—Winthrop, Eliot, and Leverett among them—where the upperclassmen lived in suites, were served their meals in oak-paneled dining halls, and studied in their own small libraries.

Had John Kenneth Galbraith had his way, White would have been invited to live in one of those houses after his freshman year, but Harvard's unofficial quota on Jews precluded that. Galbraith, then a junior professor, had taught White the basics of economic theory in "Econ A" and found him to be "my best student." So when Galbraith, as a resident tutor at Winthrop House, was asked to participate in selecting which freshmen would be accepted as house residents during their remaining three years at Harvard, he suggested White. Ronald M. Ferry, Winthrop's house master, had provided members of his admissions committee with a ruled sheet on which graduates of top private schools were the clear preference and Jewish candidates were counted in the column labeled "X." Ferry balked at Galbraith's choices. Pointing to

---

7. THW, letter to Sarah Richman, August 16, 1934, TWA, Box 1, Folder 1.
8. White, *In Search of History*, 42.

White's name, Ferry "told me we were already up to our Jewish quota," and he dismissed Galbraith's protests that White was not a Jewish name with "a hopeless gesture."[9] Throughout his Harvard career, White remained a commuter student, returning each afternoon to his Erie Street neighborhood and a nearby Hebrew School where he earned money teaching the language, culture, and history of Judaism to young boys who were as reluctant as he had once been to spend their after-school hours being drilled in the language and traditions of their forefathers.

His classmates might indulge in Saturday afternoon football games in Soldiers Field, but White first saw Harvard's team on the gridiron several decades after he graduated. Instead, White spent his time studying the fearsome assortment of characters in the Chinese alphabet and writing scholarly essays that answered ponderous academic questions such as the one Fairbank posed when he required White to write an essay detailing, "What, if any, effect did Thomas Aquinas have on modern life?" (The tutor provided his student with half the answer in a brief cautionary note: "if you say none, then you're wrong.") Harvard invigorated White, challenged his agile intellect, and gave him a sense of achievement. Just after he completed his freshman year, an acquaintance who was soon to enter the university asked White about his principal academic interest. With his propensity for the grandiose statement well formed even then, White—who was standing on the steps of Widener Library—raised a fist toward the sky and declared, "I am majoring in history! I want to lead a revolution."[10]

White's political orientation during his Harvard years was decidedly liberal but hardly radical. Looking back on his youth, White characterized himself as a "mild Marxist," but there is little evidence to suggest that he spent much time espousing Marxist doctrines. Although he had joined campus protests against President Roosevelt's naval rearmament program, he had also tried to join the Reserve Officers Training Corps in his senior year. Because Harvard's ROTC requirements stipulated that students enroll in the sophomore year, White settled for auditing ROTC classes during his final semesters—an undertaking that taught him not only the fundamentals of military strategy but also how to ride a horse, a skill he would soon put to use in China.

9. John K. Galbraith, *A Life in Our Times*, 51.
10. THW, letter to John King Fairbank, December 17, 1936, TWA, Box 1, Folder 2; Irving London, personal interview, July 14, 1992.

He found that Communists were "as thick as fleas" at Harvard, but he had little time or forbearance for the radical politics in which some of his wealthier classmates dabbled during the mid–1930s. When those well-off political activists preached their doctrines to the Dudley Hall commuters, White found their entreaties both patronizing and condescending. They were, White recalled to a friend years later, "the rich boys. . . . They tried to organize us poor boys very clumsily as if we were a minority race or depressed proletariat—many of us were Jewish—and we reacted as all poor and ambitious students did by saying, 'Fuck you.' I was saved from Communism because I was jealous of their good fortune and the girls they could take out to parties."[11]

In a later decade, he would be denounced as a Communist, or at least a fellow traveler, but although he embraced the tenets of socialism early in his life, White seldom found any redeeming qualities in Soviet-style communism. "Russia is a Socialist state doing evil," he wrote in the late 1930s. "I think the reason is that socialism without democracy leads to vicious ends and that democracy comes first in the list of human necessities."[12]

The struggle against fascism in Spain engaged White and many of his contemporaries in the mid–1930s. Together they talked excitedly about the military uprising in Burgos, the general strike in Saragossa, and, later, the long Battle of Ebro during the summer of 1938. White was also an impassioned Zionist. At Harvard he was a leader in the Avukah (Torch) Society and helped to organize boycotts of German-made wares at Boston stores in response to the growing anti-Semitism in Germany.

In his preoccupation with good grades, White realized soon after he graduated, he had missed the real riches of a Harvard education. "I would give ten years to have Harvard to do over again," he lamented in a letter to his younger brother, who was soon to enter Harvard. "There are great men pouring out their wisdom there—go listen to them . . . damn it, I wish I had done that." The people one meets at Harvard, White advised his brother, were more important than the courses. "They're all brilliant young men there and they'll be running America some day. . . . Try to keep out of the path of the stinking, long-maned aristocrats from the Back Bay and New York; but go out of your way to meet the boys who have brains."

11. THW, letter to Mary, Gladys, and Robert White, August 24, 1940, TWA, Box 2, Folder 12; White, letter to Philip Horton, June 8, 1951, TWA, Box 9, Folder 16.
12. THW, letter to Mary and Gladys White, October 17, 1939, TWA, Box 1, Folder 21.

And although White himself had majored in history, he good-naturedly threatened to disown his brother if he did likewise. The future, he insisted, was in science. "History makes a civilized man; and science makes a useful one. You must be useful first, then civilized."[13]

With his degree, he later realized, he had become the "beneficiary of all the Establishment had packed into the Harvard processing system." Later, he would represent those Establishment interests in his work as a journalist, and finally, he himself became a full-fledged member of that Establishment. When he graduated in 1938, he was awarded Harvard's prestigious Frederick Sheldon Traveling Fellowship, a fifteen-hundred-dollar stipend meant to finance a year of travel. With it, White planned to make his way to China. Shortly before he left America on that long journey, White's first byline appeared on an editorial in the *Michigan Daily*, the student newspaper published at the University of Michigan, where White engaged in intensive Chinese language training the summer following his graduation. In that editorial, White endorsed the proposed Ludlow Amendment, which would have prohibited Congress from sending American soldiers to fight foreign wars without the consent of the people, calling the measure "sane and simple." Recalling World War I, he wrote that American participation had cost the nation $40 billion and retarded its social progress. That war, White claimed, demonstrated that American military forces could bring no lasting peace to Europe.[14] He never expressed any similarly pacifist sentiments in any subsequent American conflict. Another article he wrote for the *Michigan Daily* that summer warned of the dire international consequences that would result if the Chinese city of Hankow, critical to the country's transportation and communications network, were to fall to the Japanese.

With his language studies behind him, White heeded John King Fairbank's advice, and before departing on his traveling fellowship he struck an arrangement with *Boston Globe* publisher Laurence Winship. As he traveled through Europe, the Middle East, and on to China, White was to send occasional "mailers" for which he would be paid a minimal honorarium. He traveled to Europe in a third-class cabin aboard the *President Roosevelt*, an "old scow," as White described it. He ate and wrote his way across the Atlantic—his weight shot up seven pounds and, using the typewriter that had been Fairbank's farewell gift, he wrote page after page of the details of what he called his

13. THW, letter to Robert White, December 10, 1939, TWA, Box 1, Folder 21.
14. White, *In Search of History*, 53; THW, "The Ludlow Amendment: A Force for Peace," TWA, Box 1, Folder 3.

uninteresting life out of a wish to clarify his thinking and to record his childhood memories for pure sentiment. Erie Street, he recalled, was a happy Jewish bazaar, a street that "literally sang." But its sordid, dirty, and ugly side was equally fresh in his memory. Erie Street, he concluded, was an experiment in social adaptation. Its residents had been torn out of Middle Europe and set down "in the most vibrant community of 20th century life—America. These people were undergoing a quadruple revolution all at once; an industrial revolution, a religious revolution, a political revolution and most of all a social revolution."[15] The biggest revolution he would witness in his life awaited him—the revolution in China.

White arrived in London a week after the signing of the Munich Pact and watched trenches being dug in Hyde Park as the city prepared for war. Later, he joined thousands of Parisians on the Champs Elysées to celebrate Armistice Day. Although Germany was not on his itinerary, the shadow of its persecution of the Jews hung over White's travels. In a more somber moment, he found all Europeans hateful: "They're mean and barbarous; evil to the core. I hate them with all the blood and spirit in me; . . . Curse them! they're animals, beasts. God Bless America."[16]

White's long affection for the Zionist movement drew him to Palestine where, as he wrote to Fairbank, he wanted "to see for myself what the place looks like, whether there's a possible 'out' there for the terrific pressure on the Jews of Central Europe." He sent his first mailer to the *Boston Globe* from the Middle East: a series of impressions of the simmering conflict between Arabs and Jews, an article that illustrates the penchant for interpretation and prediction that would characterize so much of White's later work. Writing from Palestine late in 1938 as eighteen thousand British troops struggled to maintain their authority in the face of an increasingly violent Arab rebellion, White optimistically predicted their strategy "should succeed in bringing complete peace to the land by Christmas. . . . There is trouble in almost every corner of the [British] empire," White concluded, "and Palestine is at present the No. 1 imperial headache."[17] The piece earned him eight dollars and his first byline in the *Boston Globe*. With a clipping of the story that reached him when he arrived in Hong Kong, White conferred on himself the title of Far Eastern correspondent for the *Globe*.

15. THW, sixteen-page diary entry, undated, TWA, Box 193, Folder 1.
16. THW, letter to Mary and Gladys White, November 14, 1938, TWA, Box 1, Folder 6.
17. THW, letter to John King Fairbank, October 31, 1938, TWA, Box 1, Folder 12; Theodore H. White, "From a Bostonian in Palestine," *Boston Globe*, December 12, 1938.

White had come to journalism with a better education than the average newsman of his era. According to Leo C. Rosten's 1935–1936 survey of journalists covering Washington, D.C., only 51 percent were college graduates.[18] And since the Washington assignment, according to Rosten, generally was earned by competence and seniority, it is safe to conclude that nationally, even fewer journalists were college educated. Henry Luce's cadre of mostly Anglo-Saxon, Ivy League–educated men—whose ranks White was to join a few months after he arrived in China—was the exception rather than the norm in American journalism, particularly newspaper journalism. Unlike the average beat reporter whose formal education ended with a high school diploma, Time Inc. staffers were educated at America's great universities, often in the humanities and liberal arts.

On his three-week voyage from Port Said to Hong Kong aboard a Norwegian freighter, White mused at length about his future, wondering in several longhand, ungrammatical notebook entries what direction his life would take. In a remarkable bit of self-analysis, White pondered:

> What will happen to me in China? There are two ways of life open to me: A. moral—live clean, honest, peaceful, no harm to anyone. B. cut corners, make money. . . . So what? I say now I want to do these things: to live in China as a journalist. But I want to live comfortably. . . . My ideals are squirming, soft things, live and vital and honest—but unformed, unprotected by a hard shell. I am afraid I will always be in danger of compromising with comfort at the expense of my ideas.[19]

Those "squirming, soft" ideals were about to be tested. White arrived in China in the early days of 1939, the year of the hare on the Buddhist calendar. American missionaries had preceded White by about one hundred years. They had sentimentalized America's role in China and had endowed their countrymen with an emotional stake in the politics of China. Efforts to Christianize the Celestial Empire were familiar in America to Protestant and Catholic churchgoers alike, who had been asked for decades to help finance God's work in the Far East. The principal source of funds for America's Protestant missionaries, however, came not from the nation's Sunday collection plates but rather from the business enterprises, whose interest in commerce far outweighed an interest in the salvation of pagan souls. The missionaries themselves were aware that converts to Christianity

18. Leo C. Rosten, *The Washington Correspondents*, 159.
19. THW, reporter's notebook, 1938–1939, TWA, Box 50, Folder 1.

might also ultimately become converts to capitalism, and some "did not hesitate to hint that the Christianization of heathen lands would produce much commercial benefit, either because they believed this or because they wanted to stimulate business donations, or probably both." As one European observer, quoted by Barbara Tuchman in *Stilwell and the American Experience in China*, commented, the American missionaries may or may not have had an impact on China, but "they certainly made an impact on the United States."[20]

Another powerful force in fostering admiration and sympathy for China among Americans was Pearl Buck's best-selling novel *The Good Earth*, published in 1931. A warm and poignant story of a peasant family's struggle to survive nature's endless tests, the book gave Americans an uncommon glimpse of life among China's 463 million people. *The Good Earth* won the Pulitzer Prize for fiction and was part of the body of work that earned Buck the Nobel Prize for Literature in 1938. The book sold 1.5 million copies, became a Broadway play, and was made into a movie in 1937. In Depression-scarred America, this sentimental tale told by a missionary's daughter helped produce what the China scholar Harold Isaacs called "an age of admiration" for China.[21]

It was doubtless that same widespread admiration that led the *New York Herald Tribune* to engage Madame Chiang Kai-shek as a columnist in 1937 soon after the Japanese began bombing Nanking, then the capital of the Chinese republic. Using a format similar to Eleanor Roosevelt's syndicated column, "My Day," the *Tribune* published material presented as diary entries in which Madame Chiang recorded her thoughts as she visited various battlefields in China.

Those portrayals may well have contributed to the overwhelming support Americans felt for China in its struggle against Japan, which had first occupied Manchuria in 1931 and then begun an invasion of key Chinese cities in 1937. A public opinion poll conducted in 1939 indicated that 74 percent of the American people sympathized with the Chinese. Of the remainder, only 2 percent favored Japan, while the other 24 percent said they sympathized with neither side. In addition, America had a growing public and private economic stake in China, one that had roots in the nineteenth century. Indeed, in America's president one could see the embodiment of the

20. Arthur Schlesinger Jr., "The Missionary Enterprise and Theories of Imperialism," in *The Missionary Enterprise in China and America*, ed. John K. Fairbank, 345. Barbara Tuchman, *Stilwell and the American Experience in China, 1911–1945*, 188.
21. Harold Isaacs, *Scratches on Our Minds*, 157.

country's economic and emotional ties with China. Franklin D. Roosevelt's maternal grandfather, Warren Delano, was a ship owner who made a fortune in the China trade before he was thirty. Although most of his investments were wiped out in the financial panic of 1857, he amassed a second—and even larger—fortune in the opium trade by the early 1860s. Franklin's mother, Sara, sailed to Hong Kong aboard the square-rigger *Surprise* when she was just eight years old, a voyage that took four months. She made another voyage to China when she was in her early twenties. Years later, according to Franklin Roosevelt's biographer, Nathan Miller, Sara's only son "never wearied of her tales of life at sea on the long voyage around the Cape of Good Hope." As president, however, Roosevelt disapproved of the foreign penetration of China and believed the Western powers had to stop treating Asians as inferior.[22]

By the beginning of the twentieth century, the four major western European nations (France, Great Britain, Germany, and Italy) along with Japan and Russia had partitioned China's coastal regions into their individual areas of economic influence. Those so-called treaty ports or concessions were individual fiefdoms in which Chinese laws were superseded. Out of an apparent concern that these nations might prevent the United States from enjoying equal access to the lucrative China trade, Secretary of State John Hay proposed America's Open Door policy. All nations, according to Hay's reasoning, should have equivalent access to commerce and development rights in China. Hay's recommendation was sent to leaders of China's six principal trading partners in 1899 and five of the six pledged some measure of compliance—the exception was Japan. Hay announced approval of his proposal in March of 1900, and in the opening decades of the twentieth century American investments in China steadily increased. By 1936, American manufacturers, bankers, real estate interests, and utility companies had invested nearly $300 million.[23]

By 1939, when the *Boston Globe*'s self-appointed Far Eastern correspondent arrived in Hong Kong, there was widespread interest in China all across America, even though a deepening isolationist fervor was taking hold as Europe moved closer to war. White quickly made his way to Peking—then under the control of the Japanese—where he spent two months engaged in additional language studies. Away from the language school classroom,

22. *The Gallup Poll: Public Opinion 1935–1971*, 1:159; Nathan Miller, *F.D.R.: An Intimate History*, 13; Tuchman, *Stilwell*, 239.
23. Jonathan Spence, *The Search for Modern China*, 382.

he pursued his fledgling career in journalism, regularly attending press conferences at Japanese army headquarters.

In April 1939, the *Boston Globe* published another of White's mailers, this one datelined Shanghai. In it, he speculated on the likelihood of a Soviet-Japanese war and concluded that it depended entirely on the emerging political situation in Europe. "In the opinion of the Japanese Army, a Russo-Japanese war in the Far East this Spring depends solely on the European situation. . . . The Amur Valley simmers," White wrote, "as it has for almost a decade, with restrained hostility, but the Amur Valley, like the rest of the world, waits upon decisions made in Berlin."[24]

On a stop in Hong Kong in March 1939, White followed the advice of friends and made inquiries about a position with the Chinese government. To his great surprise, he was hired immediately and sent to Chungking to work in the Ministry of Information, where he assisted in the preparation of news for release in America.[25] The nine-month interlude that ensued marks a brief but fascinating period in White's professional career, a period when he was simultaneously a propagandist for the Chinese government and a correspondent for several major news organizations. Here again, White's career is a window through which to examine the professional behavior of journalists. Although contemporary journalism ethics codes would doubtless judge White guilty of ignoring the commandments of his profession in simultaneously serving two masters, those same codes are silent on the issue of alternating one's service to those same masters. In the decades between White's employment with China's propaganda ministry and the 1990s, journalists have played alternating roles as observer of government and servant of government. Benjamin Bradlee is one of the more noteworthy examples—in Paris in the 1950s, he worked first for *Newsweek* and later for the U.S. State Department in the American Embassy. Before Pierre Salinger became White House press secretary in the Kennedy administration, he worked for *Collier's*, and after its demise he joined the U.S. Senate Rackets Committee during its investigation of Teamsters' boss Jimmy Hoffa. After the Kennedy assassination and an unsuccessful campaign for public office, Salinger became a correspondent for the American Broadcasting Corporation.

24. Theodore H. White, "Russo-Japanese War Now Just a Remote Possibility," *Boston Globe*, April 28, 1939.
25. THW, letters to Dean Hanford, July 30, 1939, and August 6, 1939, TWA, Box 1, Folder 19.

When White joined the propaganda ministry in 1939, the Chinese were being badly beaten by the Japanese. Japan's army had set up a puppet government in China's resource-rich province of Manchuria in 1931 and later in the decade had successively taken control of Shanghai, Nanking, Peking, Tientsin, Canton, and Hankow. Following the fall of Nanking in 1938, the Nationalist government had retreated to Chungking, the city that would be White's home, on and off, until the end of World War II. "I arrived with a naivete that now, in retrospect, seems unbelievable stupidity," he wrote to a friend years later. "I was going to help win the war against the Japs. It was easy to be heroic then, for Chungking was an open, defenseless city and they bombed it day after day through the summer heat and the more we scratched and pimpled and blistered and hungered, the more we felt heroic."[26] A visitor's guide to the wartime capital published by the government billed Chungking as "a city of double celebration," but in White's descriptions of its mud, slime, and fog, there appeared to be little reason to celebrate. For more than two years, the Japanese had scored significant military successes, but in the public opinion war—where images rather than artillery made the difference—China maintained an easy lead. It was on that battlefield that White joined the fray, becoming a supervisor of five office staffers and a team of fifteen or twenty field correspondents whose work he would direct on behalf of the propaganda ministry. White's duties also gave him a voice in the censorship decisions made about the stories written by American newsmen, including dispatches written by such major figures as F. Tillman Durdin of the *New York Times* and Arch Steele of the *Chicago Tribune*.

White well understood the role he would play in Chungking. His boss, Hollington K. Tong, was a University of Missouri and Columbia University graduate who had become China's first American-trained newsman. Tong's official title was vice minister of information. In the eyes of at least one American journalist, Holly Tong not only directed all "Chungking information work" but was also "a loyal slave to Mme. Chiang," the powerful wife of China's leader.[27]

White's position with the Ministry of Information, he explained to his family, was "a queer sort of job." He would be responsible for ensuring that no valuable information inadvertently slipped out to the Japanese through foreign correspondents in Chungking. More importantly, however, he was

26. THW, letter to Philip Horton, June 8, 1951, TWA, Box 9, Folder 16.
27. Emily Hahn, *China to Me*, 84.

to "turn out the proper stories to elicit the proper and desired response in all the various circles so important to China, the American liberal crowd, the missionary–Red Cross–Philanthropy gang, the commercial men of money, etc, etc, etc." In short, the Chinese government was paying him four hundred Chinese dollars a month (or sixty-five U.S. dollars) to manipulate public opinion in America, a position which, he found, had "a peculiar Alice-in-Wonderland quality."[28] Now, he would see history being made from inside the government. Even as he took the job, however, he was hoping to land a position as a cub reporter in the United Press office in Shanghai.

One of the cornerstones of the Chinese propaganda system, White soon realized, was the care and feeding of American missionaries. While American correspondents' dispatches focused largely on the bombings, the Ministry of Information—using a dozen different channels—churned out stories of hunger, of relief work, of children and orphans in need of shelter, all targeted at those who traveled the missionary circuit and then returned to America to give lectures. "Special stories," White called them, stories designed to pluck at the heartstrings. "I was very soon recognized as not being quite the type they wanted," White recalled years later. "They liked me, and found me competent, but also cynical and garrulous so I was never elevated to any part of their major secrets."[29]

Years later White said he had wondered when he took the information ministry job if this was a way to help in the fight against fascism or whether it would "forever disbar him from American journalism."[30] But at the time, the main misgiving he expressed in letters to his family and friends was whether employment violated the terms of his Frederick Sheldon Traveling Fellowship from Harvard. However, even in his role as propagandist, he continued to pursue work as a journalist in American, Australian, and English media. The *Boston Globe,* the *Manchester Guardian,* and the Australian Broadcasting Commission regularly received White's dispatches. And indeed when John Hersey, who was about to become *Time's* Far Eastern editor, arrived in Chungking looking for a stringer, none other than F. Tillman Durdin of the *New York Times* and Robert Martin of the United Press told him the young, energetic Teddy White over in Holly Tong's office would be an appropriate choice.

28. THW, letter to Mary and Gladys White, April 24, 1939, TWA, Box 1, Folder 17; THW, letter to Dean Hanford, July 1939, TWA, Box 1, Folder 19.
29. THW, letter to Philip Horton, June 8, 1951, TWA, Box 9, Folder 16.
30. White, *In Search of History,* 65.

White was initially skeptical about this "young milking lad" on a tour of Chungking. Although he and Hersey soon cemented an enduring friendship, White was initially suspicious of this inexperienced young man who, by an accident of birth, would never confront the hardships that had rutted White's own path in life. In his mind, class and religion had conferred on Hersey privileges that were denied to the sons of impoverished Jewish immigrants. In a letter to his family, White expressed his seldom-voiced envy of the ease with which the well born established their place in the world—a feeling that continued to burden him despite his own considerable successes. Hersey, he wrote, would be *Time*'s Far Eastern editor because "he had the right kind of parents and the right kind of luck; and in addition to the fact that he went to the right kind of schools, he is very good looking, and tall and very attractive personally."[31]

Time hired White in June 1939, with the understanding that he would be paid for material used from the weekly political analyses he would mail to New York from Chungking. With his long, richly detailed dispatches, White soon ranked among *Time*'s most garrulous correspondents. His editors made no stipulation that he quit his post in Hollington Tong's office. And although Tong approved of his connection with *Time*, he insisted on seeing all White's reports before they were mailed off to New York. "Quite fair from his viewpoint but not so fair from ours," White wrote to Hersey. "It would be a mistake, I realize now, to paint the Chinese as white as angels or to portray the future of this war in too-roseate terms; it would lay the people of the States open to disillusionment that they have suffered in several outstanding cases."[32] Unfortunately, the American people were being disillusioned again, and White was about to become a contributor to that disillusionment.

Years later, Hersey said he doubted that White knew much about professional standards in those early days of his career. "Teddy was a youngster, not long out of college when I arranged for him to be a stringer for *Time*, and though he had already made friends with some of the journalists in Chungking at the time, I wonder whether he had much chance to come to understand, or even wonder about, professional standards of journalism." Hersey said, however, that White's arrangement with *Time* was unique. "I dare say it was most unusual for a correspondent of an American journal

31. THW, letter to Mary and Gladys White, June 2, 1939, TWA, Box 1, Folder 18.
32. THW, letter to John Hersey, July 21, 1939, TWA, Box 3, Folder 1.

to be working for a foreign government, and it may have been a blind spot on my part to suggest that he string for the magazine I worked for."[33]

In an early letter to David Hulburd, who, as chief of *Time*'s news bureau, was his boss, White had already confessed his commitment to China and its cause: "The chief fault that you are liable to find with my production is a pro-Chinese bias and a Chinese enthusiasm." That bias, however, apparently meant little to *Time*, for the magazine frequently used material from his weekly reports as background in its streamlined accounts of events in China. Both Hulburd and Hersey expressed delight with his work in letters to Chungking. In a demonstration of their approval, within two months White's stipend was sweetened. In place of the ten-dollar honorarium that *Time* originally paid for each of his thousand-word dispatches, the magazine put him on a monthly retainer of twenty-five dollars and promised him an additional minimum of twenty-five dollars for his weekly backgrounders. He was, as he wrote to his family, "aces high" with *Time*—the only other *Time* correspondent on retainer was the man in Berlin, he told them.[34]

Driven in part by a sense of loyalty to China, and in part by his continuing need for money, White remained with the information ministry, even when the job became tiresome and troublesome, as it did following his five-week trip through central and northwestern China in the fall of 1939. Few reporters had ever ventured to Sinkiang, which White described as "the most romantic spot in Central Asia," and where he learned that Soviet troops had invaded and occupied the ethnically mixed province in which the Chinese were a minority. With Moscow in control of its oil and mineral resources, the region had become a virtual Soviet buffer state. Japanese aggression, however, had locked Moscow and Chungking in an unlikely alliance during the 1930s. Aware that Japanese expansion in China had not only diminished the threat of Japanese aggression against the Soviet Union but also weakened the Kuomintang's offensives against the Chinese Communists, the Soviet Union had come to Chiang's aid. In a Sino-Soviet nonaggression treaty signed in August 1937, the Soviet Union agreed to refrain from participating "in any communistic activity in China which was antagonistic to the present Chinese government" and promised to "lend no support to any independent communistic Chinese military forces." In

33. John Hersey, letter to the author, February 1, 1993.
34. THW, letter to David Hulburd, June 9, 1939, TWA, Box 3, Folder 1; THW, letter to Mary and Gladys White, October 31, 1939, TWA, Box 1, Folder 21.

1938 and 1939, for example, Joseph Stalin had approved a total of $250 million in loans to Chiang's Nationalist government. White returned to Chungking, anxious to write to *Time* about the events that he alone had uncovered in Sinkiang. Hollington Tong, however, forbade it, warning him, "if anything is printed, we'll deny it." In a letter to Fairbank back at Harvard, White explained the basis of Tong's objections: "The whole story is that China today cannot afford to jeopardize Russian aid by letting anything be printed about Russia's position in China."[35] Reluctantly, White kept his silence.

He was, however, able to write about a subsequent trip, a six-week journey to northwestern China to cover the war fronts for *Time*. On a leave of absence from his job in the information ministry, White made his way by bus, rail, and horseback to towns behind the Japanese lines—Sian, Loyang, Paochi, and the Shansi front—the last reaches of interior northern China free of Japanese occupation. En route with the Chinese horse cavalry, he discovered what he called the "pure Chinese," those unadulterated by the Western influences that characterized residents in China's port cities. In the remote provinces the Chinese were not surrounded by Europeans as they were in the port cities; they had not been educated in American universities. Nonetheless, the people he encountered along the way clearly understood the importance of America to their well-being. White discovered "the name of America is a key to every door of China." In one town, school children were called out to the streets to greet him with songs. Banners in Chinese and English underlined that enthusiasm: "Welcome to the American Journalist, Mr. Theodore H. White. Friend of the Resistance."[36] White was, indeed, a friend of the resistance.

One of the many reports White wrote about that trip earned him a highly rare credit line on the pages of *Time*; it was said to be the first time that the magazine ever gave a special correspondent a byline. In an unusually long story about the Chinese victory over Japanese troops in northern China's Shansi Province, *Time* described how White was "the first white man to visit parts of the province in 15 years." White's article, which appeared in *Time*'s December 18, 1939, issue, concluded with an observation that might have been written in Hollington Tong's office: "The present Chinese Army has

---

35. Joseph E. Davies, *Mission to Moscow*, 134; Robert C. North, *Moscow and Chinese Communists*, 183; THW, letter to John King Fairbank, November 28, 1939, TWA, Box 2, Folder 6.
36. THW, letter to Mary and Gladys White, November 16, 1939, TWA, Box 1, Folder 21.

spirit. It glows. The men are willing to die. They mix and tangle with the
Japanese with a burning hate that is good."[37]

White had been in China almost a year when he wrote those words,
and by then it was clear to him that he would never return to Boston and
teach history as he had imagined when he left home in 1938. *Time* notified
him that his monthly retainer was to be increased. So, on the same day
that his byline appeared in *Time*, White put aside his fears that leaving the
publicity bureau would be construed as "running out" on China and wrote
Hollington Tong a letter of resignation. Although he felt "bound by the
ties of duty and affection," he said ethical considerations demanded that
he leave the payroll of the Chinese government if he was to be a journalist
for *Time*:

> I have eased my conscience by telling myself that I will be a far more
> eloquent friend of China and one with greater professional integrity if
> I wrote of China, as I feel about China in *Time*'s columns as a journalist
> unattached to the payroll of the Chinese government. It would be unfair
> to *Time* magazine to offer to write for them on a permanent basis and
> yet allow my name to be found on the Chinese government's list of
> employees.[38]

The magazine had increased his retainer following the trip, but nowhere
in all the congratulatory correspondence that passed between White and
his editors in New York was there any demand that he quit his work as
a propagandist. In casting his lot with *Time*, White—in the eyes of some
observers—had left the employ of one propaganda agency only to land in
another.

37. White's rare byline in *Time* is mentioned in W. A. Swanberg, *Luce and His
Empire*, 184; Theodore H. White, "Eagles in Shansi," *Time*, December 18, 1939, 22.
38. THW, letter to Hollington Tong, December 18, 1939, TWA, Box 1, Folder 22.

Chapter Two

· · · · · · · · · ·

. . . **The Making of a** Time **Man**

That's exactly it . . . that's the function of

enlightened journalism, to lead, to put in

what ought to be.—Henry Luce

White became a *Time* employee just a few months after the magazine had named Generalissimo and Madame Chiang Kai-shek its "Man and Woman of the Year." Skepticism had characterized *Time*'s initial appraisal of Chiang when he had assumed leadership in China in 1927. He had first appeared on *Time*'s cover on April 4 of that year, and although the accompanying article praised the new generalissimo's success in uniting China, it included a cautionary warning about his ties to Communists: "His purpose is to accomplish, by *any* means (including Bolshevism where prudent) all that is implied by the threadbare but kindling phrase 'China for the Chinese.' " Other articles in those early years were similarly lukewarm. Chiang was, for example, chastised as temperamental and for having a "mind as changeable as a woman's" in a 1929 article. Later he was scolded for his failure to halt the growing Communist movement in China. However, when Chiang converted to Christianity in 1930, *Time* took one of its familiar verbal flights of fancy and hailed him as "the most exalted man in China."[1] Applied to China's leader in the early years of his rule, the descriptive phrases that were *Time*'s stylistic trademark applauded Chiang as "stalwart" and "full of cogent wisdom" or derided him as a "pygmy" and "high strung."

White's new boss, Henry Luce, had become a national voice by the late 1930s, one whose conservative-centrist ideas on foreign and domestic policy were to become a model of mainstream thinking in the years of postwar consensus. The reach of his magazines made him a genuine American press lord at a time when the great press lords of a prior century had left their empires to a new and often less colorful generation. Luce, like Pearl Buck, was a "mishkid," the child of Presbyterian missionaries who had grown up in China. His father, Henry Winters Luce, had forsaken an opportunity for the comfortable life of a lawyer in Scranton, Pennsylvania, the prosperous mining center where he had been born. The elder Luce was drawn instead to theology and saw in the vastness of China "an unparalleled opportunity for conversion." Luce and his wife went to China in 1897, and their first child was born there the following year. In his missionary work, Luce was part of a movement that beheld China as a laboratory in which to establish the virtues of America's "sentimental imperialism."[2] The elder Luce went to China to convert its heathen hordes and worked to create Christian schools and colleges to accomplish his mission. China and its salvation became his son's mission, too. But Henry Robinson Luce believed he had to save China not from the false gods his father had sought to vanquish, but from its Japanese invaders. Luce was already using his magazines in the service of that mission when White joined his staff in 1939.

Although it is impossible to measure to what degree, White's notions about the role of a reporter in a democratic society were surely influenced by Luce. *Time* was fifteen years old when White became an employee. Luce's success with *Fortune* in 1929, followed by the spectacular triumph of *Life* seven years later, elevated him to the ranks of an American powerhouse, a man whom presidents and policy makers were careful to court. An abiding faith in American capitalism and the missionary zeal cultivated during his childhood in China made Luce determined to stamp his values and viewpoints on the American public through his magazines. When his frustrated Washington bureau chief, Felix Belair, berated Luce for his dogmatism and

1. *Time,* April 4, 1927, 18; November 18, 1929, 34; November 3, 1930, 25.
2. James L. Baughman, *Henry R. Luce and the Rise of the American News Media,* 9. Fairbank, *The Missionary Enterprise,* 138.

for using his magazines to tell readers not what was, but what he believed ought to be, Luce excitedly insisted, "That's exactly it, Felix." Enlightened journalism was supposed to lead. In writing "what ought to be" rather than what was, Luce maintained, his magazines were fulfilling the noblest tradition of journalism.

From the beginning, Luce had also scoffed at the notion of objectivity, calling it a myth or fad. Objectivity, the magazine declared in its twenty-fifth anniversary edition, tends "to kid the reader into a belief that he is being informed by an agency above human frailty or human interest." Nor did the magazine attempt to be impartial. "Fairness" was its goal, Time declared. "What's the difference between impartiality and fairness? The responsible journalist is 'partial' to that interpretation of the facts which seems to him to fit things as they are. He is fair in not twisting the facts to support his view, in not suppressing the facts that support a different view."[3]

Only on rare occasions did the magazine use its correspondents' verbatim accounts of events on the world scene. More typically, Time's newswriters synthesized those dispatches with material from other resources to produce the reports that appeared in the magazine. Time had originated the idea of summarizing the news for "busy men" in March 1923, in its first issue. In its early years, Time writers simply rewrote articles from newspapers, recreating abbreviated summaries of the news for its own columns in a narrative, story-telling style. Later, the magazine developed its own research staff whose work supplemented correspondents' dispatches. By the time White became a Time correspondent, the magazine was establishing its own worldwide news-gathering organization, which provided original material used by its staff writers—along with press association and newspaper reports and material assembled by the magazine's research team—to produce the distinctive weekly summaries of world events. With several noteworthy exceptions, White's often lengthy dispatches from China were not published in their original form. They were instead processed into narrative, Time-style reports, just as dispatches from the magazine's correspondents in Moscow, Tokyo, Paris, Berlin, and other international capitals were.

There appears to have been no discernible change in Time's "interpreta-tion of the facts" in China after White had quit his job in Hollington Tong's office. Indeed, in tone and style there is little to distinguish the magazine's China coverage in the final months of 1939 from its subsequent tone after White left the information ministry. Echoing the same praise for the spirit

3. *Time*, March 8, 1948, 66.

of the Chinese army, several months after White's return from Shansi, the magazine applauded Chiang Kai-shek much in the way that White's bylined dispatch had:

> Generalissimo Chiang Kai-shek's Government is one-party, his author-
> ity total. His People's Political Councils are scarcely more representative
> than Adolf Hitler's Reichstag. But what sets China apart from stock-in-
> trade totalitarian states and what has kept the people of Britain, France
> and the U.S. behind her is that China wants to be a democracy. . . .
> Chiang Kai-shek believes his people must hang on the vines a little
> longer before they will be ripe for democracy.[4]

Similarly, in a lengthy dispatch written in July 1940 to mark the third anniversary of Japan's aggression against China, White described Chiang as "the symbol of unity, idol of the people" and praised "his fragile, energetic, moral wife, whose New Life Movement supplied China with its backbone of courage." In his private, unpublished notes, however, White reflected on Chiang's other dimension: "He is a man of shrewdness but not deep understanding," White wrote of Chiang in July 1942 after attending a grad-uation ceremony at Chungking's Central Training Academy, "in many ways a great man and also still a goddamned ignorant superstitious peasant."[5] And in his private correspondence, White derided Madame Chiang's New Life Movement as simply another instrument through which the government could exercise its iron-fisted control over the people.

On the fourth anniversary of Japan's 1937 assault on China, White's report to *Time* extolled China's army and made one of the magazine's frequent pitches for American aid. "China's best troops belie all the old saws about Chinese cowardice and indifference. These are husky, shaven-pated sons of the soil who, when they must, storm concrete casements with nothing but hand grenades. . . . Chinese officers of the line think they could achieve success . . . but they are still forced to fight an 18th-Century war without even having the 18th-Century weapon, artillery."[6]

Certainly China's wartime censorship restrictions limited what might be written. By the end of the war, White joined with other correspondents in Chungking to protest the draconian limits Chiang's government imposed

4. *Time*, April 22, 1940, 31.
5. *Time*, July 8, 1940, 23; THW, notes dated October 4, 1942, TWA, Box 55, Folder 18.
6. *Time*, June 16, 1941, 25.

on dispatches from Chungking. Early on, however, he appeared to have a measure of sympathy for the censors' lot. Although White had complained about the limits Tong had placed on him before he quit the propaganda ministry, not long after he left that job, White seemed to pardon China's censors in a dispatch to *Time*. "It is difficult to develop the same type of hatred of censorship in Chungking that may exist in European countries. . . . The rigid and annoying cable censorship that prevails on all the wires is offset to some extent by clever policy in treatment of foreign correspondents." The publicity board, White's dispatch explained, fed and lavishly entertained the foreign correspondents, reasoning that "a contented correspondent is far less likely to turn out bad copy than a disgruntled one."[7]

White's dispatch did not reveal that government officials routinely showered extravagant gifts on correspondents as well. Years after he left China, White explained to a friend that gifts were fairly routine "because China is a gift-giving country." Americans who received those gifts, however, "kept their mouth shut about it. You didn't solicit gifts—they arrived and were loaded on you and you were a churl to [give] them back." T. V. Soong, who was China's prime minister, brother-in-law of Chiang, and a man whom White greatly admired, once sent him an ivory Buddha figurine, "one of the finest I've ever seen," after White wrote a piece about Soong. Following his marriage, White said Soong sent him a museum-quality painting that dated from the Sung dynasty. "Once before leaving China, Madame Chiang summoned me to her presence and gave me a jade medallion, bang just like that. You can't say to people like her—shove it up your ass. . . . But that was the type of gift they gave to a small fry like me."[8]

In his early years in Chungking, however, White's loyalty to China in large part grew out of his fervid opposition to fascism. That opposition shaded his work and the work of other correspondents well into the early 1940s. Certainly he was influenced by the merciless daily bombings that began each April and ended in September when fog and rain had once again made Chungking impregnable to Japanese aircraft. Because Chungking was a defenseless city, those bombings engendered a measure of hatred toward the Japanese among all who survived the brutal raids. One of the most vicious Japanese attacks came on May 4, 1939, the first such raid that White experienced. A woman's body was blown through the window of his rooms at the Friend's Mission in the city, but White was at the press office at the time

7. THW, dispatch to *Time*, March 25, 1940, TWA, Box 53, Folder 11.
8. THW, letter to Charles Wertenbaker, July 4, 1951, TWA, Box 8, Folder 25.

of the raid. Emily Hahn, whose dispatches from Chungking appeared in the *New Yorker*, explained that correspondents who endured those bombings developed "a sense of duty toward Chungking." White's sentiments were more savage: "I want to see Tokyo bombed just once before I die," White wrote to his family. "I want to know that all the babies with split heads I've seen in Chungking are somehow marked off the list as paid. I want to know that some Japanese journalist has sat on a hill outside Tokyo and seen hundreds of refugees running, bleeding and crying as they run."[9]

Those sentiments inevitably colored the dispatches White sent from Chungking to *Time*'s New York offices. Despite the wickedness White saw in Chiang's government, he continued to equivocate and even ignore reality in his news reports while his doubts were expressed in his private correspondence. In a letter to John King Fairbank, White wrote in 1939, "As for China, the longer one stays here the more confused one gets. . . . One sees behind the good and the heroic, to see the corruption, graft, intrigue, administrative stupidity, cowardice and greed of the officials. And one begins to doubt." In a subsequent letter written in March 1940, White defined the undesirable alternatives Chungking correspondents faced. "You either become a cynic completely and join the boys at the bar in their drunken haze. Or you become part of it and act. . . . We can't say what we know today, because it may injure a people who we are trying to help; and tomorrow no one will be interested in what we have to say; and it won't be true anyway."[10]

In Emily Hahn's China memoir, published in 1944, she described White as "a large part of Chungking as far as the Fourth Estate was concerned." She characterized him as "conscientious and in his work he had a broad clear field, without rivals." In an observation about White's initial reporting compared with his later work, Hahn wrote:

> He came out East full of illusions and warm hopes of the leftist party in China, and although he still holds many of his early convictions he has had to go through a period of bitter disillusionment. Nowadays I think we ought to consider Teddy as a leading expert on many of China's lesser-known territories and we can trust what he says, almost completely. Then, I thought that his reports were too highly colored by what he wanted to see rather than what he actually saw.[11]

9. Hahn, *China to Me*, 132; THW, letter to Mary and Gladys White, December 31, 1940, TWA, Box 2, Folder 14.

10. THW, letter to John King Fairbank, undated, TWA, Box 2, Folder 6; THW, letter to John King Fairbank, March 29, 1940, TWA, Box 2, Folder 23.

11. Hahn, *China to Me*, 142.

White and many American journalists in Chungking depicted China's struggle against Japan as a simplistic crusade, one that pitted democracy— or at least the promise of democracy—against fascism. As a propagandist, White had worked to palm off that idea among foreign correspondents in Chungking. Later, as a correspondent himself, White persisted—long after he knew better—in casting the conflict's major players as uncomplicated representations of good and evil. "Out of sympathy with her resistance or investment in her affairs," Barbara Tuchman explained, "correspondents, missionaries and other observers concentrated on the admirable aspects and left unmentioned the flaws and failures. . . . They overpraised Chiang and once committed to his perfection regarded any suggestion of blemish as inadmissible."[12] Recalling the war years in an interview several years before his death, White said that had the Japanese and the Germans triumphed in World War II, all of Western civilization would have been doomed. How could the journalist's role as truth-teller supplant that more compelling responsibility to serve as a defender of Western civilization? With the admirable goal of China's salvation at the root of White's purported transgressions, what is the proper yardstick against which to measure his behavior? If we believe now—as the vast majority of people did in those troubled years before and after America entered World War II—that the triumph of America and her allies was paramount, then White's professional conduct is not only defensible, it is commendable.

In an October 1940 letter to John Hersey, White explained his political transformation:

> I started off ardently and enthusiastically pro-Chinese; and I still re-main pro-Chinese, but my first ardors have cooled quite a bit; and my enthusiasms are tempered by a great many facts. . . . *Time's* philosophy is that it is the man that makes news. It's one with which I don't quite agree—but Lord God, when I think of the men who direct China, their weaknesses, their stupidities, their prejudices to the fate of the people they direct, then I'm almost convinced that *Time's* philosophy of man in relation to history is right.[13]

White's partisanship with the Chinese in their struggle against the Japanese reflected what by then had become a well-established tradition among some American war correspondents. Journalists had frequently taken sides

12. Tuchman, *Stilwell and the American Experience*, 188.
13. THW, letter to John Hersey, October 2, 1940, TWA, Box 2, Folder 23.

in the conflicts they covered; whether it was out of expediency or ideological commitment, the result was the same. In the Spanish-American War, for example, journalists became partisans to the degree that some of them participated in battles against the Spanish army. Richard Harding Davis took up arms and went to the firing line against the Spaniards with Theodore Roosevelt's Rough Riders at Las Guasimas. He had taken command, "like an officer," according to the citation he was later awarded.[14] In "The Death of Rodriguez," which may be Davis's most famous dispatch to the *New York Journal*, he told the story of a Cuban rebel publicly executed by a firing squad. In Davis's portrayal, the Cubans were virtuous insurgents engaged in a noble struggle for freedom.

In the conflict that had absorbed White and his fellow students at Harvard in the mid–1930s, journalists who covered the Spanish Civil War were similarly engaged. Just as correspondents in China later believed that backing Chiang Kai-shek put them on the side of justice and liberty, American correspondents in Spain believed in the Republican cause. Martha Gellhorn, who covered the war between the Spanish Nationalists and Republicans for *Collier's*, echoed the sentiments held by many of her colleagues when she insisted that supporting the Republican cause was the only legitimate choice. Ernest Hemingway—whom Gellhorn soon married—shared her view. "We knew, we just knew that Spain was the place to stop Fascism," Gellhorn had said. "This was it. It was one of those moments in history when there was no doubt."[15]

In China, ignoring the Nationalist government's misdeeds and mismanagement was apparently essential to the cause, just as overlooking atrocities committed by Spain's Republican fighters was fundamental to the depiction of them as righteous crusaders. Later, Hemingway acknowledged to his editor, Maxwell Perkins, that the war in Spain was a "carnival of treachery and rottenness on both sides." But Hemingway, unlike White, never wrote about that dual treachery in his role as a correspondent.

Nowhere is White's dedication to China's cause better illustrated than in his role in creating the Harvard Club of Chungking in 1941. White and a group of twenty-four Harvard alumni in Chungking established the club in January 1941, intending to lobby American lawmakers to suspend trade with Japan as a way of aiding China. In a letter to T. V. Soong, who had graduated in Harvard's class of 1915, White explained how the group had elected

14. Fairfax Downey, *Richard Harding Davis, His Day,* 157.
15. Phillip Knightley, *The First Casualty,* 192.

Soong president of the new organization while White himself was serving as secretary for English correspondence. At that organizational meeting the members drafted a message urging members of Congress to use "all means short of war but powerful enough to halt Japanese aggression. . . . We appeal to you in the name of humanity and civilization." White acknowledged to Soong that it was unorthodox to elect him without consultation, but the urgency of debate in Congress over the future of American trade with Japan left the group with no alternative. The Harvard Club, White concluded in his letter to Soong, served to underline the friendly relations between China and America.[16]

In this way, White, along with many of his colleagues in Chungking, became a self-appointed policy maker, a journalist who would try to determine the outcome of events rather than simply report those events. In his chorus of praises for Chiang Kai-shek and the Kuomintang government, White was joined by a number of renowned voices both in Chungking and Washington, D.C.

The *New Republic*, for example, was as ebullient as *Time* in its applause for China's leadership. Just a month after the Japanese bombed Pearl Harbor, the magazine waxed purple about Soong. "Brilliant soldier," "financial expert and democratic statesman," "China's Alexander Hamilton," were among the accolades the article heaped on Soong. His family, the piece continued, had "the most amazing accumulation of brains and power in the modern world." Chiang was similarly exalted as a visionary.[17]

Martha Gellhorn wrote a similarly rhapsodic piece about the Chinese army several weeks later in *Collier's*. Gellhorn, who had traveled through China with Hemingway in the spring of 1941, praised the army's "surprising and thorough job of practical military education." Although Gellhorn noted that the army was the poorest paying government service, its members, she reported, were a highly committed, well-disciplined, and effective force. "Nothing but treachery could defeat them," Gellhorn concluded. "They [the Japanese] would have to find some tricky political way to win this war."[18]

Several months later, *Collier's* once again extolled the wisdom and virtue of China's leadership, claiming that it had inspired among the peasants

16. THW, letter to T. V. Soong, January 11, 1940, TWA, Box 2, Folder 7.
17. Ernest Hauser, "T. S. for Victory," *New Republic* 56 (January 26, 1942), 111–12.
18. Martha Gellhorn, "These, Our Mountains," *Collier's*, June 28, 1941, 44. White met with Gellhorn and Hemingway twice during their Chungking visit but passed up a third invitation to join them for breakfast because "I don't like Hemingway. His wife is a nice girl" (THW, letter to his family, April 1941, TWA, Box 2, Folder 26).

patriotism, unity, and the spirit to fight. "The old warlords have been swept away, and these new movements worked like lightning, cleaning up villages, stimulating towns, giving the people spiritual impetus and a new view of life and responsibilities."[19]

Collectively, then, the American press corps determined that China's cause must triumph, and their reports about events in the Far East were fashioned to achieve that outcome. No less than those journalists who covered the Spanish Civil War, these men and women in Chungking were loyalists. They believed, to be sure, that they were ministering to the cause of democracy, but in performing that service they misinformed the people whose democracy they purported to serve. In persuading the American people that Chiang was a noble and democratic leader, they helped to lift American expectations beyond the boundaries of reality. A certain naive arrogance characterized their work, for clearly, though perhaps unconsciously, they appeared to believe that the reality they created in their reports could, in fact, be realized in China. Inadvertently, they submitted to Luce's improbable dictum on enlightened journalism: They "put in what ought to be." In hindsight, it is obvious that the reality the Chungking press corps created in those dispatches could not be realized in China. The distortions in those dispatches left Americans with false expectations about China and its future, expectations that were dashed at the end of the decade when the Communists triumphed.

Although the constitutional guarantees of a free press clearly empower the media to make the kinds of policy decisions its representatives made in China, the purpose of those freedoms can clearly be sabotaged when journalists collectively decide that their work should accomplish a particular policy goal. Whether that is ever acceptable professional conduct is a question for which there is no easy answer.

For more than three years, White would continue to cast China's leaders as democratic and well intentioned even though he had clear evidence that indicated just the opposite. Despite his deep feelings for China's peasants, for example, for years White chose not to write about the abuse he saw them endure at the hands of their government:

> It's [sic] the stories that don't get out that count in this country. . . . The Generalissimo runs this country (I think—though he may be slipping) and about him are a thousand little men all running about on hands

19. W. H. Donald, "China Can't Lose," *Collier's*, September 13, 1944, 13.

and knees trying to get a pat on the head from him. The Generalissimo
will order an attack on a city and though it is impossible to recapture
a place, two generals will throw away the lives of four or five thousand
men in 24 hours trying to bear back first honors to him.[20]

The agonizing White did over a book he wrote about China for Random
House in 1940 is a demonstration of how those conflicting allegiances bedeviled him. The manuscript of that book is evidence that White's quandary
was self-inflicted and existed independent of the pressures of Luce's ideas
and opinions about China. John Hersey had promoted the book idea with
his acquaintances at Random House, and White received a small advance.
Tentatively entitled "Ploughshares into Swords," White's book, which was
never published, recounted his travels in northwest China and assessed
contemporary Chinese politics. Even before he undertook the project, White
realized its potential dangers. Writing to his sister in 1940, White sum-
marized his problem: "If I can write this book and retain my intellectual
honesty, then I will do it. . . . I could spill all I know about China, but
then I would injure China's cause in America and forever close its gates to
my future return. I could write a poor book and spoil forever what little
intellectual prestige I may have already acquired."[21]

He produced a book nonetheless. He completed it in mid–1940, but was
enormously troubled by the result. It was a highly personal narrative of his
travels and impressions of China combined with analyses of the country's
industrial capacity, its military power, and its universities. His opening
chapter, "By the Light of the Silvery Moon," recounted the savage Japanese
bombing of Chungking in May 1939, and in a subsequent chapter he
described in horrifying detail the tortures that Japanese soldiers inflicted on
Chinese peasants. He conceded that the complaints by Communist leaders
about how the Nationalists had left their army woefully underequipped to
fight the Japanese "seem to be true." White was also mildly critical of the
pervasively American character of China's Nationalist government: many of
its members had been educated in American universities. But in his description of China's leadership, White again dissembled. He praised Madame
Chiang's beauty and likened her good deeds to those of an American club-
woman. Of her husband, White wrote, "Chiang has dominated the history
of China for nearly two decades and [his] personal record is one of the most

20. THW, letter to John King Fairbank, March 29, 1940, TWA, Box 2, Folder 23.
21. THW, letter to Mary and Gladys White, undated fragment, TWA, Box 2, Folder
14.

positive and virile of any government leader today. . . . Since 1937, he has
been a national and not a party leader and today the man who symbolizes
China. . . . Perhaps the greatest compliment that can be paid him is to say
he had lived up to his responsibilities."[22] The outcome of his attempts to
protect China's relationship with America and maintain his own position
with important Nationalist news sources while he simultaneously revealed
some of the less savory details of Chinese politics left White in despair.

Believing that his intellectual and journalistic integrity was at stake, White
feared the worst. "It is not a good book," White told his family. "In so far
as it is interesting and honest, it injures China; in so far as it pussyfoots
about, it is not interesting." In a later letter he explained that he had sent
the book off to Random House despite his misgivings but added that he
was ashamed of it. "I had their contract and wanted the money; the lure of
publication. And so I sold my soul down [the] river," he wrote. "The book
is not a dishonest book. Everything I wrote in it is true, but it is only half
the truth. I painted a China in that book so pure and virtuous that anyone
who knows anything at all about it will just snicker and write propagandist
after my name."[23]

In still another letter to a business associate, White explained the bind in
which this book placed him, the same bind that many American journalists
in Chungking faced—how to tell the truth without compromising China's
efforts to defeat Japan:

> Two things I saw as fundamental to writing this book: to say nothing
> at all that might help the Japanese (and this automatically ruled out all
> military and industrial criticism): and to say nothing that might hurt the
> cause of China in American eyes (this automatically made impossible
> the telling of the rank corruption, inefficiency and stupidity that exists
> in high places in Chungking today). Whether it was ethical journalism
> or not to attempt to suppress facts of interest to the American people—I
> don't know. But I feel, and felt then, that Japan must be defeated, that
> America must help China, that anything which soured the American
> people on the Chinese cause was a disservice to democracy and all the
> suffering millions of a great nation. Mind you I did not write a single
> line in my book that wasn't true. But the omissions weigh heavily on
> my conscience.[24]

22. THW, "Ploughshares into Swords," unpublished manuscript, TWA, Box 61,
Folders 1 and 4.
    23. THW, letter to Mary and Gladys White, June 1, 1940, TWA, Box 2, Folder 10,
    24. THW, letter to Gerson Herzel, October 4, 1940, TWA, Box 2, Folder 13.

To White's great delight the book was never published, even though an internal memorandum at Random House indicated its editors liked the manuscript:

> White's writing, needing the blue pencil only lightly applied, is basically journalistic. . . . The author has almost a gossipy quality which makes for good reading. It maintains the romance of strange people (which is good for our war nerves) and yet brings these people into our personal orbit. White has a mind that cuts to the essentials, that picks out basic problems of action and thought.[25]

White's own concerns about having failed to provide an accurate portrayal of China and its politics had nothing to do with the fate of his book. Instead, concern over how publication of "Ploughshares into Swords" would affect a new book by Edgar Snow—also scheduled to be published in 1941—ultimately resulted in a decision by Random House to scrap White's book. The success of Snow's 1938 book about China's Communist movement, *Red Star Over China*, made his the more commercially promising project. So, although Random House editors believed White had written a "comprehensive and completely impartial story of China today," fears that their star author might be overshadowed dictated that White's book remain unpublished. "I'm so happy," he wrote his sister of the Random House decision. Had the book been published, he said, it "would have dogged my footsteps all the rest of my natural life." He concluded by telling his sister never to show the manuscript to John King Fairbank. In Emily Hahn's China memoir, she recounts that White told her once he had reread the completed book he "realized it was all padding except for a little bit, most of which wasn't true. A book like that isn't worth printing," White had told Hahn, "so I withdrew it." With a note of unmistakable admiration, Hahn maintained, "Very few of our fraternity would have been as honest as Teddy in like case . . . I like Teddy a lot for that decision. It marked his entry into the adult world."[26]

White first met the boss of Time Inc. nearly a year after his book project was shelved. *Time*'s New York office cabled Chungking to inform White that Luce and his wife, Clare Booth Luce, would arrive on May 6 for what became

25. Random House manuscript report initialed KB, August 4, 1940, TWA, Box 2, Folder 25.
26. THW, letter to Mary and Gladys White, October 30, 1940, TWA, Box 2, Folder 13; Hahn, *China to Me*, 143.

a sentimental journey back to the land of his childhood and a business trip to visit his growing staff, which by then included White and the *Life* photographer-reporter team, Carl and Shelley Mydans. White anticipated the visit with considerable trepidation. "It's always fine, of course, to have a chance to work in close proximity to the big boss," White wrote to his family several weeks before the Luces arrived. "But I know Mr. Luce will disagree with me politically and it will be hard to keep my mouth shut. Mr. Luce will probably also want to use me as an office boy and I don't know whether I can do that or not." With their mutual passion for China, however, Luce and White cemented an immediate and enduring bond. Around the Chungking Press Hostel, the compound where the foreign press corps lived, there was considerable speculation about how White—who habitually addressed people by their first name—would greet Luce. They decided that White most likely would walk up to his publisher at the airstrip and begin, "Hello, Mr. Luce. I'm Teddy White. Now, Harry, what we're going to do today is . . ." And that, legend has it, is precisely what White did say.[27]

Luce landed in China several months after his controversial but prescient essay, "The American Century," had been published in *Life*. America, according to Luce's essay, should provide a model for the rest of the world. Just as the missionaries of his father's generation had sought to impose their Christian God on China, Luce proposed that America's economic, social, and cultural values be imposed on the rest of the world. With its wealth, generosity, and know-how, America, Luce wrote, was duty bound to recreate the world in its own image.[28] Although Luce's essay did not receive the widespread acclaim he expected, it was a remarkable description of the world as it would emerge in the aftermath of World War II.

That, however, was still years in the future when Henry and Clare Luce arrived in Chungking after a long flight from San Francisco. Chiang Kai-shek and Madame Chiang, ever mindful of the influence and power Luce and his magazines could wield among American policy makers, honored him with personal audiences and lavish banquets. The Chinese government, White would later explain to an associate, saw Luce as a "great natural resource like a hydroelectric project or a gold mine or a fertile valley. It was something they counted on."[29] Luce's return was a joyful homecoming; a Christian government—which had been his missionary father's dream early in the

27. THW, letter to Mary and Gladys White, April 19, 1941, TWA, Box 2, Folder 26; David Halberstam, *The Powers That Be*, 69.

28. Henry R. Luce, "The American Century," *Life*, February 17, 1941, 61.

29. THW, undated letter to Joseph Liebling, TWA, Box 8, Folder 5.

century—was leading China. Now, that government paid homage to its greatest friend in the Western world.

It was Theodore White who took Luce into the streets to see the China of his youth. Together they toured Chungking's downtown marketplaces, moved around by rickshaw, and took time out only when the air raid sirens warned of an imminent Japanese attack and drove them to seek refuge in one of the city's many air raid shelters. White's Harvard-honed Chinese outdistanced his boss's language skills, which had grown rusty from years of disuse. Luce was fascinated and charmed by White, the short, energetic son of immigrants, who, like Luce, had grown up in poverty—Luce in the genteel poverty of the Presbyterian ministry, White in the gritty streets of Dorchester. White's knowledge of China and his passion for its people enchanted Luce. Witnessing the Chinese in their fight against a brutal invader seemed to convince Luce that America's future was somehow bound up with that of China, and "there was never any pretense of objectivity in *Time* columns from then on about the war in Asia."[30]

After thirteen days in Chungking, Luce told White to pack his bags and return to New York with him. White would be returning to America for the first time in three years. He soon became Henry Luce's "fair-haired boy." His first assignment was to produce a series of four stories about China and its war effort for *Fortune.*

White worked for thirty-five days and traveled to Washington, D.C., several times to compile research and do interviews for those stories. There, he met dozens of Chinese officials linked to China's defense and economic interests and to T. V. Soong. T. V., as he was known, had arrived in Washington in the summer of 1940. Soong's mission was to pry loose more American aid for China's government. "I cannot . . . recall anything sinister about that month," White wrote later. "Time Inc. had decided to throw every bit of its weight behind China. I agreed that China had to be supported and that the story of that war had to be told fully. And the Chinese threw everything into our laps." In his conversations with aides to President Roosevelt, White discovered that Soong and his minions were perceived by members of the Roosevelt administration as leading a Chinese version of FDR's New Deal, making them all the more attractive as recipients of U.S. aid. "It shocked me then for there was no New Deal crowd whatsoever in China, and certainly T. V.'s men did not qualify by any stretch of the imagination. But I imagine

30. Halberstam, *The Powers That Be,* 70.

that line was peddled all over Washington by the former New Dealers working for TV who tried to convince their maturing New Deal friends still in government that they were the wave of the future."[31]

The resulting four stories that appeared in *Fortune* in September 1940, however, further illustrate White's disinclination to reveal all he knew about China. Even in New York, where he was well removed from the censors who had made it impossible to write truthfully in Chungking, White continued to put aside the grave doubts he had expressed in so many letters and portrayed the Nationalist government as worthy. Those stories made no mention of the misperception among American leaders that a "New Deal" style government was running China. Instead, White proved that he was able to heave hyperbole with the best of Time Inc.'s wordsmiths. He wrote of Madame Chiang, "It would be impossible to exaggerate her loveliness. . . . No photograph does her justice because her beauty—aside from perfection of feature, a complexion that puts cosmetics to shame, and about the best figure in free China—is electric, incandescent and internal." Similarly, in a *Life* profile of Chiang published in March 1942, White hailed the generalissimo as China's hero. Pronouncing Chiang "an honest man," White declared, "Under his leadership China made such magic strides toward self-consciousness."[32]

Once America entered the war, the need to maintain the fictions that had been created about China became all the more important—for a while, at least. White was at his desk in *Time*'s Rockefeller Center headquarters writing about the tensions in Asia when he learned of the Japanese attack on Pearl Harbor. He was, he remembered years later, "gleeful" to be at war with Japan. He and his colleagues made airplanes with sheets of paper on which they had written, "The Japanese are bombing America," and sailed them out their office windows to the crowds of Christmas tree gawkers below. Long convinced that despite what Japanese diplomats might be saying in Washington, D.C., America would inevitably be forced to fight Japan, White was certain "it was the right war, a good war, and it had to be fought and won." Luce's father, the Presbyterian missionary who had spent much of his life trying to Christianize China, died in his sleep hours after the Japanese attack. When White offered his condolences to Luce the next day, to his

31. THW, letter to Philip Horton, June 8, 1951, TWA, Box 9, Folder 16.
32. Theodore H. White, "China the Ally," *Fortune*, September 1941, 50; Theodore H. White, "Chiang Kai-shek," *Time*, March 2, 1944, 71.

amazement the publisher was dry-eyed; he brushed aside the expressions of sympathy, saying, "He lived long enough to know that we were on the same side as the Chinese."[33]

The attack on Pearl Harbor also meant that White would be released from the increasingly uncomfortable confines of *Time's* organizational pecking order and could return to China, this time in a U.S. military uniform as a war correspondent. Back in the Far East early in 1942, White ranked as one of the elite among the dozens of journalists accredited to cover the war in the Pacific. The prestige and power of *Time* along with his status as a veteran on the China beat combined to make White a correspondent with high-level access in both Chinese and American circles. He was on a first-name basis with many of China's top officials. On more than one occasion he sipped tea and brandy with Madame Sun Yat-sen, widow of China's revered leader who had died in 1925. American Ambassador Clarence Gauss shared many of White's views about China. White considered Chou En-lai, Mao's representative in Chungking whom he had first met in 1940, as an old friend. And a number of American foreign service officers were among his newer friends. He would soon become a trusted confidant of General Joseph Stilwell, commanding general of the U.S. forces in the China-Burma-India theater. In short, he enjoyed the kind of access that later made journalists vulnerable to manipulation by American government officials.

Once again, he took up residence in the Chungking Press Hostel, a compound of four mud-and-bamboo, gray-painted buildings where he lived with every other foreign correspondent assigned to Chungking. A fluctuating population of between twelve and thirty foreign correspondents lived in the compound, which was surrounded by a bamboo fence and guarded at its single entrance by policemen. Each correspondent was assigned a small room, and although the comforts they enjoyed were unknown to most Chinese, by American standards, the living conditions ranked as primitive. White's efforts to ward off boredom included a habit of playing his trumpet first thing in the morning—a practice that irritated his neighbor, Harrison Foreman, a famous British journalist who had once explored the inner reaches of Tibet. They took their meals together in a common dining room, retreated to their rooms to write, and submitted their stories to the government censors who were ensconced nearby. At night there were boisterous parties that, according to White, were attended by "the gayest,

33. White, *In Search of History,* 154; THW, undated letter to A. J. Liebling, TWA, Box 8, Folder 25.

most cosmopolitan crowd on the face of the globe." Airmen, Frenchmen, spies, racketeers, munitions men, gamblers, and minor-league diplomats all joined with the correspondents and consumed crocks of vodka and orange juice. "It was," White wrote, "the most curious institution for the collection and dissemination of news in the history of journalism."[34]

The political situation White found when he returned to Chungking had changed little. Chiang's Nationalist government was as inefficient, corrupt, and savage as he remembered. The nation's peasants, those who survived the continuing ravages of disease and malnutrition, still lived in relentless poverty while the country's largely Western-educated leaders lived in splendor. But using the same rationale that the U.S. government used to justify its acquiescence in meeting Chiang's frequent requests for multi-million-dollar loans and military assistance, White and other journalists believed in the need to ensure Chiang's political survival. Despite his obvious weaknesses, Chiang gave China the appearance of a united front, which was essential to the defeat of Japan. Like so many others in his generation, the intensity of White's hatred for fascism allowed him to overlook Chiang's inadequacies. The generalissimo, according to the prevailing wisdom, was the only force in China capable of beating back the Japanese. That myth, however, was about to unravel.

In less than a year, White became one member of the Chungking press corps who tried, often unsuccessfully, to disclose the truth about China. The constraints of military censorship and Luce's notion that China's and Chiang's interests were synonymous created increasing tension between the two men who so loved China. Later, White would discover that after having created a false image in the public consciousness, correcting that image was enormously difficult.

White changed his mind about Chiang early in 1943 when he was one of the few Western witnesses to a famine in Honan Province. Thereafter, White became increasingly unable to misrepresent events in China. White learned that Honan's thirty-two million peasants were starving from a young diplomat in the American embassy who had quietly shown White letters from missionaries in the province who described the catastrophic dimensions of the tragedy. No Chinese reporter dared to make the trip—criticizing the government could destroy one's career, if not one's life. So White, accompanied by Harrison Forman of the *London Times,* flew to northern China, took the Lunghai railway to Honan, passing through Japanese artillery fire

34. THW, draft of unpublished Press Hostel story, Box 60, Folder 70.

along the way. In normal times, wheat, corn, soybeans, millet, and cotton grew in the province's fertile soil. However, a drought had withered those crops in 1942, and by the winter of 1943 the people were dying.

For two weeks, White encountered the grisly effects of famine. Hundreds of gaunt and emaciated peasants crowded into the Tunghseintien railway station, huddled in the cold and waiting to board the boxcars that would take them from their drought-stricken homes. As he traveled by handlebar car to the provincial capital of Loyang, White saw the frozen and occasionally mangled bodies that had fallen from the passing trains. From Loyang, he set out on horseback with an American Catholic missionary from Iowa. Most villages were deserted, but in those that were not, White heard the dying cries of abandoned babies and saw dogs digging bodies from sandpiles and eating the flesh from corpses. There were reports of the living eating the dead and of starving parents selling their babies. White's horror soon changed to indignation, however, when he concluded that although nature had inflicted this famine, it was the government that had let these people die. Military and civilian officials had continued, despite the famine, to impose heavy grain taxes, and although there were surpluses elsewhere in the country, none had been sent to Honan in time to avert this catastrophe. Thus, through a combination of miscalculation, neglect, and indifference, an estimated two or three million peasants died of starvation.

White poured his wrath into a story for *Time.* Inexplicably, most of his outrage-filled report, which he sent from the first telegraph station on his route back to Chungking, reached New York uncensored. When it appeared in *Time* in March 1943, Madame Chiang, who was in the United States on one of her extravagant cross-country fund-raising trips, asked Henry Luce to fire White. Luce refused, "for which I honor him," White noted in his biography.[35]

To his great credit, White desperately sought help for the people of Honan after his return to Chungking. To anyone who would listen, White poured out his fury on behalf of China's starving peasants. "I began to burn up everyone I knew," he wrote to a friend. In White's unconcealed disgust, there was an echo of the lessons his Socialist father had tried so hard to teach him. "It makes you almost mad when you realize how the rich cheat the poor and how the army steals the grain and how no one gives a good goddam about death."[36]

35. White, *In Search of History,* 154.
36. THW, letter to Annalee Jacoby, May 3, 1943, TWA, Box 4, Folder 21.

Aware though he was that his role as the self-appointed savior of Honan's peasants overstepped the boundaries of his professional role, White was unable to quiet his rage. He badgered officials at the American Embassy to help. "Something must be done," he wrote in an entreaty to Madame Sun Yat-sen imploring her to intercede with her brother-in-law, the generalissimo.[37] He beseeched China's defense minister and pleaded with the head of the nation's legislature to get relief supplies to Honan. Apparently stung by his charges that corrupt government officials had exacerbated the famine in Honan, Chinese leaders in Chungking countered that White was a Communist. "Before I knew it, my God, the town was up in arms against me." In a letter to his editor at *Time*, White explained how he "started raising hell" and conceded, "I know it is not my place to create free public opinion or constitute myself as a one-man free press. But I had to do something." Finally, at the insistence of Madame Sun, Chiang agreed to see White.

Seated in the long, dark room where he traditionally received visitors, the generalissimo stroked his chin and betrayed no emotion as he listened to White's harangue. Describing the scene, White wrote, "I gave him the works, [I] told him of how corrupt his government was," deliberately oblivious to how indecorous it might seem for a foreign correspondent to berate a head of state. Chiang grunted occasionally but then he tried to deny White's allegations. "First he didn't believe my story about the dogs digging bodies out of the sand. Then I made Harrison Forman show him the actual pictures. . . . That woke him up."[38] Heads began to roll, White reported to his editors in New York. The censor who had let his dispatch slip through went to prison.

In an apparent response to White's famine story, trainloads of grain began arriving in Honan Province, soup kitchens were opened, and millions of Chinese dollars poured in from Chungking for famine relief. But the Nationalist government also took steps to ensure that embarrassing stories would be kept hidden in the future. In May 1943 the government imposed new regulations forbidding any Chinese to give information to a foreign correspondent unless authorized to do so by the government. In addition, measures were taken to discourage travel by foreign correspondents and to punish those Chinese who disclosed information about conditions outside Chungking. As a result, White and other correspondents organized a press association—with drama critic turned war correspondent Brooks Atkinson

37. THW, letter to Madame Sun Yat-sen, April 2, 1943, TWA, Box 4, Folder 20.
38. THW, letter to David Hulburd, April 15, 1943, TWA, Box 3, Folder 24.

of the *New York Times* as its chairman—to protest the new restrictions, but since the Chinese government did not regard the group as legal, working conditions continued to worsen for the Chungking press corps.[39]

With censors constraining any attempt to write candidly about China's internal political turmoil and Luce's editors on the foreign desk beginning to question the accuracy of White's dispatches, he turned to the battlefields, which ironically became a kind of safe haven. Combat was a relief from the frustrations of Chungking politics and from the relentless haggling with his editors. He flew supply missions over the Hump with the Air Transport Command, an airlift over the Himalayan Mountains that began in April 1942 after the Japanese seized the Burma Road and blocked China's land supply route. Later, he flew on Air Force bombers as they raided Hong Kong, the Hainan Islands, Burma, and Formosa. The daring and valor of the American soldiers made great stories, and White found their comradeship a refreshing antidote to the intrigues that surrounded him in China's capital. White flew so many dangerous bombing missions that he was awarded the Air Medal for "meritorious achievement in aerial flight."

On his intermittent trips back to Chungking, White continued to fret over the welfare of the Chinese people, as he had done after witnessing the Honan famine. Less than a year after that story had made him a pariah in Chungking, White once again sought help from his influential friend, Madame Sun Yat-sen, with whom he occasionally shared a glass of brandy and his books by Ernest Hemingway and Somerset Maugham. Having learned from an American doctor who made Friday afternoon calls at a tuberculosis clinic in Chungking that the electricity was routinely turned off in the city's downtown area, hampering her work with the patients, White asked Madame Sun to intercede. "I am shamefully sorry that I bother you so frequently about small matters," White wrote to Chiang's sister-in-law. "But it was really your intercession that got the Honan famine straightened out last spring and saved thousands of lives. And the tuberculosis rate is so bad, and so many of my friends' families are suffering of it that I would like to see everything possible done to mitigate the plague."[40]

On a visit to New York during the spring of 1944, White pushed Luce to tell the real story about China. White was convinced that Chiang's command "hindered rather than helped our war against Japan. The s.o.b. was not only wasting millions of Chinese lives, for which I wept, but the bastard was

39. "Chinese Censorship and the Foreign Press," *Amerasia*, March 3, 1944, 67–68.
40. THW, letter to Madame Sun Yat-sen, January 24, 1944, TWA, Box 4, Folder 20.

causing thousands of Americans to expose themselves to danger, thousands to die." With his anger over the Honan famine still unassuaged, White wrote, "*Life* Looks at China," an attempt to correct some—but clearly not all—of the misguided impressions of China that he had earlier helped to create. After considerable wrangling, Luce approved a story that condemned Chiang's Kuomintang government but avoided any condemnation of Chiang himself. The Kuomintang, White wrote, combined "the worse features of Tammany Hall and the Spanish Inquisition." The article, as White described it to an associate years later, suggested "that Chiang was OK but the guys around him were bad, that if only he would reform his government we would love him."[41] White's article marked one of the last occasions on which Luce would let his Far Eastern correspondent have his say on the deteriorating political situation in China.

Even then, however, unimaginable though it may seem, White's diary entries indicate he still felt some compulsion to protect Chiang. In September 1944, for example, he spilled his fury at Harold Isaacs into a long diary entry. Isaacs, then a correspondent for *Newsweek* in China, had criticized White's *Life* article as "dishonest" and a "whitewash." It would be impossible, White lamented, to write an attack on Chiang. "I was furious. I refuse to accept his morality; . . . I believed what I said; I did not stress his overwhelming faults because now is not the time. My job was to give the American people some facts to work with. It's impossible for me to write as a revolutionary with the facts and theories as they are now."[42]

Once he returned to Chungking, White's growing disenchantment with Chiang inevitably led to disenchantment with *Time* and its editorial policies. Increasingly, his dispatches were heavily edited and sometimes changed altogether. Late in 1944, White hung over his desk in the Chungking Press Hostel a sign that read: "What is written in this office has no relation to the things that appear in *Time* magazine."[43]

And in the Chinese capital, the Nationalists increased pressure on White and other journalists whose stories cast increasing doubt on the integrity of Chiang and his government. In a crude effort to discredit dissident members of the foreign press corps in Chungking, a book by a Chinese newsman in the capital attacked certain American and British journalists whose stories had

---

41. Theodore H. White, "*Life* Looks at China," *Life*, December 18, 1944, 39–40; THW, undated letter to A. J. Liebling, TWA, Box 5, Folder 8; THW to Liebling, Box 8, Folder 25.

42. THW, diary entry dated September 9, 1944, TWA, Box 193, Folder 2.

43. Halberstam, *The Powers That Be*, 79.

provoked displeasure in government circles. Thomas Chao, an American-educated, Chinese newsman who was Reuters bureau manager and some-one White had once respected, portrayed Chungking's foreign press corps as "whoring, drunken ignorant men" whose lifestyles made the veracity of their dispatches suspect. The inflammatory book is an illustration of the lengths to which Chiang's government went to silence its critics. A top member of China's Ministry of Information wrote the introduction, which pilloried representatives of the Associated Press, *Life*, the *London Times*, and the *Manchester Guardian* along with White, who, according to Chao, "has little talent but esteems himself highly." Chao claimed that *Time*'s man in Chungking had grown fabulously wealthy by stealing from his expense account and that he sunbathed nude on the Press Hostel lawn—a practice that allegedly offended his colleagues.[44] White contemplated suing for libel, but put aside the idea because he thought the case would drag on for months in the courts.

By late 1944, as White struggled to temper the glowing image he had helped to create for Chiang and the Nationalist government, Chungking represented only one of the fronts on which he did battle. The other front was in New York. Not long after John Hersey had hired White as a *Time* stringer in 1939, Luce hired Whittaker Chambers, onetime member of the American Communist party and courier for Soviet military intelligence. By the 1940s, Chambers had abandoned those radical allegiances and embraced anticommunism with a fervor that soon made his name a symbol of zealotry. Chambers, who was promoted from back-of-the-book editor to foreign news editor in August 1944, believed that some *Time* foreign correspondents, either out of sympathy or naivete, were writing positive appraisals of communism from abroad. White's dispatches, along with those written by John Hersey in Moscow, Walter Graebner in London, Charles Wertenbaker in Paris, and John Osborne in Rome, were routinely altered or completely rewritten by Chambers to reflect his belief that world conquest was the Soviet Union's goal.[45]

Even Luce on occasion was forced to concede that Chambers might be going too far. Chambers believed White and his colleagues had become too enamored with the Communists. The Chinese Communists, Chambers insisted, were not the "agrarian reformers" that some observers perceived, but rather "the Number One section of the Communist International."

---

44. THW, dispatches dated October 2, 1944, and October 7, 1944, TWA, Box 56, Folder 11.
45. Baughman, *Henry R. Luce*, 145.

From Chambers's perspective, it was "a struggle to decide whether a million Americans more or less were going to be given the facts about Soviet aggression or whether those facts were going to be suppressed, distorted, sugared or perverted into the exact opposite of their true meaning." White and his fellow correspondents saw it as an unconscionable intrusion into their editorial prerogatives, and he rejoiced in the news that Hersey was said to have told Luce in a face-to-face confrontation that "Pravda gave a fairer picture of international relations than *Time* magazine. Good for Johnny." Several of *Time*'s overseas correspondents, men for whom Luce had deep respect, revolted against Chambers and demanded his removal after his attack on American correspondents in China following White's trip to Yenan, where China's Communist forces had their headquarters, in the fall of 1944. Finally, Luce relented and made a move to tame Chambers, who, Luce wrote in 1945, "has to some degree failed to distinguish between, on the one hand, the general revolutionary, leftist or simply chaotic trends and, on the other hand, the specifically Communist politics in various countries."[46]

General Joseph Stilwell had also helped to fuel White's loathing of Chiang through much of the war. In the crusty, unsentimental general, White found a soulmate who recognized that China's problems were rooted in the Byzantine machinations of its Nationalist leadership. The West Point–trained soldier, who as commanding general of the China-Burma-India theater was charged with transforming the Chinese army into a force that could aid in conquering Japan, saw Chiang as the obstacle to his success. "The trouble in China is simple," the legendary Vinegar Joe declared to White during their first interview in the summer of 1942. "We are allied to an ignorant, illiterate, peasant son of a bitch."[47] White was stunned. He had never heard anyone in the American military denounce Chiang in such harsh terms. Stilwell greatly admired the tenacity and courage of the common Chinese soldier, who, he believed, was ill-served by the country's political and military leaders.

White so admired Stilwell's intellect, patriotism, and candor that the general soon became one of his heroes. So when, at Chiang's insistence, President Roosevelt relieved Stilwell of his command in the fall of 1944, White interpreted the episode as yet further proof that Chiang was a malevolent tyrant. White endorsed Stilwell's contention that "every major blunder

46. The anecdote about John Hersey is mentioned in Whittaker Chambers, *Witness*, 498; and in THW, letter to Annalee Jacoby, undated letter written in 1945, TWA, Box 4, Folder 21. For Luce's comment on Chambers, see Baughman, *Henry R. Luce*, 146.
47. White, *In Search of History*, 134.

of this war is directly traceable to Chiang Kai-shek." In an uncharacteristically subversive move, Stilwell broke army protocol to ensure that the story about his departure was publicly told. For several days before Stilwell left China on October 21, 1944, White and Brooks Atkinson, the *New York Times* drama critic who spent the war years reporting from the Far East, were given the run of the general's headquarters and allowed to read the "eyes alone" cables he received from Washington, D.C. Years later White recalled Stilwell's invitation as a revelation. "It was my first sense of the American press as the supreme court of political appeals—that this man should violate his military oath of secrecy. . . . He wanted us to know the way it really was."[48]

Atkinson, who was anxious to write the story of Stilwell's recall away from the eyes of Chinese censors, left Chungking with the general aboard the military transport plane known as "Uncle Joe's Chariot" and carried with him White's story for *Time.* White had stood on the muddy airstrip and waved as they flew away that Saturday afternoon. "The only comparable emotional exhaustion I have ever suffered was after the death of Papa," he told his family in a letter several weeks later.[49]

The *New York Times* ran Atkinson's story on its front page on October 31, 1944. That article marked a breakthrough in American press coverage of China, according to Tuchman. Stilwell's recall, the story declared, "represents the political triumph of a moribund, anti-democratic regime that is more concerned with maintaining its own supremacy than in driving the Japanese out of China. America is now committed at least passively to supporting a regime that has become increasingly unpopular and distrusted in China," one that maintained its power with the help of three secret police services, concentration camps, and severe curbs on free speech. Atkinson characterized Chiang as "bewildered and alarmed by the rapidity with which China is falling apart," and explained that "he feels secure only with associates who obey him implicitly. His rages become more and more ungovernable and attack the symptoms rather than the causes of China's troubles."[50]

Atkinson's article opened the floodgates for American newspapers. Overnight, it seemed, the news media changed its collective mind about America's ally in China: "Every correspondent or former correspondent in CBI [China-Burma-India theater] wrote all the things he had not been permitted

48. Ibid., 176.
49. THW, letter to Mary and Gladys White, December 3, 1944, TWA, Box 4, Folder 25.
50. Brooks Atkinson, "Stilwell Recall Bares Rift with Chiang," *New York Times,* October 31, 1944.

to publish for years." Editorially, the *New York Times* characterized General Stilwell's recall as a crisis, one that required internal reforms of the Nationalist government. "It would seem that we were entitled to ask Chiang Kai-shek to take steps which would make the sacrifice of American as well as of Chinese lives as small as possible," the *Times* editorial declared.[51]

Newsweek's story on the Stilwell recall—headlined "One Man's Fight against Corruption"—paralleled the *New York Times* account. "Any interpretation of the recall which lays the blame exclusively on Stilwell fails to take into account the essential dynamics of the situation," *Newsweek* reported. "Stilwell fought a losing battle against inertia, corruption, inefficiency, and questionable motives." The *New Republic* declared that Stilwell's recall "can only be considered a defeat for democratic hopes and aspirations with regard to China. . . . Chiang has proved himself unequal to the task of reforming and democratizing the Chungking armies."[52]

Thoburn Wiant of Associated Press—who had been assigned to Chungking and Burma—wrote: "Democracy does not exist in China. . . . There are secret police, concentration camps and firing squads for those who dare to speak, or write, or act out of turn. For years," Wiant concluded, "China has been falling apart." The American public had not been informed, Wiant declared in the article, which appeared in the *New York Times* just one day after Atkinson's front-page story, in part because of Chinese censorship, but also "because Washington held out the hope that the mess could be cleaned up." Stilwell, according to Tuchman, had long lamented what he called the phony propaganda about China and had frequently wondered about the consequences when the American public learned the truth. The answer was simple and surprising. There were no consequences. Nothing happened. In spite of the shrill questions finally asked by the press, official policy remained steadfast.[53] The Roosevelt administration maintained its commitment to the plan to have China fill the power vacuum that the defeat of Japan would leave in the Far East.

On the pages of *Time*, the reaction to Stilwell's departure was predictably muted. Although White's dispatch—which paralleled Atkinson's interpretation of the events—made it back to the magazine's New York offices, the story that appeared was cleansed of White's criticisms of the Nationalist

51. Tuchman, *Stilwell and the American Experience,* 506; "A Crisis, Not a Failure," *New York Times,* November 4, 1944.
52. Harold Isaacs, "One Man's Fight against Corruption," *Newsweek,* November 13, 1944, 44; "Why Stilwell Has Gone," *New Republic,* November 6, 1944, 581.
53. Thoburn Wiant, "China in Dictator's Grip," *New York Times,* November 1, 1944; Tuchman, *Stilwell and the American Experience,* 508.

government. Rather than chastise Chiang as the *New York Times* had done, *Time*'s rewritten version of White's report rationalized the generalissimo's behavior and warned against insisting that he come to terms with the Communists. The story—written by Fred Gruin and edited by Whittaker Chambers—declared General Stilwell's recall clumsily terminated an embarrassing episode but not the basic situation from which it resulted. The story said China's dictatorship, which was "ruling high-handedly in order to safeguard the last vestiges of democratic principles in China, was engaged in an undeclared civil war with Yenan, a dictatorship whose purpose was to spread totalitarian Communism in China."[54] The story also praised Chiang's patience and scolded Chiang's critics. Although the Nationalists had repeatedly been urged to come to terms with the Communists, "Nobody ever urged the Chinese Communists to come to terms with Chungking." The *Time* story also criticized Atkinson's *New York Times* article and fired a shot at Edgar Snow and other correspondents whose sympathetic reports about the Chinese Communists overlooked the censorship, secret police, and concentration camps in Yenan.

From White's perspective, *Time* had printed "a tissue of lies and fabrications. They hauled in the Red menace, the Russian bogey, pandered to China," White claimed in a letter to his family. He was incredulous: how could Luce, a man whom he considered a friend, squander and so misrepresent one of the great inside stories of the war? Feeling as if he had been sold out by his own brother, White fired off still another angry cable, this time telling Luce he planned to resign. In a series of conciliatory telegrams, Luce admonished White "to keep his shirt on," and provide him with the details of any factual errors that the Stilwell story contained. With his fury temporarily quieted, White decided to stay on, hoping that "perhaps they will be forced to tell the truth in the future." What confounded him and made him shrink from the thought of leaving *Time*, he explained to his family, "is the fact that I like Harry Luce so damned much as a person."[55]

Looking back on those days in Chungking nearly forty years later, White concluded, "We were all very young ignorant men, unskilled men. . . . We lived on the slope of a volcano; we could see it steaming, record an eruption now and then, knew the landscape was heaving and all of us sensed that this volcano would blow its top."[56]

54. "China," *Time*, November 17, 1944, 40.
55. THW, letter to Mary and Gladys White, December 3, 1944, TWA, Box 4, Folder 26.
56. Walter Sullivan, "The Crucial 1940s," *Nieman Reports*, Spring 1983, 31.

An unusual gathering of China scholars and members of the Chungking press corps was sponsored by the Center for Asian Studies at the University of Arizona in 1982. Among other questions, the participants discussed whether the press had done an adequate job in alerting Americans that popular support in China for the Nationalists was vanishing and that Communist victory was inevitable at the end of the 1940s. Although White did not attend, many of his colleagues did and together they relived those convulsive days in Chungking. Their session concluded with the participants indulging in a bit of unrestrained self-congratulation. "All told," declared Henry Lieberman, a former *New York Times* man, "we did a pretty goddam good job." John King Fairbank, however, offered a more sobering assessment of the performance of those individuals who might have alerted Americans to the real nature of the upheavals in China. "We all tried but we failed in one of the great failures of history," Fairbank said. "We could not educate or communicate. We were all superficial, academics, government officials, journalists."[57]

But perhaps the most chilling assessment of all came from John S. Service, one of the key foreign service officers in Chungking who was later blamed and blackballed as one of the individuals responsible for the purported loss of China to the Communists. Service saw the profound consequences of the misconceptions that academics, government officials, and journalists helped to nurture: "If the United States had been able in 1945 to shed some of its illusions about China, to understand what was happening in that country and to adopt a realistic policy in America's own interests, Korea and Vietnam would probably never have happened."[58]

57. James C. Thomson Jr., "China Reporting Re-Visited," *Nieman Reports,* Spring 1983, 33.
58. John S. Service, *The Amerasia Papers,* 191.

Chapter Three

. . . .

. . . The Making of a
Consensus Journalist

All of us in those days entertained the illusion
that we could make events march in the direction we pointed, if we pointed clearly enough.
—Theodore H. White, *In Search of History*

The image of Mamoru Shigemitsu, Japan's foreign minister,
limping in obvious pain across the veranda deck of the *USS Missouri* seared
itself into Theodore White's memory on a late summer morning in 1945.
As Emperor Hirohito's representative, Shigemitsu was about to concede his
nation's unconditional surrender in World War II. Dressed in a morning
coat and black silk top hat, Shigemitsu had struggled up a rope ladder on
his wooden right leg and now hobbled toward General Douglas MacArthur
to sign the surrender document laid out on a baize covered table. Not a
single hand aboard the crowded battleship reached out to help the crippled
old statesman. Decades later White would still recall those moments on
September 2, 1945, with savage glee. For the rest of his life, White would
warm to the memory of having seen the Japanese humbled and humiliated.
"Hell," he once said as a smirk swept across his jowly face, "it was better than

sex."[1] Shigemitsu's pain somehow evened the score for all the maimed and dead Chinese children White had seen in Chungking after those merciless Japanese bombing raids.

White's hatred of the Japanese persisted for decades. On the fortieth anniversary of that surrender ceremony, he wrote in a *New York Times Magazine* cover story that America had mistakenly been too generous and too merciful with the Japanese in the aftermath of World War II.[2] With the ceremony aboard the *Missouri* concluded, White would soon shed the uniform and the rank of captain that correspondents held during the war, but Japan's tyranny, first against China and later against America, had made it his permanent enemy. Having grown up in a home where his mother forever rejoiced in having been born "in the good old U.S. of A.," White would never relinquish the value system that made him a patriot first and a journalist second. America's enemies would always be White's enemies whether their flags were emblazoned with the rising sun, the swastika, the hammer and sickle, or—as he perceived in a later generation—the peace symbol. He had initially found much to admire in the Chinese Communists. By the late 1940s, however, White developed an abhorrence for communism along with a powerful allegiance to the cold war consensus that limited America's foreign policy alternatives for decades after World War II. "America's best interests," or White's perception of them, framed his reportage.

Early in his career those presumed interests had dictated that Chiang be portrayed as honorable and pure. Later those same interests demanded that Chiang's misdeeds be exposed, and White did so with a zest that raised questions in conservative circles about his loyalty. Finally, those same patriotic impulses led White and so many other mainstream journalists in America to embrace the ideology of the cold war, an ideology that blinded them to the possibility that in orchestrating the nation's foreign policy agenda, the government could use the canons of objective journalism to control America's supposedly "independent" press. For much of his career, White seemed unaware that his brand of patriotism and his participation in "insider journalism" helped to create a consensus in American political life. Policy decisions were debated in private, hashed out among policy makers, and often presented by journalists to the public without debate or dissent in the press or elsewhere. Conformity was to become the norm in

1. Theodore H. White, personal interview, May 5, 1982.
2. Theodore H. White, "The Danger from Japan," *New York Times Magazine*, January 17, 1954, 18.

American life by the late 1940s, and journalists, no less than other segments of society, operated within distinct political boundaries. The citizen or journalist who strayed beyond those boundaries put his or her credibility in jeopardy. White ranked among America's best-educated journalists and, like other Establishment journalists, he was unable to see that his style of journalism helped to create a world of moral absolutes by discrediting alternatives to the foreign policy status quo. That commitment to a single set of foreign policy options—an almost righteous determination to thwart the advance of communism anywhere in the world—ultimately led America to an unanticipated reckoning in Vietnam. Furthermore, White was unable to see that members of his own government could and did use him to create illusions that harmed the nation he was so intent on serving.

Although White briefly joined that circle of diplomats and scholars who challenged the wisdom of America's inalterable support for Chiang and its strident opposition to China's Communist movement after the war, by 1950 he had cast himself not as an adversary but rather as a partner of his government. In his journalism of the postwar years, White would become the embodiment of what Daniel C. Hallin saw as "the historical trade-off" between reporters and the government they covered:

> Journalists gave up the right to speak with a political voice of their own, and in turn they were granted a regular right of access to the inner counsels of government. . . . The press was recognized as a sort of "fourth branch of government," a part of the informal constitution of the political system; and it in turn accepted certain standards of responsible behavior. These standards involved not merely renouncing the right to make partisan criticisms of political authority, but also granting to political authorities certain positive rights of access to the news and accepting for the most part the language, agenda, and perspectives of the political "establishment."[3]

Obviously, it would be unfair to evaluate White's reportage and that of his generation without considering the impact of World War II on their professional lives. There is no doubt that the existence of indisputable evils in the leadership of Germany and Japan and the habit of working with censors had an enduring impact on professional standards. Hitler and Hirohito made loyalty to America an easy assumption for journalists. The censorship of the war years had developed in them an ingrained habit of

3. Daniel Hallin, *The Uncensored War*, 8.

protecting American interests. Perhaps it was inevitable that those lessons journalists learned so well during the war years would later apply in equal measures to their postwar reporting.

Although America's war in the Pacific ended on that September morning in Tokyo Bay, White's personal battle with Henry Luce over the portrayal of China's politics in *Time* continued unabated. White wanted desperately to tell the truth about the turmoil and revolutionary ferment that was gripping China, believing that it was in both America's and China's best interests. That desire would cast him in a minor role in the last major foreign policy debate to preoccupy America until the Vietnam war. The hegemony of the postwar consensus would soon place questions about the appropriateness of accommodating Communist movements well outside the boundaries of acceptable political debate. America chose to ignore the Communist government of China after it seized power in 1949—even though it represented nearly a quarter of the world's population—just as American presidents had once tried to ignore the Communist government of the Soviet Union by refusing to establish diplomatic relations for nearly fifteen years after the Bolshevik Revolution.

Time's interpretation of events in China had continued to rankle and embarrass White right up until the war's end. Whittaker Chambers's heavy-handed editing and continuing suspicions of Communist conspiracies—all directed, he believed, by Joseph Stalin—during the year he worked as *Time*'s foreign news editor had repeatedly angered White. In Chambers's own words, "The driving force of my work at *Time* has been a sense of mission, of calling to clarify on the basis of the news, the religious and moral position that made Communism evil."[4]

From White's perspective, *Time* was instead dishonoring itself—and him —with what he now considered dishonest reporting. For months, an exchange of long and indignant cables had buzzed between Chungking and New York. White's wrath would boil up, as it did after the Stilwell story, and Luce would mollify him with yet another of those soothing telegrams reminding White of their common purpose in the struggle between democracy and fascism. "I deeply regret the pain and embarrassment you have endured in the past few weeks," Luce cabled White in a year-end message late in 1944, "and we hope that nineteen forty five will be the best year ever for you and for *Time* in our Asiatic assignment." *Time* would byline

4. Terry Teachout, ed., *Ghosts on the Roof,* xx.

his combat stories, and effusive congratulatory cables followed from *Time* editors in New York. Not long after the German surrender in June 1945, Luce cabled White, "have been much impressed by your dispatches of the last few weeks . . . now that VE day has passed the editors promise me they will get busy catching up on the subject of China. It is indeed exciting to read the phrase, 'last summer in Chungking.' "[5]

Still, the magazine's policies continued to embarrass White. Even away from Chungking, on the front with American soldiers—trips that provided some respite from his ongoing quarrels with his publisher—the magazine's policies haunted him. To America's fighting men, he told David Hulburd, "*Time* is completely valueless as a reliable news source." He had been asked to speak to a group of sick soldiers at a hospital in North Burma, White explained to Hulburd. "There were several hundred men there. They put a lot of questions to me and then one of them got up and said, 'Well, what do you think of that Stilwell story in *Time?*' I had to say that I thought the story was factually incorrect. I writhed when I said that in public."[6]

White was in Manila on the day the atomic bomb was dropped on Hiroshima; he called it "a day of terminal madness and joy." When he talked with General Douglas MacArthur two days later, the old warrior declared the bomb meant not only that World War II was over, but that all wars were over. "Men like me will be obsolete," MacArthur declared. "There will be no more wars, White, no more wars."[7]

With the Japanese defeated, White reasoned, exposing the sins of China's Nationalist leaders would no longer jeopardize the Allied cause. With that critical concern assuaged, only White's publisher remained as an obstacle to thwart that goal. But there would be no cordial message from Luce to his Far East correspondent on VJ day as there had been several months before on VE day. It seemed to White that Luce, whose emotional second home was China, had somehow convinced himself that China and Chiang were identical, and thus "any enemy of Chiang's was an enemy of China's and vice versa." The only other people who had the same idea, White believed, were "Madame Chiang, Chiang himself, and the secret police." In his preoccupation with facts and factual correctness, White thought Luce overlooked the reality that facts are like bricks and "with bricks you can build a temple to god, or you can make a brick shithouse. And in his China

5. Henry R. Luce, undated cable to THW, TWA, Box 52, Folder 2; Luce, undated cable to THW, TWA, Box 52, Folder 19.
6. THW, letter to David Hulburd, February 9, 1945, TWA, Box 3, Folder 31.
7. White, *In Search of History*, 224.

stories he used most of the facts his correspondents sent to build a brick shithouse."[8]

Luce, on the other hand, sensed in White too much sympathy for China's Communist movement, especially after he had journeyed to Yenan following Stilwell's departure from Chungking. White had traveled to the Communist party's headquarters aboard the same military courier plane that carried John Paton Davies, a bright young Foreign Service officer who was trying to determine what help the Communists could provide if American army forces landed on the coast of China. Like so many other American journalists who had preceded him to Yenan, White was captivated—particularly by Chou En-lai, who had earlier charmed him in Chungking. Although he had once disparaged Chou as the Communist's "cagy contact man in Chungking," White had become increasingly impressed by his intelligence and wit. During those weeks in the fall of 1944, White lived in the legendary caves among the Communist leaders, and he had long talks with Mao Tse-tung about China's past and future. White asked Mao about the danger of civil war in China, about how he expected the Kuomintang to reform itself, about his relations with the Soviet Union, and about American aid to China.[9]

Luce and Chambers, however, believed White, like others before him, had romanticized the Communist revolutionaries, portraying them as idealistic reformers rather than as the embodiment of evil. *Time* did not print White's dispatch from Yenan. In it White declared that the Communist party advocated democracy because, for them, democracy paid. Giving peasants the vote, the report claimed, ensured a Communist victory because the peasants voted Communist. Friendship with America, White further insisted, was another Communist priority, but its leaders sought that friendship, "not as a beggar seeks charity but seeks aid in furthering a joint cause." White left Yenan believing that the Communists held the key that could unlock China's future. Their achievements in establishing a vast chain of bases from China's coast and Manchuria all the way to Hankow overwhelmed him. It was, he wrote, one of "the greatest and most dramatic stories the world has ever known. Nothing in the history of modern war or politics equals the imagination, the vision or the epic grandeur of this move. The Long March besides [sic] it pales into nothingness. This is greatness. This

8. THW, undated letter to A. J. Liebling, TWA, Box 8, Folder 25.
9. White, "Ploughshares into Swords"; Transcript of THW interview with Mao Tse-tung, undated, TWA, Box 57, Folder 14.

is the future." White believed the Communist leaders were the kind of men who could redirect the locomotive of history for the good of others. That, too, was an illusion. Decades later, even White conceded that his report from Yenan was "in truth winged with a hope and passion that were entirely unreal." What he had been shown in Yenan, White later recognized, was "the showcase democratic artpieces they (the Communists) staged for us American correspondents was [sic], literally, only showcase stuff. But I know too that they were infinitely more effective than Chiang's form of despotism."[10]

By the time White left Yenan, Chou had entered his pantheon of personal heroes, joining ranks with his only other hero at the time, Stilwell. Later, John F. Kennedy would become the third and last member of that exclusive club. In each case, White eventually would come to realize that his idols had feet of clay. Stilwell, out of rigidity and honor, had stubbornly refused to accept the inevitably political nature of war. Behind all of Chou's intelligence and charm, White later discovered a capacity for cruelty. In Kennedy's character he also discovered some distasteful qualities, qualities that disabused White of the notion that men could be heroes. White, however, first learned those lessons long after he left China.

The weeks White had spent in Yenan in November 1944 would haunt him, just as they would haunt Davies and his Foreign Service colleague John S. Service. White's support for Davies during the long inquiry into their loyalty later cast additional suspicion on White's allegiances. In that mindless hunt for scapegoats that began in the late 1940s, Davies—who early on had predicted the fall of Chiang and the triumph of the Communists—along with other key Foreign Service officials took the blame among America's archconservatives for the triumph of communism in China.

Major General Patrick Hurley, who became President Roosevelt's personal emissary in Chungking after Stilwell's departure, made an unannounced visit to Yenan during the weeks White spent there. Hurley, a talkative, Oklahoma-born general whom White later dismissed as an ignoramus, had come to discuss a truce to end the strife between China's Nationalist and Communist forces that was about to erupt into a civil war. Drawing on the substance of his own conversations with Mao, White, concluding it was only proper to brief Hurley on the substance of Mao's statements, told Hurley that

10. THW, Dispatch No. 23 to *Time*, November 21, 1944, and a fragment of an undated dispatch, TWA, Box 57, Folder 15 and Box 57, Folder 26; White, *In Search of History*, 205; THW, letter to Col. Neil VanSickle, April 3, 1958, TWA, Box 14, Folder 22.

his mission was probably futile and that a peaceful end to the strife could come only if America recognized the de facto Communist government. As a result of that conversation, Hurley reported to the State Department that White was "definitely against the mission with which I am charged." The general, White believed, had misunderstood the code of American journalism. "Hurley expected an American reporter abroad to be an arm of American purpose, and thus I had betrayed him." Ironically, however, White was indeed a reporter who had invariably made himself an "arm of American purpose." The discord, it seems, emerged when White's vision of the appropriate purpose differed from Hurley's. The general's distrust for White grew and in less than a year he denounced White as "un-American" and called him a "goddam seditious little son of a bitch."[11]

Perhaps it was the years of distorted reporting out of China that left Americans unprepared for the realities of postwar Chinese politics and the fall of Chiang's Nationalist government. In their ignorance, it was easier for Americans to accept the notion of a conspiracy than it was to believe that Chiang, once portrayed as America's noble Christian ally, was, in fact, a cruel thug. Americans simply could not grasp the truth in White's observation that Washington had squandered an opportunity to prove to the Chinese Communists that America wanted peace and democracy in China. In failing to seize the opportunity, White warned, "all the people in China who want progress will be forced into the Communist camp and America will have created the thing it feared most: an organized mass of Asiatic peasants believing that America was their enemy and Russia was their only friend."[12]

As White had prepared to make his way to Tokyo for the Japanese surrender, he received a cable from his editors in New York that detailed *Time's* plans to feature the two heroes of the Pacific war in two successive cover stories. MacArthur was to be the first. Chiang was to be the second. White responded that he would write the story only if it accurately reflected polarization of Chinese politics and how Chiang's intransigence made civil war all but inevitable. It would be a mistake, White argued in a cable to Luce in which he spoke for himself and his *Time* colleague in Chungking, Annalee Jacoby, to further legitimize the tyrannical leader and his Nationalist government:

11. White, *In Search of History*, 201.
12. "America and the Chinese War," transcript of an NBC radio discussion, October 27, 1946, TWA, Box 185, Folder 1.

It is true, indeed, that Chiang Kai-shek is the key personality. . . . But if
Time Inc. adopts the policy of unquestioningly, unconditionally supporting his hand we will be doing a monstrous disservice to millions
of American readers and to the Chinese whose personal concern this
is. We hope that you will select facts in an impartial, judicious manner
warranted by the enormous dimensions of this tragedy. . . . If this is
determined otherwise we shall consider this a repudiation of ourselves
as reporters and will want to be relieved of the current assignment and
return home at least to put the case directly before the editor-in-chief
for final settlement of our status and China policy.[13]

On his journey from Chungking to Tokyo White traveled via Manila
where, taking the opportunity to avoid the Chinese censors, he cabled his
portrayal of Chiang to New York. The generalissimo, he wrote, shared personality traits with America's wartime Communist ally, Joseph Stalin. Like
Stalin, Chiang "permitted his government to impose upon the people one of
the most merciless and brutal of totalitarian systems." The Communist party,
he maintained, had simply capitalized on the misery of China's peasants to
create its following.[14] The intensity of Luce's anger was unmistakable, even
in its attenuated cablese format (which has been translated here):

We desired nothing except nonpartisan reporting. We realized this might
be an unreasonable request in view of your avowed partisanship. Your
cable 250 presents *Time* with a double news blackout. We are blacked
out by official censorship on one hand and on the other hand by
partisan unwillingness to report from a middle of road position. *Time's*
policy regarding China [is] exactly what you describe as nonpartisan
directed to middle road, democratic, peaceful solution. Such policy
obviously doesn't include efforts to overthrow the duly recognized president of China. . . . I suggest you make supreme personal effort to give
us nonpartisan news of Chiang in what we hope will be a week of
victory.[15]

With that, White was ordered back to New York. He left Chungking
anticipating that he would resolve his differences with *Time* and write the
"real" story about the war years in China. If Luce prevented him from writing
honestly on the pages of *Time* magazine, he would write a book, then return

13. Elson, *The World of Time, Inc.*, 141.
14. Ibid., 142.
15. Henry Luce, undated cable to THW, TWA, Box 52, Folder 17.

to China in time to witness the climax of the revolution. He could hardly have guessed as he packed to leave his rooms in the Chungking Press Hostel that his yearnings to return to China would remain unfulfilled for twenty-seven years.

In the context of the way White and other American correspondents in China had tailored coverage to affect the policy positions they deemed appropriate for America, it is appropriate to examine White's own assessment of the far-reaching responsibilities and power of a foreign correspondent in a speech he made to members of the Institute of Pacific Relations late in 1946. White dismissed the popular, romanticized image of the foreign correspondent in trench coat as Hollywood mythology. He criticized American editors for their preoccupation with the exotic curiosities in Chinese life. Stories about two-headed babies, opium dens, and eggs that could be made to stand on end during Tet, the Buddhist New Year celebration, he insisted, were geared more to entertainment than enlightenment. Because the foreign press corps functioned as an unofficial but independent arm of the nation's Foreign Service, it had a far more serious mission than to entertain readers, especially in wartime, White said. The American correspondent, he insisted, is part of the "apparatus of American foreign policy and national defense." Enumerating the special and unique responsibilities of the reporter on an overseas assignment, White claimed his role was quite different from that of a domestic reporter because no single reporter and no single dispatch carries the burden of telling the whole truth. The foreign correspondent's decisions, however, can influence whole patterns of international politics, he explained:

> It is surprising to the returned correspondent on a visit to Washington to find how greatly the members of Congress and those who enforce our national decisions are influenced by the casual dispatches turned out day after day from the overseas cablehead. Collectively, the corps of foreign correspondents sent overseas by private agencies are more important in shaping America's foreign policy for peace or war than is the diplomatic corps of the government itself.[16]

Since an abundance of facts surround the political life of any country, it is balance rather than accuracy that is the test of any correspondent's worth, he explained. Using the same logic that troubled him in his unpublished book,

16. THW, speech to the Institute of Pacific Relations, October 1946, TWA, Box 185, Folder 1.

White added that an injudicious correspondent could present a thousand facts, which, despite the truth of each one, could add up to a lie. The speech made no mention of the time when the urgency of conquering Japan had led White and others in the Chungking press corps to selectively arrange the facts in ways that resulted in the presentation of honest but misleading information.

That speech and other comments White made apparently rankled Luce. And *Time*'s reports from Chungking, written by Charles Murphy, rankled White. After White's return to the United States, he and Luce discussed the expanding gulf that separated their thinking on China. Luce insisted that supporting Chiang was crucial to its survival; White's anger would boil up and he would harken back to the grisly sights he had seen in Honan to illustrate the government's indifference to the suffering of millions of its people.

A so-called aide-memoire written by a *Time-Life* editor who attended one of those discussions between White and his publisher reflects the haggling that went on between them. "Whether or not you and Time Inc. can get along may depend now and then on getting specific agreement on specific points," Alan Grover wrote to White, "but it also depends much more importantly on mutual agreeableness of behavior." To placate White's displeasure about an article Charles Murphy had been assigned to write from Chungking, Luce proposed that White write a dissenting piece for *Life*. In exchange, Luce wanted a commitment from White that for a period of four to six weeks

> you do not dwell upon or accent, to the exclusion of other major points, the particular failures of the Nationalist Government in 1944 or go back to rehearse emotionally the Honan Famine. More especially . . . that you emphasize whatever you deem to be positive, constructive policy for America: that is concretely what do you recommend America should do?[17]

Finally, White took a leave of absence from what by then had become his ten-thousand-dollar-a-year job with *Time* to write his book. He teamed up with Jacoby, who had been his partner in the Chungking Press Hostel from September 1943 until the war's end. They were determined to be the first journalists to tell America to get out of China and leave that nation to find its own future. It was a tumultuous partnership, despite White's claim that

17. Letter from Alan Grover to THW, November 19, 1945, TWA, Box 3, Folder 32.

the "book rolled off the partners' typewriters almost by itself." They had a number of quarrels, in part because their personal and professional lives had been entwined for several years.

Soon after he returned from China, White also testified on behalf of friends in the State Department who were under suspicion of having attempted to overthrow Chiang's government and sabotage American policy. John Service and George Atcheson, another Foreign Service officer whom White had known in Chungking, had been accused by General Hurley of conspiring to promote a Communist takeover of the Nationalist government. White had traveled to Washington, D.C., as the spokesman for a group of Chungking journalists who had all known these men during their Chungking assignments. Among others, White spoke for Eric Sevareid and Jack Belden, telling the committee, "We were surprised at these charges against them . . . and we felt we should tell the Committee that we, as a non-partisan group of newspapermen, felt that they served our country as honorably as possible. I have an aversion for seeing my friends falsely slandered." A conspiracy against Chiang could never have existed without the press corps knowing of it, White insisted. Service, like the others, was simply "reporting the facts as he saw them." The fundamental question, White told the committee, is whether a Foreign Service officer should tailor his reports to reflect the prejudices of his superiors. Anyone who did that, White concluded, "would not only be useless to the United States but he would be dangerous."[18]

Meanwhile, White's friends were urging him to leave *Time*. Luce, they told him, was prostituting his own staff. "Why the hell don't you cut loose from Henry and get out from under the stigma of being kept by a guy who is on the wrong side," John King Fairbank wrote to White early in 1946. "I don't think you should take money from him. . . . We all have to choose sides these days as the tension mounts in the USA, and Luce is a man with the wrong instincts, judging by what he does editorially—he has prostituted the truth and his own staff for policy purposes."[19] The breach that developed between Luce and his most gifted staffers led many of them to resign. John Hersey found Luce's dogmatic brand of politics increasingly unacceptable and quit in July 1945. William Walton, *Time*'s daring European correspondent who had parachuted into Normandy with

18. Transcript of Senate Foreign Relations Committee hearing, TWA, Box 60, Folder 3.

19. John King Fairbank, letter to THW, February 3, 1946, TWA, Box 5, Folder 10.

General James Gavin and the Eighty-second Airborne Division on D-Day, quit to join the *New Republic* after the war. Charles Wertenbaker, *Time's* world battlefronts editor and head of the magazine's "invasion task force" that covered the Normandy story in 1944, left *Time* in 1947.

White's break with Luce finally came in mid–1946. He had returned to *Time* after he and Jacoby finished *Thunder Out of China*. It was then that Luce had demanded that White make a gesture of unquestioned loyalty, insisting that White declare his willingness to take any assignment in the corporation, "even if it meant serving on the rewrite desk in New York for a year or two." White, who had hoped that he might be considered for the Moscow post, refused to bend to Luce's will. In a parting letter to his publisher, White recalled a Chinese saying—"the finest of feasts must come to an end." At *Time*, he said, he had "spent some of the most enjoyable and certainly the most fruitful years of my life." Ever the believer in history, White concluded that the differences that divided them in their views of China would "be resolved by the course of history itself."[20]

White and Jacoby, it turned out, had written what became a best-selling book, one they believed finally corrected the lies and distortions that had appeared on the pages of *Time*, many of them in White's own name. Out from under the editorial control of Whittaker Chambers, and out from under the burden of his own perceived obligations to China, White wrote a candid assessment of Chiang and his government of China. He had undertaken the project with the zeal of a convert, determined to clear both his conscience and the historic record. Unlike "Ploughshares into Swords," this time, he wanted to serve history and correct the blemished record.

Thunder Out of China (1947) concluded that "China must change or die." The book portrayed the country as a vast land populated by hundreds of millions of peasants who, under the ruling Kuomintang government, lived in a police state. According to the book, what Hitler and the Nazis did to their enemies, Chiang and his coterie of Christian deputies were doing to their own countrymen and women. American diplomacy, White and Jacoby charged, was responsible for the civil war that broke out between Chiang's armies and the Communists within days after the Japanese surrender. The United States—which had long been an ally of the Kuomintang—needed to remain nonpartisan in China's internal struggle. "Economic aid from America can be useful only if it has one overriding condition—that it be granted

---

20. White, *In Search of History*, 248; THW, letter to Henry Luce, August 1, 1946, TWA, Box 3, Folder 21.

to a government in which the Kuomintang, Communists and Democrats all participate," White and Jacoby wrote.[21] Without some accommodation with the Communists, the book concluded, the Kuomintang government would collapse.

It was, of course, a rather different story than the one Americans had seen for so many years on the pages of their magazines and newspapers. Reviews of *Thunder Out of China* were mixed. Liberal publications applauded the book, conservative ones denounced it, adding still further confusion to the public perceptions of China. The *New York Herald Tribune* praised it as "an earnest, thoughtful and factual account of what went on in China in the war years and immediately after, which is the clearest, frankest and most combatively readable key to an understanding of that great and tormented country's current tragedy." On the pages of *PM*, Ralph Ingersoll's experimental newspaper of the mid–1940s, there was similar enthusiasm: "A happy combination of magnificent reporting and keen historical analysis," *PM's* reviewer declared. *Time's* review was ambiguous. "White and Jacoby make an obviously sincere and not wholly successful effort to be fair," the magazine declared. "Yet the same inner flame which made them such tireless reporters of the war gradually heats their indignation until it boils over in angry judgments."[22]

The *World Telegram and Sun,* part of the conservative Scripps-Howard chain, denounced *Thunder Out of China* on its editorial pages, calling it "Blunder Out of China" in a signed editorial written by Geraldine Fitch, an American reporter in China whose views paralleled Luce's judgments. Fitch's editorial, based on a pamphlet she had written in which she alleged that White and Jacoby's book contained numerous factual errors, declared, "I do not assume that the authors are Communist. . . . But they have imbibed an amazing quantity of Communist brew." The solutions White and Jacoby proposed for China, she added, were "naive and reactionary." William Sloane, the book's publisher, wrote to Walker Stone, a Scripps-Howard executive, protesting that the language of the editorial was both offensive and misleading. Noting that both General Stilwell and the Far Eastern staff of the U.S. State Department all regarded the book as first-rate, the letter admonished Stone to "stop seeing Communists under every bed

21. Theodore H. White and Annalee Jacoby, *Thunder Out of China,* 323.
22. Richard Watts Jr., "A Key to China—Clear, Frank and Combative," *New York Herald Tribune,* October 27, 1946; Philip Jaffe, "Inside Dope from China by Two Ex-'Time' Correspondents," *PM,* October 27, 1946; "Seven Years of Valley Forge," *Time,* October 28, 1946.

and do a little something to live up to the motto on your masthead, 'Give
light and the people will find their own way.' " The *World Telegram*, Sloane's
letter concluded, "has pinned the Communist label on Teddy White and he
is not a Communist."[23]

Roy Cohn and David Schine, Senator Joseph McCarthy's pair of hench-
men, later declared the book subversive and purged it for a brief time from
America's European libraries. Luce was soon denouncing White as "that
ugly little Jewish son of a bitch." Columns in *Time* occasionally referred to
White as a "pinko," and Luce once told an interviewer with the *Post-Dispatch*
in St. Louis that he had to fire Teddy White because he was a Communist. By
late in 1947, however, White began to sense a growing indifference toward
China. "No one in the whole U.S.A. gives a damn about China except Henry
Luce," he wrote to a friend late in 1947. "The country is bored to tears." Polls,
however, indicate that Americans were hardly disinterested. In a July 1948
poll, 75 percent of those surveyed said they were following events in China's
civil war. After Mao and the Communists came to power, 60 percent of those
surveyed in a 1951 poll disapproved of giving China a seat in the United
Nations.[24]

White's own concern for China, however, remained relentless. He continued to function in his role as a partner to the government's policy makers.
Driven by his sense of patriotism, White injected himself into America's
policy-making processes well after he left China and *Time*. A letter he wrote
in 1947 to George C. Marshall after President Truman recalled Marshall
from his mission to China to name him secretary of state illustrates the
apparent ease with which journalists assumed an advisory role. "What is
at stake," White told Marshall, "may well be nothing more or less than
World War III." It had been a grave blunder, White explained to Marshall,
to suppose that China was either a bridge or a buffer between America and
Russia. The problem of China, he continued, would be solved only on the
basis of what the Chinese people needed and wanted:

> The mainsprings of decision in this problem are socketed in the millions
> of tiny villages where the Chinese peasant, the raw stuff of politics,

23. Geraldine Fitch, "Blunder Out of China," *New York World Telegram and Sun*,
June 4, 1947; William Sloane, letter to Walker Stone, Scripps-Howard, June 9, 1947,
TWA, Box 6, Folder 1.
24. Halberstam, *The Powers That Be*, 85; THW, letter to Tillman and Peggy Durdin,
December 16, 1947, TWA, Box 6, Folder 8; *The Gallup Poll: Public Opinion, 1935–1971*,
2–3:728, 831, 924.

lives. . . . The peasant is neither a Communist, nor a member of Chiang
Kai-shek's Kuomintang; he is a dirt farmer who lives by the labor of
his hands and the most backbreaking, unremitting enslavement to his
fields. He is prey to superstition, ignorance, filth, pestilence, hunger. . . .
The great strength of Chiang lies in two great areas: first he has an army
that is the best China ever saw. It was created in its present form by your
great deputy, General Stilwell. . . . Secondly he has an almost complete
monopoly on the know-how of the modern world. The strength of the
Communists lies in their ideas. They have an army that is smaller than
Chiang's and pitifully equipped; but its morale is fantastically good.[25]

White's belief that *Thunder Out of China* and his oft-expressed opinions might actually change American policy in China, it turned out, was
mistaken. He could not make events march in the direction he pointed,
regardless of how clearly he pointed. White apparently never questioned
whether his early, often misleading reports from Chungking had shaped
expectations and thus helped to fuel the disappointment and debate over
who "lost" China. His diaries and correspondence offer no hint that he
ever wondered if a better-informed American public might have averted the
China debacle and the State Department purges that succeeded it.

The enormous attention *Thunder Out of China* received helped to give
White the rank of celebrity journalist. He was sought after on the radio
talk show circuit—"Information Please" and "Tex and Jinx," broadcast from
Peacock Alley in the Waldorf Astoria, were among the many shows on which
he made guest appearances. And his name made it into Walter Winchell's
syndicated gossip column, where it was incorrectly reported that White and
Annalee Jacoby were planning to be married.

The success of *Thunder Out of China* also brought White two enormously
attractive job offers—one as a correspondent for the highly popular *Saturday
Evening Post,* and the other as an editor of the *New Republic,* where the former
vice president and celebrated leader of America's Progressive party, Henry A.
Wallace, had just been named editor in October 1946. Because White greatly
admired Wallace, whom Truman had recently fired as secretary of commerce
for his outspoken opposition to the president's foreign policy decisions, he
chose the *New Republic* even though he would have earned twice the salary
at the *Saturday Evening Post.* In the magazine's editorial columns White
would join the company of luminaries such as Max Lerner and Alfred Kazin,
and his work would be read by America's best-educated, relatively affluent,

25. THW, letter to George C. Marshall, dated 1947, TWA, Box 6, Folder 9.

and politically sophisticated citizens.[26] In the year Wallace was editor, the magazine's circulation climbed from forty-one thousand to one hundred thousand. White hoped that in the *New Republic*'s historically liberal politics and in Wallace's editorial ambition to help "organize a progressive America," he would find a haven of free expression.

He was offered his choice of jobs—he could either aid in the reorganization and direction of the magazine or take his choice of any assignment across America. In the end, he opted for a combination of the two. In a critique of the magazine written for Michael Straight, the magazine's publisher, early in 1947, White reported that Henry Wallace "is the biggest living factor on the *New Republic* and at the same time its greatest living waste. Here I do not mean monetary waste—although that is not inconsiderable—but waste of talent and energy. . . . As a symbol of integrity and conviction, Wallace has a high promotion value to us."[27]

The magazine, however, soon became Wallace's mouthpiece for his Progressive party candidacy in the 1948 presidential election. As a result of Wallace's political aspirations as a third-party candidate in the race against President Truman and Thomas Dewey and of what White called Wallace's "self-intoxication," White soon discovered that what he wrote for the *New Republic* "had to fit that line which supported Henry Wallace's views, just as what he had written at *Time* magazine had to fit the line of Harry Luce." Ironically, although White himself was being labeled a Communist sympathizer because of his views on China, he found Wallace's associations with members of America's Communist movement troublesome and his tolerance of Joseph Stalin's expansionist foreign policy insupportable. White dismissed as naive Wallace's notion that by developing substantial trade with the Soviet Union and Eastern Europe, America might influence developments in the Communist bloc. White might have challenged some of the widely accepted sentiments about China, but he saw no legitimacy in Wallace's belief in "the willingness of the Soviet leaders to think more and more in democratic terms."[28] He found the *New Republic*'s tolerance of Soviet foreign policy as objectionable as *Time*'s tolerance of Chiang.

White left the *New Republic* in August 1947, just a few months after he married Nancy Bean, a researcher at Time Inc. who had worked in the Office

26. Richard H. Pells, *The Liberal Mind in a Conservative Age: American Intellectuals in the 1940s and 1950s*, 11.

27. THW, letter to Michael Straight, February 1947, TWA, Box 5, Folder 31.

28. White, *In Search of History*, 256; Henry A. Wallace, "Jobs, Peace, Freedom," *New Republic*, December 16, 1946, 789.

of War Information in Bombay during World War II. Although White would have liked to have been married in a synagogue, his Episcopalian fiancée had felt uncomfortable with that prospect, just as he had felt uneasy about the prospect of being married in a church, as her parents would have preferred. So they had settled on a civil service instead. White, who had gradually become estranged from the faith of his ancestors, and his bride believed that religious differences were irrelevant. But White had married not only outside his faith but also outside his social class. That difference would ultimately divide his union in ways that neither he nor she could anticipate as they exchanged vows in a Manhattan courthouse. Nancy's father was a well-to-do Connecticut business executive and her mother was a social activist, a background that led Nancy to take for granted her place at the head of the table and her right to challenge anyone in authority. White, on the other hand, harbored an abiding fear that unless he constantly proved his worthiness, he might be banished from his seat at the table.

It was also in 1947, less than a year after Stilwell died of liver cancer, that his widow entrusted her husband's diaries to White with the request that he edit them for publication. After his return from his command in the China-Burma-India Theater in October 1944, Stilwell had been warned immediately that he should say nothing to anyone about China, Chiang, or his having been relieved of his command. "Not a word," the four-star general had been told by his superiors, "this is dynamite." He had retreated to his home in Carmel, California, where he died nearly two years later. White was amazed and shocked at the contents of Stilwell's diaries. Those scrawled pages Winifred Stilwell gave him revealed a perplexing and contradictory individual. "A man of such greatness with so many smallnesses, too. Great cantankerousness," White wrote about his hero in his own diary. Stilwell, he discovered, had a mean-spirited and vituperative side, but he also had a marvelous command spirit. Stilwell's intense dislike for Chiang—whom he alternately derided as "peanut" and "the crazy little bastard"—convinced White that once the papers were published he would "never get back into China as long as Chiang Kai-shek lives." Chiang, Stilwell had written in mid–1944,

is confronted with an idea, and that defeats him. He is bewildered by the spread of Communist influence. He can't see that the mass of Chinese people welcome the Reds as being the only visible hope of relief from crushing taxation, the abuses of the Army. . . . Under Chiang Kai-shek they now begin to see what they may expect. Greed, corruption, favoritism, more taxes, a ruined currency, terrible waste of life, callous disregard of all the rights of men.[29]

In America's increasingly intolerant political climate of the late 1940s, White's work on the Stilwell diaries would again call White's loyalties into question. John Paton Davies warned him that it was the wrong time to be publishing Stilwell's papers. Davies suggested that if he were determined to go ahead, White should have the manuscript cleared by federal officials "so there is no question of violation of security legislation." White disagreed, insisting in a letter to the young diplomat that the public had a right to all the facts immediately and publishing the diaries was one of the few ways to buck the power of "the Luce-Howard machine." On the question of clearance, White told Davies that while he would happily submit the manuscript to him or some other authority whose opinions he respected, he refused to let "some stupid clerk . . . decide what is good and proper for America in Stilwell's papers."[30] It was one of the last occasions that White would exhibit such open defiance of his government.

The Stilwell Papers created a storm when it was published in May 1948. The same divergence of liberal and conservative opinion that had characterized responses to *Thunder Out of China* accompanied the publication of the Stilwell diaries. Writing for *The Nation*, John King Fairbank characterized the diaries as "the most comprehensive and pungent indictment of a Chinese potentate ever set on paper." Richard Watts wrote in the *New Republic*, "In White's skillful editing of his journals, Stilwell's story is a living, racy and important chapter in contemporary history." A review in *The Atlantic*, however, observed that Stilwell revealed himself as a man with "a one-track mind, irremediably convinced that [his] own way is the only way; a bitter, uncooperative personality. The general's insulting verdict on almost everyone he had to deal with—Wavell, Mountbatten, Roosevelt, and others—his venomous hostility to the British fighting alongside him make pretty sorry reading."[31]

Once again, White was seared with the left-wing brand. Critics charged he had distorted the dead war hero's views and put his own liberal slant

29. Theodore H. White, ed., *The Stilwell Papers*, 317.
30. John Paton Davies, letter to THW, October 6, 1947, TWA, Box 6, Folder 5; THW, letter to Davies, October 9, 1947, TWA, Box 6, Folder 10.
31. John King Fairbank, "Stilwell and Chiang Kai-shek," *Nation*, May 29, 1948, 608; Richard Watts, "Bitter Judgment," *New Republic*, May 31, 1948, 30; Charles Rolo, "Reader's Choice," *Atlantic*, June 1948, 117.

on the general's writings. Members of America's China Lobby, who were Chiang's strongest supporters in the United States, saw in White's work—particularly in the presentation of Stilwell's view of Chiang—still another effort to promote China's Communists at the expense of the Nationalist government. Detractors dismissed him as a fellow traveler, and perhaps even a Communist. Mao and Chou had, to be sure, engaged White with their intellect and wit during those October days in the caves at Yenan in 1944, but he had regarded communism with a measure of suspicion since his days as an undergraduate at Harvard, and in just a few more years, he would come to detest it as a totalitarian system of government.

By the time *The Stilwell Papers* was published, however, White and his new bride had decided to go abroad—to Paris first and then perhaps on to China, where it appeared increasingly likely that the Communists would conquer Chiang's Nationalist army. But because the brand of "left-wing" had become an appendage to his name, White recalled in his autobiography, no mass circulation publication would hire him. He had been too friendly with and too ready to defend those "China hands" in the U.S. State Department who were correctly reporting the successes of the Communists in winning over the Chinese peasants and predicting Chiang's inevitable fall. Those men, Davies and Service among them, would soon be purged from the Foreign Service as suspected Communists who had "lost" China. Finally, White settled for a position with the Overseas News Agency, which he described as "a service which was still unafraid of the growing paranoia against liberal journalists."[32]

Nearly a decade after he had embarked on his journey to China as a newly minted Harvard graduate, Theodore White once again crossed the Atlantic. Back in 1938, the nation was still lurching forward on its long recovery from the Great Depression and warily eyeing the events in Europe that would soon drag the country into another world war. Now, an age of unprecedented prosperity had dawned at home and America was assuming its role—with occasional reluctance—as a superpower in the post–World War II order. A war panic swept the country anew early in 1948 after the Soviet Union replaced the only democratic government in Eastern Europe with a Communist-controlled regime in Czechoslovakia, an act of aggression that prodded Congress into swiftly approving the Marshall Plan in mid-March. Days later, the first ship left Galveston, Texas, laden with nineteen thousand tons of wheat. And within less than two months, as the Whites embarked on

32. White, *In Search of History*, 261.

their transatlantic trip in June, there were, at any given moment, "150 ships carrying American goods and produce and know-how to Europe."[33] The cold war had moved into one of its fieriest phases, and Europe was about to be resurrected. In June, Stalin had closed off all access to Berlin, and Truman launched the massive airlift that would keep the former German capital alive for eleven months.

The Whites thereafter spent six years in Paris, and their two children were born there—a daughter in 1949 and a son in 1951. Gertrude Stein had died in 1946, but her companion, Alice B. Toklas, still held court at 27 Rue de Fleurus, the Left Bank studio that had been a haven for America's expatriate writers and artists in the 1920s. Stein had characterized them as "the Lost Generation." By late 1947, when the Whites arrived, a new generation of American expatriates had come to occupy the Montparnasse garrets that had once been home to the likes of Ernest Hemingway, Malcolm Cowley, Ezra Pound, and F. Scott Fitzgerald. The Black authors, including James Baldwin, Richard Wright, and Chester Himes, had come to escape the oppressive racism that prevailed at home. Others, William Styron, Peter Mathieson, and James Jones among them, came for the romance of it all, believing perhaps in Ernest Hemingway's contention that, "If you are lucky enough to have lived in Paris as a young man, then wherever you go for the rest of your life, it stays with you, for Paris is a moveable feast." Irwin Shaw, who had already achieved acclaim and financial success with the publication of *The Young Lions,* lived in the White's apartment building at 24 Rue du Boccador. Art Buchwald, a former Marine and fledgling columnist for the *New York Herald Tribune,* had a flat in the same building, too. The young musicians Isaac Stern and Burl Ives were among the Whites' frequent visitors. What distinguished the American crowd in Paris in the late 1940s from the American crowd in Paris after World War I were the legions of diplomats, Foreign Service officers, economists, and military men who arrived to implement the Marshall Plan and coordinate the North Atlantic Treaty Organization. These Americans came not to be nurtured by the European culture that had drawn previous generations of Americans, but rather to save it from the threat of communism and economic anarchy. And their success in reconstructing Europe in those postwar years represented America's finest hour.

White set off for Europe hoping to write about the human dramas in the continent's ruin and reconstruction. He wanted to witness the hunger and the housewives shopping on the black market. He wanted to take the pulse

33. Walter Isaacson and Evan Thomas, *The Wise Men,* 441.

of what he hoped were the dying fascist regimes, and measure the strength of Communist movements in France and Italy. Making the peace, he was sure, would take almost as long as waging the war. Although Paris was to have been an interlude on the journey back to China, White quickly found that writing about Europe was as vital as writing about China had been.

Paris had all the same grace and beauty that had captivated him ten years earlier when he had come carrying the secondhand Zephyr portable typewriter that had been Fairbank's graduation gift. In the late 1940s, the French embraced all things American and most especially those Americans who carried the embossed, tri-color press card. White traveled with Charles DeGaulle on a political barnstorming trip and found the general's egotism, pride, and hunger for power worrisome—"one of the great demagogues of history," White called him. He once partied with the Duke and Duchess of Windsor and dismissed the former King of England as "a decadent, hopeless character."[34] His weekly routine invariably included an encounter with W. Averill Harriman or Paul Gray Hoffman, the odd couple of American postwar diplomacy whose responsibility it was to implement the Marshall Plan. White was fascinated both with the magnitude of the task and with the two men Truman had chosen to set it in motion. Hoffman was the stocky, millionaire industrialist whose Midwestern roots and social conscience gave him a "plain folks" quality. Harriman was the aristocrat—a polo player, a canny emissary, and an heir to the Union Pacific Railroad fortune accumulated by his father, one of the most successful of the late nineteenth-century robber barons.

These two men yielded extraordinary power, the kind of power that had intrigued White since his undergraduate years at Harvard. Together Harriman and Hoffman would leave America's imprint on Europe. Marshall Plan dollars were buying tractors for France's wheat farmers, funding a massive land reclamation project in Holland's Zuyder Zee, draining marshes in Sardinia, and building a dam on the Rhone River. American cotton and chemicals and machinery and oil helped to revitalize Europe's industries. White watched in awe as America pulled off an economic miracle in Western Europe.

The unfolding revolution in China, he wrote to Fairbank, was "a blood-and-thunder, silk-and-opium melodrama with only two protagonists, a villain and a hero." By comparison, Europe was complicated and sometimes

34. THW, letter to Gladys and Mary White, August 8, 1948, TWA, Box 6, Folder 20; THW, letter to Gladys and Mary White, July 10, 1948, TWA, Box 6, Folder 20.

baffling—more like a detective thriller than a melodrama. "You don't know who the hero is and who the villain is until the very last act . . . there are great tides rocking western Europe now but I cannot understand them."[35]

The historic election of 1948, when President Truman, defying both the odds and the pollsters, beat Thomas Dewey, seems to have evinced no interest in White. Just as there is no indication that he voted in either the 1940 and 1944 presidential elections while he was a war correspondent in China, nothing in his correspondence indicates that he cast a vote in 1948, a pattern that was repeated in 1952. His sister, Gladys, wrote him from Boston of having voted—albeit unenthusiastically—for Truman, using the logic that a Democratic victory was better for the nation than a Republican one.

White was absorbed in his assignment to cover Europe for the Overseas News Agency. He had traveled through Eastern Europe in the weeks that preceded Truman's reelection. Universal education, full employment, and the sight of the poor eating as well as the rich gave the appearance that solid new societies were emerging in the eastern bloc. But the secret police and the Red Army sustained order in those societies, the result of which was a collective sense of terror. In the nations of Eastern Europe, an aging French diplomat in Hungary told White, "people are willing to trade dignity and liberty for things they need more, like security in their jobs or land of their own to farm, or schools for their kids."[36]

Warsaw's ghetto and Auschwitz stunned him. Confronting the hatred and cold-blooded inhumanity of the Nazis toward the Jews left him shaken and in tears. He quickly abandoned any thought of seeking out relatives who might have survived the war. "The chances are 9.5 out of 10 that every branch of our family has been wiped out in one burning camp or other," he wrote to his mother and sister. Germany, he was convinced, must never again be trusted. American insistence on rebuilding Germany—even though its underlying purpose was to thwart the advance of Soviet influence in Europe—horrified him. "Our country has goodness and liberty and generosity. But our country is giving the monster back its power," he wrote to his family. "Do I support our country knowing that perhaps someday it will mean that the gas chambers will work again? Can I continue to support the Marshall Plan when it means that my taxes go to feed the murderers

35. THW, letter to John King Fairbank, December 5, 1948, TWA, Box 6, Folder 23.
36. THW, letter to Richard and Tina Ravenholt, October 1948, TWA, Box 6, Folder 22.

who wiped out every decent liberal, every cringing Jew from Bohemia to the Ukraine?"[37]

Any dream White had of returning to China ended in 1949 when China's Kuomintang government collapsed and Chiang retreated from the Chinese mainland to the safety of Taiwan. Once Mao and the Communist armies took control of the government, China was closed to Western journalists. For more than twenty years he wrote letters to Madame Sun Yat-sen, Chou, Mao, and other Communist officials imploring them to grant him permission to revisit China. Not one of his letters was answered.

In the years that followed the Communist triumph, as Wisconsin Senator Joseph McCarthy began his search for Communists in government and America looked for scapegoats on whom to blame the debacle in China, White repeatedly came to the defense of his old friends in the State Department. In 1950, he wrote a letter to the editor of the *New York Times* in which he defended John Service, whose reports from Yenan and Chungking had correctly predicted that Chiang's government would fall. Service's case, White said, raised a fundamental issue of whether the reports of Foreign Service officers "should be tempered to conform with the prejudices of Congress at the moment."

> If Mr. Service is to be presently punished because he correctly reported that the Communists were less corrupt and more effective leaders than the mandarins of Chiang Kai-shek, the effect on younger officers in the State Department is easy to predict. . . . I can testify that he serviced the Republic bravely, brilliantly and in great hardship; he deserves its praise and honor.[38]

The *New York Times* refused to publish the letter and returned it to White saying that Service would soon have the opportunity to present his case himself. White subsequently sent the letter to the *Washington Post*, where it did appear. A year later, when Davies, whom White considered both an old friend and a model American diplomat, was once again investigated on charges of subversion in connection with his wartime assignment in China, White offered to testify or provide an affidavit attesting to Davies' loyalty.

During his Paris years, White came to the attention of J. Edgar Hoover and the Federal Bureau of Investigation. Although the praise *Thunder Out of China* received from reviewers helped to put the book on the best-seller

37. THW, undated letter to Gladys and Mary White, TWA, Box 6, Folder 24.
38. THW, letter to *New York Times*, April 22, 1950, TWA, Box 7, Folder 24.

lists and White's editing of *The Stilwell Papers* brought him laurels from some quarters, those books also put White on Hoover's list of suspected Communists. The FBI opened its file on White early in 1950 when Hoover himself asked one of his field officers for information on "Ted White accused of being member(s) of the Communist Party." In response, Hoover received a "top secret" memorandum that claimed White was "very much anti-Chiang" and "a misguided writer who had picked up a bludgeon and was going to beat the Generalissimo over the head with it." The investigation indicated that although White could conceivably be a "fellow traveler," he was probably not a Communist. That initial assessment notwithstanding, the FBI continued to assemble information about White from informants "believed to be reliable." In subsequent "top secret" reports, White is described as a "Communist sympathizer" and *Thunder Out of China* is said to "follow the Communist Party line." White's FBI file remained open until 1968 and its contents were still taken as gospel in some quarters long after he had embraced the ideology of the cold war. By mid–1965 President Lyndon B. Johnson had become convinced that the Vietnam protest movement was the work of a Communist conspiracy in which American opponents of the war were the unwitting dupes. "The communists are taking over this country," LBJ told White House aide Richard Goodwin. "Look here," Johnson admonished Goodwin as he motioned to a manila folder on his desk. "It's Teddy White's FBI file. He's a communist sympathizer."[39]

Ironically, however, by the time Hoover began assembling his file on "Ted White," White himself was on the verge of abandoning his earlier approval of China's Communist movement. Although in his autobiography he professed himself to have been "a mild Marxist" in his youth, once the Korean War began, White had lost the last shred of enchantment he had found in Yenan in the fall of 1944 when he had sipped tea and talked politics with Mao and Chou. Until the late 1940s, he had regarded the U.S. State Department and the Russians with equal suspicion. However, once the North Korean Army crossed the 38th parallel in June 1950, White developed an open hostility to communism. In Europe White saw the Communists as "lawless thugs," and in Asia he perceived them as aggressors. "The Communists had deliberately, clumsily, but with calculation, launched a violent war of conquest" in Korea, he believed. "But however stupid their command

39. Memorandum from Guy Hottell to J. Edgar Hoover, March 15, 1950, Federal Bureau of Investigation File #100–369814; Richard N. Goodwin, *Remembering America*, 402.

decision, there should have been somewhere in the world community of Communist opinion, a loyal opposition—the counterpart of the intellectual opposition that, while loyal to democracy, questions constantly any action by the world's democracies."[40] What White failed to acknowledge, even when he wrote those words years later in his autobiography, was that there was no loyal opposition—intellectual or otherwise—that questioned the actions of the world's democracies during the 1950s and early 1960s.

In the years following World War II, White joined with mainstream journalists in allowing the government to keep secrets, indeed on occasion even participated in keeping those secrets. White not only participated in, but perhaps even helped to create, the "age of consensus" that characterized American life throughout the 1950s and early 1960s. That consensus, as described by Godfrey Hodgson, led Americans of every political stripe to accept the same set of assumptions about the nation's foreign and domestic policies during the postwar era. Few doubted the essential goodness and strength of American society. That consensus, which muffled dissent on critical foreign policy issues, swept across party lines to embrace Americans for Democratic Action on the left and inhabitants of Wall Street board rooms on the right. "Not only in Washington, but in the press, on television and—with few exceptions—in the academic community, to dissent from the axioms of consensus was to proclaim oneself irresponsible or ignorant," Hodgson concluded. "That would risk disqualifying the dissenter from being taken seriously, and indeed often from being heard at all."[41]

Important historians—Daniel J. Boorstin, Richard Hofstadter, and Arthur M. Schlesinger Jr. among them—were a part of the consensus that helped to reinforce the cold war ideology. In their books and essays, these "liberals with conservative assumptions" supported the idea that America's arms race with the Soviet Union was both a necessary and appropriate response to the Soviet threat, and that Stalin and his successors were out to destroy the American way of life.[42]

Schlesinger, for example, who was emerging as one of America's leading intellectuals, was predicting in the late 1940s that "tomorrow Soviet power will surely spread everywhere that it meets no firm resistance." While he acknowledged that Russia's history made its leaders understandably anxious to secure their nation's borders, its totalitarian leaders, Schlesinger warned,

40. White, *In Search of History,* 337.
41. Godfrey Hodgson, *America in Our Time,* 72.
42. Marian J. Morton, *The Terrors of Ideological Politics,* 72.

possessed an insatiable territorial appetite. "Since 1939, the Soviet Union had added 280,000 square miles of new land. Today the satellite states of eastern Europe are being readied for incorporation into the Soviet Union itself. . . . It has gradually become clear that the totalitarian conception of security implies the elimination of all opposition or even indifference anywhere: it means the absorption of all in the central maelstrom of tension."[43]

The voices of those few observers who offered opposing viewpoints were barely audible in the cacophony of terror sounded by these highly influential consensus historians. C. Wright Mills was one of the few who resisted the tide of consensus. He deplored America's paranoid view of the Soviet Union and the widespread conformity to the cold war ideology in his 1958 book, *The Causes of World War III*. "Politicians and journalists, intellectuals and generals, businessmen and preachers now fight this war," Mills argued, "and busily create the historical situation in which it is viewed as inevitable."[44]

Essential to that consensus were journalists who shared the opinions and attitudes of government policy makers and who transmitted those views to the public. And while White might have been convinced, as he declared in his 1946 speech, that a foreign correspondent was an independent part of the nation's defense and foreign policy apparatus, as a member of an inside circle of American journalists in Paris, White became dependent on his official sources—a trap that has bedeviled generations of journalists on beats from a village council to the United States Congress because it can make them susceptible to manipulation. White and his contemporaries, by carrying over their World War II values and standards into the postwar world, helped to reinforce that consensus by becoming echoes rather than sounding boards or constructive critics of American policy. If indeed the corps of foreign correspondents sent overseas by media agencies was more important than the diplomatic corps in shaping America's foreign policy for peace or war, as White had once claimed, then he and his fellow journalists in postwar Paris must accept a share of the blame for the depth and persistence of the cold war.

Despite his own considerable differences with the State Department during the China debate, White became a confidant and friend of key American diplomats and military officials assigned to implement the Marshall Plan and oversee the creation of the North Atlantic Treaty Organization to subdue Soviet aggression in Western Europe. Ultimately, White came to embrace without question the idea that the cold war was both necessary

43. Arthur M. Schlesinger Jr., *The Vital Center*, 98.
44. C. Wright Mills, *The Causes of World War III*, 58.

and appropriate. By 1952, White conceded, he had become reflexively anti-Communist. He believed that the Communists had attacked Korea, that the Marshall Plan had saved Europe from communism, that NATO was necessary to protect American survival. And while he may have been correct in those assumptions, like so many newsmen of his generation, he was blind to the incongruity of Dean Acheson's memorable statement that summed up American attitudes in the postwar years: "We are willing to help people who believe the way we do, to continue to live the way they want to live."[45] Indeed, White probably would have endorsed the statement, for he believed that America had to maintain an offensive posture and remain in the forefront of the anti-Communist movement following World War II.

Those notions about America's place in the world squared with the views of his former boss Luce, with whom White made peace midway through his Paris sojourn. Word had reached White from staffers in *Life's* Paris office—where Nancy White had taken a job as acting bureau manager—that Luce wanted to see him. "So Teddy invited him for tea," recalled Nancy. They had agreed that she would stay in her office until Luce departed, which they anticipated would be about 5 P.M. When Luce arrived at 24 Rue du Boccador, White set one condition: "We will talk about anything in the world, but let us not talk about China," he told his former boss. Hours passed as Nancy awaited the all-clear telephone call from her husband. Finally, Luce left—in time to catch his 10 P.M. flight out of Paris.[46]

Describing the encounter in a letter to his family, White said he and Luce had had

> a long, warm chat . . . I enjoyed seeing him so much and I know he enjoyed seeing me. He's told other people about the visit. Funny, isn't it—he's the best boss I ever had; and I could go back to work for him tomorrow at about $20,000 a year . . . and yet I can't bring myself to do it, I just can't. For he'd want me to write an article saying he was right and I was wrong about China, which just ain't so.[47]

In France, White once again played the role of spectator and participant in the historical events of his age. "History spun on a turntable in Paris that year," White discovered, and in Europe, America was about to "do

45. White, *In Search of History,* 338; William Appleman Williams, *The Tragedy of American Diplomacy,* 17.

46. Nancy White Hector, taped personal interview, April 4, 1990.

47. THW, letter to Mary and Gladys White, March 28, 1951, TWA, Box 8, Folder 21.

as much good as it had done harm in Asia."[48] From Paris White put the
same interpretive spin on events that he had originally applied in his first
mailer to the *Boston Globe* written from Palestine and would later continue
to put on events in America when he began a trend-setting examination of
American politics in 1960. Rather than predict an end to the Arab hostilities
by Christmas, as he had done in 1938, from Paris he predicted the creation
of a united Europe, praised the wisdom of the Truman-Acheson foreign
policy, and applauded the French and American diplomats who were carrying out those utopian dreams for peace and prosperity choreographed in
Washington, D.C.

As Europe struggled to rebuild its bomb-shattered cities, its industries,
and its wasted economies, America's intentions seemed high-minded, its
strength unequaled, and its power to shape the future undeniable. With its
money and sheer determination, America would resurrect Western Europe.
Its successes in those endeavors inevitably made Americans feel both virtuous and invincible. To be an American in Paris after the war, with pocketsful
of America's muscular and much-desired dollars, representing a country that
was to save Europe from the chaos of the postwar era, was to enjoy a sense
of invulnerability. Like other American correspondents, White's standard of
living was considerably enriched by the favorable black market exchange
rates available to those who possessed dollars and by the military post
exchange privileges granted to accredited American correspondents in Paris.
White and his wife lived in unaccustomed luxury, employing servants and
spending their summers on the French Riviera. "Being in Paris was like
sinking into a big feather bed," Nancy recalled. "It was a totally wonderful
world. We were young and life was beautiful and we just used to take francs
out of a suitcase under the bed."

There was a parallel between the personal abundance the Whites enjoyed
in the midst of the poverty of their postwar European neighbors and the
collective abundance America enjoyed at a time when so much of the world
teetered on economic chaos. Perhaps that personal abundance blinded individuals as much as the national abundance blinded the American government to the needs, aspirations, and unique cultural identities of other, less
prosperous nations. For those Americans who witnessed the reconstruction
of Europe from the vantage point of Paris, America would seem capable
of reshaping the world in its own image—if only the Communists would
abandon their ruthless attempts at world conquest.

48. White, *In Search of History*, 262.

The reach of American culture and American power flabbergasted White. American novels were serialized in French newspapers, American-style hamburgers were served in French restaurants. France, he discovered, was utterly infected with American influence and was so heavily dependent on American largesse that the American ambassador could casually declare in cocktail party banter: "I made them [the French government] cut taxes." The French government, White explained to friends in America, was little more than the tail man in a snap-the-whip formation driven by American policy. It was impossible to judge the meaning of events in France until responses were in from Washington and Moscow. France, White declared to his family back in Boston three weeks after his arrival in Paris,

> is now a great colony of America, and it is shocking to realize that no real news comes from here any more. All I can write from here are reaction stories—reactions to American deeds, reaction to Russian deeds. [France] has lost its grip as a great nation, it is hungry, it is weak and it is powerless to make decisions. . . . It means the chief source of news here is the American embassy, and it means that instead of seeking out Frenchmen, I have to seek out American attaches and the American ambassador.[49]

Thus, there was little to distinguish the role American journalists played in the postwar world of Western Europe from the role they had played in the years between Pearl Harbor and the Allied victory. With Joseph Stalin and the Soviet Union creating—at least in the eyes of American leaders—as dire a threat to the survival of democracy as the fascist tyrants of Europe and Asia once had, news makers and news reporters once again shared a common enemy and a common goal. In telling the stories about the reconstruction of postwar Europe, White's brand of journalism would again allow him to inject himself into events, interpret events in the context of how they might affect American policy, and permit him to offer special treatment to those subjects who ranked as friends, just as it had done in China. White's stories— like those of his colleagues in the mainstream press—never questioned America's ability to usurp the power of the governments it aided, never questioned whether America could and should be the world's policeman, never wondered whether its policies had alternatives.

49. THW, letter to Victor Bienstock, July 11, 1948, TWA, Box 7, Folder 4, and letter to Mary and Gladys White, July 10, 1948, TWA, Box 6, Folder 20.

Henry Luce's American Century had indeed arrived! Compared to all the rest of the human family, most Americans were "just plain rich" after World War II, just as they had been when Luce wrote his editorial sermon on the nation's responsibilities in 1941—"rich in food, rich in clothes, rich in entertainment and amusement, rich in leisure, rich." And America had become "the dynamic center of ever-widening spheres of enterprise."[50] American generosity, American technology, and American power ordered the world—just as Luce had said they should. America had established its dominance and was exporting its free enterprise system to much of the world, creating a decidedly capitalist, military, and imperialist epoch. In the late 1940s, White became one of its most demonstrative cheerleaders. Like other journalists of his generation, he bought into the ideology of cold war, a mind-set in which international events were reduced to an uncomplicated set of confrontations—democracy versus totalitarianism, freedom versus tyranny, black versus white.

That mind-set shaped White's vision of the world and America's rightful place in it. In his work first for the Overseas News Agency and later for *The Reporter*, White demonstrated his own comparatively moderate zeal for the American way. He considered ONA "the outstanding moral agency in the world." The French and Chiang, he wrote to a friend, "are sons of bitches to us and our correspondents need practice no whoring neutrality to them; we tell the truth, we hate tyranny and terror."[51] Occasionally ONA's leftist leanings and ties to Jewish interests made White uncomfortable. But it was ONA's shaky finances that led White to end his association with the agency in 1950.

Later that year, White began writing for *The Reporter*, a two-year-old "liberal" magazine established by Max Ascoli, an exiled Italian intellectual and antifascist who had taught law at the University of Genoa before fleeing to America in 1931 with the help of the Rockefeller Foundation. In New York, he became dean of the New School for Social Research and later married Marion Rosenwald of the Sears, Roebuck Rosenwalds. "We are publishing *The Reporter*," Ascoli wrote in the magazine's first edition in April 1949, "because we think there is room in the United States for a type of reporting free from obsession with headline news and from the conceit of opinions." He was one of the first publishers to attack the demagoguery of Senator Joseph McCarthy but was as fervent an anti-Communist as the Wisconsin

50. Luce, "The American Century," 61.
51. THW, letter to Victor Bienstock, May 16, 1948, TWA, Box 7, Folder 1.

senator. Like White, he embraced the idea that America should assume
the role of world arbiter and standard-setter. At its peak, *The Reporter* had
210,000 readers—many of them policy makers and academics.

White was intrigued by both the publisher's intellect and the fortnightly's
readership. Ascoli ran the magazine like a penny-pinching despot, but those
flaws paled in the glow of his intelligence, courage, and curiosity. Unlike
Luce, who had been convinced that men made history, Ascoli saw institutions at the fulcrum of change. He was an editor "who sought meanings,
large meanings, and always preferred the institutional to the personal in his
pages."[52]

White enjoyed continuing success in the business of inspiring confidence
in people. Members of America's diplomatic corps became his friends. The
Marshall Plan administrators were among the men he most admired, the
military leaders of NATO became his dinner partners, and European leaders
were his guests at off-the-record luncheons.

In his autobiography, White described the journalistic practice of those
he dubbed the "inner few," an elite circle of journalists who cast themselves
as surrogates for the entire American people and demanded that men of
state explain themselves—off the record. Whether he was in Chungking
or Paris or Washington, D.C., White managed to make himself a member
of some exclusive circle, even though, after he left China, he seldom had
an official or full-time affiliation with a premier mass-media organization.
Nonetheless, White made himself part of the select inner few in Paris, a
circle that he ranked as first-rate. "The best 'inner few' gathering of reporters
I can remember was ours in Paris. It had its *New York Times* man, Harold
Callender; its CBS man, David Schoenbrun; its *Time* magazine man, Frank
White; its *U.S. News and World Report* representative, Robert Kleiman; and
several lesser personalities, all presided over by the dean of the Paris press
corps, Preston Grover of the Associated Press." Thanks to some help from
his friend Schoenbrun, White could also count himself as a member of
that circle, even though his small, often cash-strapped news agency hardly
ranked among America's major news organizations.

For five years, as White explained it in his autobiography, this select group
of reporters met with Europe's key statesmen at off-the-record sessions
and "filtered much of the politics of Europe as our guests wished them
to be reported to the American public." The European luminaries invited
to meet with this inner circle included René Pleven, France's premier in

52. White, *In Search of History*, 377.

1952, Gunnar Myrdal, Sweden's eminent sociologist, and Pierre Mendes-France, the French premier who decided to abandon Vietnam. White also participated in long, off-the-record discussions with Dean Acheson, Dwight D. Eisenhower, John Foster Dulles, George Marshall, and George Kennan. At one of those sessions in March 1952, "a private, off-the-record, all-secret" luncheon at the home of Associated Press correspondent Preston Grover, Eisenhower, then commander of NATO, confided in White and seven of his fellow "insiders" that yes, he would be a candidate for the presidency later that year. The general had conscripted them that afternoon to help him decide about the best and most gracious way to submit his resignation. None of those eight reporters, however, wrote a story about Ike's plans. "Somehow, without meaning to, we had all become bound to confidence so we could not break the story from Paris of his resignation—and knew our Washington counterparts would break it instead," White recalled in his memoir years later. "But we did not care."[53]

Benjamin Bradlee, who was in Paris during White's years there, defended the practice of insider journalism, explaining that "there had to be some system to form a group that foreign leaders could talk to. In every country this was true." Membership in those inner circles, Bradlee explained, most often had to do with the organization a journalist represented. It invariably included the American wire services, its major newspapers—most notably the New York Times and the Herald Tribune—and the news weeklies. There was no collusion, Bradlee said, nor did members of the group make any collective decisions on what stories to write or how to cast those stories. But while each reporter interpreted events independently, their shared ideas and common viewpoint colored the reporting of members of the inner circle of American newsmen in Paris. "You would get interested as a group in things," Bradlee said. "We were all attracted to the people who were trying to build a European union. Jean Monnet was a hero to us. We liked Eisenhower and David Bruce. Our friendships set an agenda for us."[54] They had, in short, what might be considered a consensus within the consensus. Their stories thus tended to echo and reinforce one another. Because they all shared the same viewpoint, similar ideas reverberated through their stories. To look at those reverberations in just a few examples of their stories with Paris datelines is to begin to understand how consensus journalism worked to circumscribe the boundaries of acceptable political debate.

53. Ibid., 330, 352.
54. Benjamin C. Bradlee, personal interview, January 22, 1993.

When White wrote about Jean Monnet, the French political economist, in dispatches to the Overseas News Agency in the late 1940s and early 1950s, he lionized him as an intellectual and idea broker in ways that paralleled the writings of his colleagues in the inner circle. White's gift for hyperbole often outdistanced that of the other American correspondents in Paris. "Hyperbole," he often told his wife, "is the garment of truth." Nonetheless, it is clear, as Bradlee explained, that they all shared a common view. White declared that Monnet, as the mastermind of a plan for European economic and political unity, was "a wizard, all things to all men, a dynamo of efficiency, firebrand among thinkers and some kind of a cookie pusher among diplomats." Harold Callender, chief of the *New York Times* Paris bureau, held Monnet in similar esteem and applauded the role he was playing in creating an economic union in Europe. In 1950, Callender wrote that Monnet "may be called the outstanding integrator of our time," and explained that "He finds satisfaction and enjoyment in translating an idea into reality. To this end he is capable of vast, almost passionate concentration." In a story written nearly three years later, Callender praised Monnet's "intellectual boldness" and called his work "statesmanship of a high order." And in a burst of hyperbole that rivaled White's, Callender applauded Monnet's work: "His conceptions are at once bold and far-reaching yet measured and balanced, revolutionary yet shaped by an acute sense of practical politics. He has the clear logical mind characteristic of his country, but unlike many other Frenchmen he never lets his logic run away with him."[55]

In June 1950, *Newsweek* joined in the round of media applause for Monnet. In a cover story that described Monnet as a "spark plug," the magazine praised him as "Europe's No. 1 idea man." The story described Monnet as "a short wiry man with a quick, intelligent face and eyes as searching as the questions he constantly asks. He is a careful listener and files away information in his orderly memory." Several years later on the pages of *U.S. News and World Report*, Monnet was characterized as "one of Europe's brainiest men" and the magazine explained to its readers that, "the U.S. likes to back Monnet because he gets things done with American-like vigor."[56]

55. THW, dispatch to Overseas News Agency, TWA, Box 70, Folder 11; Harold Callender, "Architect of the Coal-Steel Pool," *New York Times Magazine*, June 11, 1950, 15; Harold Callender, "Monnet—Prophet of a United Europe," *New York Times Magazine*, February 8, 1953, 14.

56. "Coal, Steel, and the Monnet Spark Plug," *Newsweek*, June 19, 1950, 30; "People of the Week," *U.S. News and World Report*, April 16, 1954, 14.

White and his fellow insiders were similarly enamored with Pierre Mendes-France. Writing for *The Reporter* in 1954, White described the career of France's newly elected premier as "a chain of such brilliant and solitary achievements." He was, in White's telling, "the darling of the nonconformist left, the standard bearer of those who yearn for a new popular front."[57]

Time was likewise ecstatic: "A man of fresh ideas and heartening determination," a man with a reputation for thoroughness and clarity had taken over the government of France, the magazine declared. Mendes-France, according to *Time*, "brought a transfusion of young, fresh blood into the trouble-hardened arteries of French government." Later in 1954, when the French premier made a six-day visit to the United States, *Time* reiterated its approval. Mendes-France, it said, "dispelled most of U.S. officialdom's lingering suspicions that he was a neutralist at heart and all too willing to flirt with Russia. U.S. negotiators learned to respect his tough-minded realism, and ordinary bystanders compulsively burst into applause as he passed."[58]

Once again, the *New York Times* was also enthusiastic. Callender described Mendes-France as "an intellectual and as such is painfully aware of the inevitable disparity between thought and action, especially in politics," and praised him as "a man of studious and methodical habits and his cautiously critical approach to the problems of his time causes him to make up his mind about them only very slowly."[59]

David K. E. Bruce, who twice served as America's ambassador to France, was similarly admired by members of the inner circle. White would cement a deep and enduring friendship with Bruce, who had graciously responded to White's frantic plea for help when his brother, Robert, a research scientist with the U.S. Air Force, was questioned as a security risk as "the brother of an individual reliably reported to be a Communist." The blight of McCarthyism had finally penetrated Theodore White's comfortably insulated life in Paris. Preposterous though the charges seemed, the Air Force Loyalty Board demanded answers from his brother, who was then working on a sensitive project at the Massachusetts Institute of Technology. Never mind that White himself had been cleared by the FBI, the Department of Defense, General Dwight D. Eisenhower's headquarters, and the European Command in

57. Manuscript of THW profile of Pierre Mendes-France, TWA, Box 74, Folder 10.
58. "The Man of Change," *Time*, June 28, 1954, 27; "Home Is the Hero," *Time*, December 6, 1954, 37.
59. Harold Callender, "French Premier with a Deadline," *New York Times Magazine*, June 27, 1954, 10.

Germany, and that he held NATO press card No. 6; Robert had to answer the charges in ten days or lose his job. Bruce was quick to intercede. He telephoned Robert White for the details of his case and promised "to get on it immediately." In a thank-you note to Bruce several days later, Theodore White wrote, "That was the quickest answer to a call for help I have ever received." White considered Bruce "the very model of what was best in the old American Establishment."[60]

Late in 1951, White wrote a freelance profile of Bruce, but he was left without a publishable story when Bruce was named undersecretary of state early in 1952. However, when President Eisenhower reappointed Bruce to the ambassadorial post in 1953, White's story came to life once again and was published by the *Times* early in 1954. White's praise for Bruce was no less lavish than his praise for Monnet. Bruce was "the hottest property on the diplomatic circuit today," according to White, who credited him with "the throttling of French inflation in 1949," and described him as "the ablest current American performer in the romance and glitter scene."[61]

Any argument against insider journalism will find no more sterling an illustration of its potential for compromising objectivity than in the correspondence that passed between reporter and subject as White prepared the original version of his Bruce profile in 1952. In a letter accompanying a draft of his story, White asked Bruce to read it carefully, "for I should like it, first, to be accurate and, secondly, to cause you as little discomfort or displeasure as is possible."[62] And apparently since Bruce's wife, Evangeline, who had studied Chinese history with John King Fairbank during her years at Radcliffe, had also developed a friendship with White, she too received a copy of the story from White along with a note that admonished her to read it carefully, especially those paragraphs that related to her activities as the ambassador's wife. David Bruce obligingly responded with a six-page, handwritten memorandum which was accompanied by his annotated copy of White's manuscript.

The ambassador's comments ranged from a request that he be described as "rich" rather than "very rich" to the rather good-humored admonition that White avoid portraying Bruce's "fling in newspapering [as] unsuccessful!

60. Gladys White, letter to Nancy White, May 5, 1952, TWA, Box 9; Robert White, letter to THW, May 13, 1952, TWA, Box 10; THW, letter to David Bruce, May 17, 1952, TWA, Box 10, Folder 7.

61. Theodore H. White, "Portrait of an Ambassador to a Dream," *New York Times Magazine*, January 17, 1954, 15.

62. THW, letter to David Bruce, January 18, 1952, TWA, Box 10, Folder 7.

I thought it was very promising, but wanted to fry other fish." White's exaggerated praise of Bruce's aristocratic wife was an echo of the hyperbole he had once heaped on Madame Chiang. He waxed purple over her exquisite figure and explained that "Paris couturiers consider her the finest display case for their wares." Indeed, Christian Dior had once designed an entire wardrobe for Mrs. Bruce for one of her trips back to the United States as a way of advertising his original designs, White's profile explained. "Like Cinderella, Mrs. Bruce sent them back after the trip," according to the manuscript. The ambassador's comments on the story, however, cautioned White that using Dior's name might cause both the designer and Mrs. Bruce some embarrassment and advised him to seek Evangeline's permission. In a later draft, White substituted "one of the great houses" for Dior's name.[63]

Bradlee insisted that most reporters, even in those more innocent times, would have considered it unthinkable to ask a subject to read and edit a story before publication as White had done with David Bruce. It was, however, something White would continue to do with some frequency in subsequent years.

NATO also rated a place on White's "much admired list." Three and one-half years after its creation, White offered the opinion that it had "shaken down into an efficient, functioning institution—the closest approach to an international governing body the world has ever known. It now in 1952 had a highly effective military arm, a somewhat less effective but still valuable civilian arm, and the mechanism for gearing together in common purpose the separate fragments of a common civilization."[64]

An echo of alarm about the Soviet Union and its aggressive intentions emerged as a common theme in stories members of the inner circle wrote in the early 1950s, and thus justified to them the need for NATO. *U.S. News and World Report,* for example, occasionally seemed preoccupied with questions about the expectation of war, about Soviet military strength, and about Europe's defenses. The magazine sometimes used the question and answer format with Robert Kleiman, its regional editor in central Europe, as a way of presenting information about the political situation on the continent. "Russia's Germany Makes Gains" announced the headline on a 1950 report about the Soviet occupation of East Germany. What did East Germans think of Russia, what is the state of East German industry, did

63. David Bruce, memorandum, "For Teddy," January 20, 1952, TWA, Box 71, Folder 24.
64. THW, untitled manuscript for *The Reporter,* December 9, 1952, TWA, Box 71, Folder 22.

the people expect war, did young people take communism seriously, the *U.S. News* editors asked their man in Europe. Kleiman said the country's industrial progress had been terrific and thanks to Communist-controlled trade unions, there were no labor problems. Using police controls, he explained, the Communists were tightening their grip throughout the country. "Tighter political controls will aid in the protection of Soviet communication lines if Russia decides to invade West Germany . . . [and] make it easier for the Communists to remain in power if Russia withdraws from Germany," Kleiman observed.[65]

In another "interview" with Kleiman less than a year later, the *U.S. News* editors questioned him about Soviet strength in Europe. An editor's note that preceded the questions and answers wondered, "Is Russia getting ready for World War III?" Observing that war-weary Europeans lived "under the threat of Stalin's armies," the editor's note asked, "If the shooting starts, which side will they [the Europeans] be on?" Airfields under construction throughout East Germany were of a sufficient size to accommodate bombers, Kleiman explained, but he added the comforting observation that the disparity between Soviet and Allied troop strength "has been vastly overestimated."

A story by Callender in the *New York Times Magazine* early in 1951 also raised a sense of foreboding about the isolationist impulses emerging in both Europe and the United States following the outbreak of war in Korea. Both the Marshall Plan and NATO, Callender explained, were motivated less by American generosity than by the nation's strategic interests. A free Europe was vital to the United States, the story warned in language that became commonplace during the cold war, because "its conquest by the Soviet Union might shift the productive balance of power against us."[66]

White was similarly preoccupied with the specter of Soviet conquest, and his writing emphasized the brutality and harshness of life in the Soviet Union. Carbons of those stories in his archive echo a blend of loathing, fear, and consternation toward the Soviet Union that are no less strident than the anti-Communist rhetoric of John Foster Dulles.

In 1953, for example, he warned of an impending doomsday scenario created by the startling increases in Soviet economic growth. Although the

65. "Russia's Germany Makes Gains," *U.S. News and World Report*, October 13, 1950, 19.
66. Harold Callender, "Why a Free Europe Is Vital to Us," *New York Times Magazine*, January 2, 1951, 5.

"Communist contagion" had been initially sterilized by the Soviet Union's abysmal standard of living, it was, White advised, within the power of Soviet rulers to close the gap between the powers within a decade. "A continuation of Soviet economic expansion and present European stagnation," he warned, "offers the Soviets an almost ironclad guarantee of ultimate superiority." Seeing only malevolent intentions in Soviet policies, White conjectured that Soviet leaders would follow a strategy of economic wreckage, "buccaneering on the world market" by dumping its surplus wheat and its abundant gold supplies in ways that would upset the world's monetary standards. "The Soviet Union, however glib its future protestations of peace and amity may be, has as its sole, continuing objective the destruction of our kind of world."[67]

While that story, which appeared in *The Reporter* on May 26, 1953, characterized the Soviet Union as a major threat, its theme contradicted the ideas White articulated in still another manuscript entitled "The Education of Joe Stalin." While there is no indication that this second article was ever published, its contents reveal the depth of White's commitment to the cold war ideology. The legend of Joseph Stalin's infallibility, White claimed, is the product of the "stupendous myth-building of his state," a propaganda mechanism that has duped the Russian people and hypnotized Stalin's enemies in the outer world. White's manuscript went on to cite the Soviet leader's foreign policy blunders. Stalin miscalculated badly when he assumed that America had neither the will nor the power to intervene in Korea—a blunder that resulted "not only in defeat in Korea but in the vast rearmament of the Western alliance all around the globe," White insisted. And in what appears to be a rather remarkable oversimplification of postwar history, White claimed that Stalin had misread America's instinct for friendship and mindlessly created an enemy "in the most powerful nation on earth." Finally, White denounced Stalin's support in the 1920s for that "corrupt scoundrel," Chiang.[68]

White continued to give voice to the ideology of the cold war in his highly praised book *Fire in the Ashes,* an assessment of Western Europe at midcentury published in 1954. The reconstruction of England, France, and Germany under the relentless threat of Soviet aggression was White's principal focus. In his opinion the Soviet Union had bungled in Europe, and

67. THW, manuscript of "The Challenge of Soviet Economic Growth," TWA, Box 72, Folder 4.
68. THW, manuscript of "The Education of Joe Stalin," TWA, Box 70, Folder 5.

no peace with it was possible. *Fire in the Ashes* was promoted as a book that would deepen one's "pride in being an American." Reviewers praised it as an "urgent, rewarding and readable book," and applauded its "enlightened anti-communism." In an amusing irony, one that White could hardly have appreciated at the time, his publisher sent an advance copy of the book to J. Edgar Hoover, promising that he would find it to be "one of the most devastating exposes of the philosophy and policies of Communism that you've ever read." An unsigned margin note on the letter advises Hoover: "I suggest no reply."[69]

Correspondence in White's FBI file indicates that in late 1953, when the letter from his publisher, William Sloane Associates, Inc., was written, the bureau still suspected that White might be a Communist, and it continued to pass those suspicions along to other government agencies for more than a decade. It is uncertain whether White knew that the government he so revered was keeping a confidential file on him, one that described him as "a Communist sympathizer, a fellow traveler, and a writer whose articles were pro-Soviet."[70] Had either Hoover or his agents paid even scant attention to White's writing, they might have come to a very different conclusion.

White was clearly part of the system of shared values that existed between news makers and news reporters, a system that resulted in a form of journalism that resembled the function of the chorus in ancient Greek drama. White and his colleagues in the Paris inner circle often operated with the same procession-like movements required of the Greek chorus that served to reinforce the principal themes of the events being played out on stage. Thus, journalists became a presence at stage right, tendering comments on the dramatic developments of the cold war, foreshadowing, on occasion, some future doom, and adding lyric decoration to the gesticulations of the principal actors at center stage. Like the men who populated those choruses at the Theater of Dionysus in Athens during the fifth century B.C., insider journalists helped to create illusions that reinforced the status quo rather than challenged it. The influence of the Paris insiders reached well beyond the readership of their own prestigious publications. Because they were generally considered to be the leaders of their profession, their views and interpretations of events were invariably echoed by journalists in the less exalted media leagues.

69. Letter from William Sloane Associates, Inc., September 9, 1953, Federal Bureau of Investigation, File #100–369814.
    70. Ibid.

That is not, of course, to say that there were no voices of dissent. *I. F. Stone's Weekly* and *The Nation* both espoused liberal ideas and continued to question government policies. Similarly, the *National Review* began giving voice to conservative doctrines in 1955. But with their meager circulations, those journals had little impact alongside mass-circulation powerhouses whose readers numbered in the millions. With the exception of those few years in the late 1940s when he wrote for the liberal *New Republic* and Overseas News Agency, and in the early 1950s, when he wrote for *The Reporter,* much of White's work appeared in mass-circulation publications— *Time, Life, Collier's, Fortune,* and the *New York Times Sunday Magazine.*

I. F. Stone, that keen-eyed Cassandra of the left who continued to question his government even in the face of the overwhelming chorus of consensus, understood how the press had been co-opted. Although few people listened to him in the 1950s and early 1960s, time and distance have weighted his observations with special eloquence. "Most of my colleagues," Stone wrote in 1955, "agree with the Government and write the accepted thing because that is what they believe; they are indeed—with honorable exceptions—as suspicious of the non conformist as any group in Kiwanis." While White and other consensus journalists saw in the Korean conflict a necessity to contain communism, Stone saw aggressive instigation by the United States. Stone rejected the government's official explanation that North Korean forces had unexpectedly crossed the 38th parallel and attacked South Korea. He believed instead that the United States had provoked the attack that led Truman to commit ground forces in Korea in June 1950, and that MacArthur had forced the Chinese to enter the war some months later with his reckless forays close to the Yalu River. Stone gave voice to those ideas in his book, *The Hidden History of the Korean War,* but it languished in manuscript form for more than a year because publishers in both America and England found the subject too controversial. When it was finally published in the spring of 1952 by the Monthly Review Press, which was run by Paul Sweezy and Leo Huberman, the editors of the socialist *Monthly Review,* the book was largely ignored by the mainstream press and its publishers were called before America's infamous witch-hunt committees.[71]

Stone protested against the cold war ideology. He denounced America's defense policies during the Eisenhower years, lamenting that Democrats and Republicans were equally committed to the arms race. Stone, in contrast,

---

71. I. F. Stone, *The Haunted Fifties,* 176. Andrew Patner, *I. F. Stone: A Portrait,* 15; James Aronson, *The Press and the Cold War,* 109.

saw the arms race as "the line of least resistance . . . a grandiose WPA for perpetual prosperity until the bombs go off." Stone was also a lone and largely ignored voice in the early 1950s, when he revealed that the U.S. Department of Defense had entrusted to Henry Luce's editors at Time Inc. the creation of a booklet on nuclear war and civil defense. Stone not only found that link between the government and a presumably independent media enterprise inappropriate but also wondered why no news organization had questioned the contents of the booklet, which, he charged, ignored the real costs of nuclear war.[72]

Like many of his colleagues in journalism and associates in government, White dismissed Stone and his work as part of a lunatic fringe. But White, like others, also felt a touch of sentiment for Stone's crusading spirit. "Izzy is a round, puffy little guy, easily hurt, he's had a hard time," White wrote to a friend in the early 1950s. But he disdained Stone's style of journalism every bit as much as Stone disdained the style of consensus journalists. Stone's book, White wrote soon after *The Hidden History of the Korean War* had been published, "amuses the hell out of me." When they had met some years before in Paris, Stone had been writing about the war in Korea, White explained in a letter to an associate at *The Reporter.* "I asked him how in hell he could cover the Korean war from Paris. . . . He said nobody except him ever read the daily communiqués on the Korean war which appeared in the *New York Times* (which arrived here three days late). Just by reading the communiqués carefully, he could discover things that nobody else had even dreamed about and so he was reporting Korea, from Paris, via three-day-old *New York Times.*" White concluded that although he hadn't read Stone's book, if it included that same style of reporting, "it sure gives me a laugh."[73]

Stone, in turn, disdained insider journalism because he believed it created unacceptable risks for journalists who were drawn into the seductive inner circles where White and other key American correspondents in Paris found so many of their stories. "The private dinner, the special briefing are all devices for managing the news," he wrote in 1955. White, of course, would have dismissed Stone's conclusion just as he had dismissed his reporting style. The consensus, Stone believed, robbed journalists of their constitutional freedom. He took issue, for example, with a speech Supreme Court Justice William O. Douglas made at Occidental College in which he declared there was no room for the crusading journalist in Russia. Drawing on his

72. Aronson, *The Press and the Cold War,* 317.
73. THW, letter to Philip Horton, February 23, 1953, TWA, Box 11, Folder 23.

own personal experience, Stone maintained that the growing climate of conformity and intolerance in America left precious little room for the crusading journalist here.[74]

It was only when Stone's opposition to American intervention in Vietnam as an immoral and imperialistic quest entered the popular consciousness that he earned a measure of respectability beyond his narrow band of followers on the political left. Despite his initial opposition to American involvement in Vietnam, White was never to share Stone's thinking about the immorality of American intervention in Southeast Asia. America had to stand firm, just as it had done in postwar Europe, White believed; it had to halt the expansion of communism and demonstrate its willingness to spill blood in the face of Soviet-backed aggression. The illusions of omnipotence that White had helped to create during the postwar years in Europe were the illusions on which America based its misguided policies in Vietnam.

Despite, or perhaps because of the hardships he endured in his youth, White believed unequivocally in his country. He doubtless agreed with Franklin Roosevelt when he said in 1936, "The very air of America is exhilarating." White carried that opinion with him to Paris, and through his journalism he helped to shape the way Americans viewed the outside world in the 1950s. In that view, according to Robert Dallek, Americans saw their country involved in "a contest between darkness and light, oppression and freedom, evil and good, in which one side or the other must eventually win. Rollback, liberation, massive retaliation—all suggested the apocalyptic nature of the struggle in which the country felt itself involved."[75]

It is, of course, easy to imagine how the combination of American power and its noble aspirations had the capacity to captivate both individuals and the nation. White returned to America in 1954 carrying with him a vision of his country as the world's infallible moral leader. His views of politics and power, his notions about America and its place in the world, and his concept of the journalist's role in a democracy were cemented in Chungking and Paris.

Teddy and Nancy White had sailed from LeHavre aboard the *Ile de France* with their two children and a French nanny. During one of their last interludes at their villa on the French Riviera, they had learned that *Fire in the Ashes* had been chosen by the Book-of-the-Month Club as its October selection. With the slow demise of the Overseas News Agency resulting in intermittent paychecks and the shadow of his China writing still limiting

74. I. F. Stone, *The Truman Era 1945–1952*, 216.
75. Robert Dallek, *The American Style of Foreign Policy*, 191.

the magazines that would accept White's work, the family's spending had steadily outpaced earnings through most of their years in France. So when Nancy heard the news of the book club decision, her joyous observation was, "Well, at least it means we're living within our income again." With their years as expatriates concluding on this wave of success, they returned to America "as if we were the Scott Fitzgeralds coming home again."[76] An enthusiastic review in the *New York Times* appeared on the very day when White's ship docked in New York harbor, adding a note of triumph to his homecoming.

America's new political realities, in which even as ardent a patriot as White could be suspected of disloyalty, quickly invaded his life in New York. As he had on several prior occasions, White volunteered to testify on behalf of John Paton Davies, who was, in 1954, once again being investigated for alleged Communist connections. This time, White's own loyalty became the issue. Questions were raised about a long-ago "pep talk" he had given a unit of dispirited Black troops building a road in North Burma. All White could remember a full decade later was that he had probably told the troops that after they had helped to "knock off the racist Nazis in Europe and the racist Japanese in Asia, we would all go home and knock off racists in the United States."[77] He had gone to Washington, D.C., to defend his old friend, but White found himself under interrogation. Had he tried to organize a revolt among those troops in Burma? Was his wife a Communist? How about Annalee Jacoby, his coauthor for *Thunder Out of China*? And just why had he attended those meetings with suspected subversive groups in 1946 and 1947?

For a brief time, White was denied a passport, as was the standard for Americans suspected of supporting Communist movements. He was obliged to defend himself to a State Department official. Nancy White remembers that "he was paralyzed with fear" as he prepared to explain his activities before a passport hearing officer.[78]

First at *The Reporter* and later at *Collier's*, White wrote the "big stories": the Army-McCarthy hearings; the security investigation of J. Robert Oppenheimer, the nuclear physicist who developed the atom bomb and was later denied security clearance. He wrote, too, about the connections between oil money and politics in Texas and about the migration of America's Blacks to northern cities. In mid–1956, he set out to write a lengthy story about the presidential election race between Adlai Stevenson and President

76. White, *In Search of History*, 360.
77. Ibid., 385.
78. Nancy White Hector, personal interview, April 23, 1990.

Dwight Eisenhower. He had intended to entitle the piece "The Making of the President—1956." But *Collier's*, one of several outstanding American magazines that would be victimized by the ability of television to deliver mass markets to advertisers, collapsed before White could complete the story. Years later, he told Timothy Crouse—who was writing a book about how the media covered the 1972 presidential election—"There I was . . . ready to go for the massive summary of the 1956 campaign, and here I am out of a job and no place to write it."[79]

For nearly three years, White abandoned journalism for fiction. He wrote two novels, *The Mountain Road*, based on his wartime experiences in China and *The View from the Fortieth Floor*, a roman à clef that tells of the demise of *Collier's*. Both books were favorably reviewed in the late 1950s. Populated as both books are with heroes and villains, White's stories had great appeal in Hollywood—Jimmy Stewart played the hero in *The Mountain Road*, and Gary Cooper paid eighty thousand dollars for the movie rights to *The View from the Fortieth Floor*. White's novels recreated in fiction that same monochromatic world of good and evil that had been so conspicuous in his journalism for nearly two decades. The action of those novels—featuring men with the power and authority to make life-altering decisions on behalf of people for whom they have taken responsibility—gave voice to the ideas that were at the foundation of White's worldview. The nonfiction heroes of his campaign histories would later take shape as similarly moral, God-fearing, righteous characters.

The Mountain Road was praised by no less a literary light than Ernest Hemingway. White and Hemingway's mutual friend, Major General Charles T. Lanham, with whom both men corresponded for many years, repeated a passage from one of Hemingway's letters that said, "I liked Teddy White's book. . . . It was a good story and I enjoyed it. Hope he does a good novel on the Crowell-Collier thing. His book was much better than the reviews indicated. I remember him from Chungking." White's old friend, John Hersey, applauded the book, too, calling it "a well-made book, indeed. You're a natural-born story teller, you bastard (80% of all invective, as you know, stems from envy, and I envy the naturalness of your yarn-spinning)."[80]

The Mountain Road draws on White's familiarity with China in a fast-paced, suspenseful war-era adventure. White's hero, Major Phillip Baldwin,

79. Timothy Crouse, *The Boys On the Bus*, 34.
80. Charles T. Lanham, letter to THW, September 29, 1958, TWA, Box 15, Folder 2; John Hersey, letter to THW, March 26, 1958, Theodore White Papers, John F. Kennedy Library.

who is the head of an army demolition unit, confronts the last frantic Japanese push through southeast China in 1944. His orders require him to delay the Japanese invaders and it is left to his discretion whether to accomplish that by destroying strategic points along the only road of escape. A moral predicament emerges because that winding mountain road is choked with starving refugees. So Baldwin becomes a prototype of the individual in crisis, who during his week-long journey begins to understand the beauty and horrors of China's past. A Chinese general and an American-bred Chinese woman who accompany Baldwin on this journey give voice to the conflicting ideologies between old and new China. "My novel is about virtue triumphant, proving that Americans are fundamentally men of good will, who screw things up only by accident, but generally are on the side of the angels," White wrote to his old friend Paul Hoffman.[81] In the plot of *The Mountain Road*, White had found a way to voice the morality that had been the guiding framework behind the stories he wrote as an American journalist in postwar Europe.

Despite his success with his first novel, White remained ill at ease—his first love was journalism; fiction made him uncomfortable. His journalistic persona, White explained in a letter to friends, sometimes awakened him at night and ridiculed him as "a fool, a wastrel, a sell-out, a monster. . . . I let that fellow talk me into doing a piece for *Life* this summer on the Rockefeller campaign and enjoyed the reporting of it more than anything else since *Collier's* folded."[82] White, however, held his journalistic persona at bay for more than a year while he completed another novel. The rewards he reaped from that book allowed him to once again become a political journalist.

The View from the Fortieth Floor, which made him enough money to abandon fiction, was White's thinly veiled account of the collapse of *Collier's* and its sister publication, *Women's Home Companion*. The magazines became "Trumpet" and "Gentlewoman" in White's novel, both run by the "tall, smooth, Roman-nosed" publisher, John Ridgley Warren. In the tale of the demise of this flamboyant publisher's fictional magazine empire, cold business philosophies and financial hanky-panky are played off against employee loyalty and commitment. White saw in American business the same qualities that he saw in American politics—inherent drama and excitement.

81. THW, letter to Paul Hoffman, July 1, 1957, TWA, Box 14, Folder 4.
82. THW, letter to Robert and Jane Kleiman, August 28, 1958, TWA, Box 14, Folder 22.

Former associates at *Collier's* were offended by White's book. They recalled the magazine not as a nest of intrigue, but as an idealistic adventure in which young war veterans, including the likes of Pierre Salinger, Cornelius Ryan, Peter Maas, and Robert Massie, saw themselves on a crusade into quality journalism. Penn Kimball, a *Collier's* national affairs editor whom White had first known at *Time* and later at the *New Republic,* saw himself and the magazine as the 1950s incarnation of Henry Luce and Briton Hadden when they launched *Time* in 1923.[83]

Critics were circumspect in their praise for *View,* but Hollywood loved it. Gary Cooper was smitten. He wanted the film rights so that he could play the lead. The legendary Irving "Swifty" Lazar called White with the offer one night at his club, the Century, and demanded an immediate answer. Eighty thousand dollars. Say yes or no now, Swift demanded. White grabbed at the offer. That "Hollywood money," as he later called it, would buy for White the freedom "to resume the only profession I was ever really proud of."[84] The result of those longings was a book that would transform political journalism in America. He turned a presidential election race into a tale of heroes, suspense, and adventure; a story infused throughout with White's idealized vision of America. He succeeded in transforming the grubby business of a political campaign into an epic that featured large and noble personalities who would lead America through its large and noble mission to save the world from communism. And in the process, Theodore White continued to create illusions.

83. Penn Kimball, taped personal interview, April 11, 1990.
84. THW, letter to Tillman and Peggy Durdin, October 7, 1959, TWA, Box 15, Folder 21.

Chapter Four

. . . .

. . . The Making of a Mythical President

When that book came out it was like Columbus
telling about America at the court of Ferdinand
and Isabella. Goddam thing was an unbelievable
success. —Theodore H. White, quoted in *The
Boys on the Bus*

The story begins at midnight. Conflict and suspense start building in the opening sentences, which speak of mystery, power, and secrets. Plot and characters start to take shape in hazy outlines. The focus sweeps from a New Hampshire village across the American landscape, then travels back through history to Rome and Athens—all on the first page. With its vast panorama, its drama, and its detail, *The Making of the President 1960* hardly unfolds in the way books about democracy and politics traditionally did in the early 1960s. That, however, is precisely what its author, the novelist and reporter Theodore White, intended. America was unique, he believed, "so very different that most Americans scarcely recognized the nature of their history."[1]

1. Theodore H. White, *America in Search of Itself*, 99.

107

White had set out to write a textbook describing the vast process of the American presidency; his mission was "to write [about] public affairs—but differently."[2] The book that resulted from White's aspiration vividly illustrated how those thorough, objective, stenographic presidential election reports that had traditionally appeared in the nation's leading newspapers had overlooked part of the essence of American politics. White believed that the mechanics of a presidential campaign held the intensity of an action-packed, wide-screen thriller. In a candidate's style, White believed, one could discern personality, and personality ultimately determined the quality of leadership.

In contrast, in its stories about the 1960 race, the *New York Times* and the *Washington Post*, for example, followed the customary practice of covering what might be characterized as the "public campaign" while they ignored what went on behind the scenes, which, until the appearance of White's book, might easily have been considered the "private campaign." A sampling of nearly two hundred campaign stories from the *New York Times* and the *Washington Post* reveals that the newspapers seldom ventured beyond the public record. In applying the long-tested techniques of police beat reporting to the business of politics, the *Times* and the *Post* coverage of key events in the campaign—candidates' announcements, primary elections, party conventions, televised debates, and closing days—suggests that its overriding mission was to create an official historic record of the campaign, rather than to aid voters in making an intelligent presidential choice. White's book, however, succeeded in demonstrating that although an official record of the public campaign might have historic value, a look at the private campaign offered a vastly more compelling story, one that could serve to better enlighten voters about the men who sought to lead America.

An analysis of the issues and anecdotes that White used to portray the race between John Kennedy and Richard Nixon shows that while White's perspective broke new journalistic ground, it also helped to create a mythic identity for the new president, one that enlarged the presidency and ennobled the man who achieved it. With his focus on personality and strategy and in using the techniques of fiction, White cast the winner as hero and nurtured grandiose visions of America itself. In the process, he created further illusions about American life. White's book also incorporated the essence of insider journalism and consensus ideology, demonstrating convergence of two important strains in mid-twentieth-century journalism.

2. White, *In Search of History*, 453.

White's work changed the ground rules that determined how journalists covered presidential elections. The result would be a new era in the history of the media and American politics.

The Making of the President 1960 not only introduced a new genre of political reporting but also was a departure from books about elections and the presidency. White's book became the oracle of the 1960 campaign, a reference point for other historians writing about the Kennedy years. Arthur M. Schlesinger Jr. deferred to White in *A Thousand Days,* saying, "I can only add a few notes from the outside to White's compelling portrayal of the campaign." Theodore Sorenson bowed to "the astute Theodore White" in *The Kennedy Legacy,* for his analysis of how the Kennedy campaign had devised a strategy to use volunteers in a way that made them feel wired into the power system of American life.[3]

For years, White had looked with a sense of wonder at America's peaceful, orderly political process. Compared with the turmoil and upheavals he had witnessed in China in the 1940s and Europe in the 1950s, White saw majesty in America's political system. For White, a presidential election—that single day when the American voters spoke about their leadership—counted as one of democracy's sacraments. Politics was the mechanism that linked individuals to power, and White's long fascination with power reached all the way back to his impoverished childhood in Boston. His vision of America was an intellectualized and sophisticated replica of his mother's simplistic view of America as "a grand and glorious place." White's awe for the country and its distinctive system of political leadership is reflected in some of his early musings about his election chronicle:

> In Russia the succession is determined in the classical fashion of tyrants —the aspirant strikes for the throat of the tyrant and if he wins he becomes a tyrant, if he loses he loses his head. And so in China, too. Again, in such countries as England and France it is almost impossible to mistake the shape of the next leader, he has come up slowly through the party escalator. And he is there. In America, not so. . . . Power here is intangible, though nothing less real—it is power to hurl missiles, plunge the world to death, tax, demote, promote, create, alter, refashion the nation. Yet you can't isolate this power because it belongs to the people. Probably ten men go to sleep tonight dreaming that they may go to sleep in the White House a year hence. But none will be killed

3. Arthur M. Schlesinger Jr., *A Thousand Days,* 19; Theodore Sorenson, *The Kennedy Legacy,* 45.

for having tried. So in our country you have one of the most subtle,
puzzling, sophisticated political processes of choice of leadership the
world has ever seen. The process itself is almost unknown to the men
who participate in it.[4]

Viewed from White's angle of vision, politics was a noble and glorious
calling, not a grubby, compromise-filled business of ego and greed as some
perceived it both then and now. In place of the back rooms, the odorous
cigars, and the furtive deals that others associated with politics, White saw
grandeur and limitless possibilities. He was fascinated by the personalities of
those backroom characters. He believed all their deals were not necessarily
nefarious. And he wanted to know the brand names of their fat cigars. White
introduced the idea that character mattered in a president, that personal
style was an important measure of a man, and that campaign strategy
proffered a glimpse of leadership skills. Moreover, White had the ability
to put the election into a historical context. By explaining America's past—
using presidents from Jefferson to Eisenhower to illustrate where we had
been as a nation—his stories took on the sweep of history. Then he set
those personalities and events in the vast panorama of the 1960 census, and
skillfully explained such emerging patterns in American life as the population explosion and resulting suburbanization, shifting employment trends
from a blue collar to white collar workforce, the vanishing American farmer,
and ethnic, religious, and racial divisions. In short, he saw in presidential
politics an all-American morality play with large characters; a vast landscape;
a series of dramatic confrontations; and a virtuous hero cast as a latter-day
cowboy armed with ideas, riding a jet plane in search of votes, intent on
saving America.

The success of White's book is in its narrative, which is both intellectual
and visceral. For a book to reach beyond the commonplace and become
"great," White once explained to a friend, it "must be bound together by
more than a chronology, or fine language or prismatic facets of personality.
A book, to be a great book, must have a unity, a dramatic unfolding from a
single central theme so that the reader comes away from the book as if he
had participated himself in the development of a wonder."[5]

White's 1960s campaign history succeeded in creating the sense that he
was everywhere, that he had an eye and an ear inside each campaign. That

4. THW, memorandum dated January 14, 1960, TWA, Box 100, Folder 3.
5. THW, undated letter to Theodore Sorenson, TWA, Box 22, Folder 17.

was accomplished with the help of the dispatches of *Time* reporters, whose weekly files, he knew from his own experience as a correspondent on the magazine, were far more detailed than the brief reports that appeared in the magazine's columns. White's old friend, Richard Clurman, who was *Time*'s chief of correspondents, broke his own rule that forbade the use of correspondent files outside the magazine and allowed White to see those weekly reports.[6] With *Time*'s unused material, his own journalistic eye, and some well-placed connections within campaign organizations, White produced a book that reached deep below the surface of the campaign. And unlike his colleagues, White chose to write about that private campaign. White's gift was not only revealing what lay behind the scenes of a campaign but also pointing out its obvious but often-overlooked details: moments of decisions to run, the campaign staff, and the machinations candidates employed to win.

So *The Making of the President 1960* became a tapestry in which history and journalism are interwoven. What White achieved was a book that had Tocquevillean qualities; it was simultaneously a civics lesson and an adventure story. As it turned out, 1960 became a turning point in American history; it was destined to become a landmark year, much as the elections of 1800 and 1860 had been. As a result, White's book was a snapshot of America at a pivotal moment in its history, a moment that marked a divide between the perceived normalcy of the Eisenhower years and the cataclysmic disorders of the 1960s. There were, to be sure, other books about presidents and elections, but none quite compared with White's blend of journalism and history seasoned with the flavors of fiction.

The American presidency has fascinated and bemused writers for nearly two centuries. With its unique powers, novel system of checks and balances, and complex selection process devised by the founding fathers, the office of the president has been a source of endless study by historians and political scientists. Curiously, the man who so popularized American presidential politics was himself largely unfamiliar with the intricacies of that system until just a few years before he wrote his best-seller. Because his early career in journalism had taken him abroad, he knew much more about the forces that shaped governments in Chungking, Paris, and Bonn than he did about power in Washington, D.C. When he returned to America in 1954, White was not unlike two famous travelers from an earlier century—Alexis de

6. Richard Clurman, personal interview, March 22, 1990.

Tocqueville and James Bryce—who had also looked at America's political system with a sense of wonder.

Tocqueville had marveled in *Democracy in America* at how a mood of agitation and intrigue grips the people in advance of an election. The nation, he wrote, "glows with feverish excitement; the election is the daily theme of the press, the subject of private conversation, the end of every thought and every action." But that mood is quickly replaced by calm once the vote is cast: "Who can refrain from astonishment that such a storm should have risen." James Bryce, the Scottish traveler whose appraisal of America followed Tocqueville's by half a century, was similarly awed by a presidential election: "Nowhere does government by the people, through the people, for the people, take a more directly impressive and powerfully stimulative form than in the choice of a chief magistrate by fifteen millions of citizens voting on one day."[7]

White's book caught the wave of a resurgent fascination with the presidency that developed in the mid–1950s. The presidency had previously captured the interest of book publishers during Woodrow Wilson's two terms as president in the early twentieth century and later during Franklin D. Roosevelt's years in the White House. Writing in *America in Our Time,* God-frey Hodgson credits Clinton Rossiter's acclaimed analysis of the nation's highest office with this renewed interest in America's leadership. Rossiter's view of the modern presidency, written in 1960, held that Roosevelt created it, Harry Truman defended it, and Dwight D. Eisenhower inherited it. In the postwar years, particularly during Eisenhower's presidency, America assumed its status as a superpower and, in the words of Winston Churchill, took its place "at the summit of the world." By the 1950s, Rossiter wrote, the president's stature in the world "grows mightier every year. For some time to come, the President of the United States will also be the president of the West."[8] White not only shared that view but also helped popularize it.

Richard Neustadt's *Presidential Power,* also published in 1960, observed that by the close of the 1950s, the presidency had grown into an unwieldy institution operated by two thousand men and women. The central problem of the presidency was whether the man at the top of that bureaucracy could harness the system rather than be harnessed by it. And yet in the public perception, Neustadt said, the presidency was growing more expansive.

7. Alexis de Tocqueville, *Democracy in America,* 1:136; James Bryce, *The American Commonwealth,* 2:221.
8. Clinton Rossiter, *The American Presidency,* 40.

"Everybody now expects the man inside the White House to do something about everything. Laws and customs now reflect acceptance of him as the Great Initiator, an acceptance quite as widespread at the Capital as at this end of Pennsylvania Avenue."[9] That, too, was an idea that White helped to popularize.

White's book, in turn, would further widen those expectations both because of its reach and because of the way he romanticized the presidency. And since White's book was popular history, it reached a far larger audience than the more scholarly tomes by Rossiter and Neustadt. As a result, according to Godfrey Hodgson, White's chronicle of the 1960 election was an important element in a renewed focus on the man who occupied the Oval Office. "His book was perhaps only less responsible than the princely style of its hero for the fascination with the presidency that so many educated Americans seem to have felt in the first half of the sixties."[10]

In advance of the 1960 election at least, publishers appeared to believe that political books looked like moneymakers. One reviewer complained about "the publishers and a host of hopeful authors who in the last six months have dumped a greater poundage of campaign biographies and primers of political science on the reading public than this reviewer can remember in any other election year."[11] John A. Wells wrote *The Voter's Presidential Handbook,* which described the history of the presidency complete with "Who's Who" style biographies of the nine men who were most prominently mentioned as presidential aspirants. Malcolm Moos and Stephen Hess covered much of the same material in *Hats in the Ring,* an informative but more entertaining description of the succession of leadership in America.

Those books had appeared prior to the election, their purpose being instructive rather than historical. No writer had ever traced the mechanics of a single presidential campaign back to the contenders' first aspirations to that office. As a result, there is little in the way of precedent with which to compare White's 1960 epic and nothing to portend its success. Once an election was over, publishers lost all interest in it.

The 1960 election had receded into history when White's four-hundred-page account of that pivotal race appeared in bookstores around the country on July 4, 1961. John F. Kennedy had already been president for six months,

9. Richard Neustadt, *Presidential Power,* 6.
10. Hodgson, *America in Our Time,* 100.
11. Cabell Phillips, "Light Horses and Dark," *New York Times Book Review,* May 22, 1960, 6.

and the gaiety and dash of his New Frontier was being threatened by an atmosphere of international crisis. The Bay of Pigs invasion had ended disastrously; Premier Khrushchev was threatening to halt access to West Berlin; the deteriorating situation in Laos looked as if it might require American military intervention. White had problems finding a publisher; a dreary book about presidential politics would never sell, argued representatives of William Sloane Associates, Inc., the house that had previously published White's best-selling books. Random House was similarly skeptical, and Bennett Cerf, its president, declined the project. So did Peter Schwed at Simon and Schuster. Indeed, White himself called it "a non best-seller" and never imagined the book would sell 4.2 million copies. Although his previous books, both fiction and nonfiction, had become best-sellers and Book-of-the-Month Club selections, White anticipated no such success for this project. On a visit to Cambridge, Massachusetts, in the fall of 1959, White told Schlesinger, whom he had known since their days as Harvard undergraduates in the class of 1938, of his plans to write a book about the election, one which Schlesinger said White believed would "only be of interest to scholars. He told me, 'I know I won't make any money on it at all.' "[12]

Recounting his early thinking about the project in a letter to his old friend John Hersey, White wrote that he had told his wife, Nancy, "What I wanted to do most was to report the presidential campaign of 1960 in my own way but that I couldn't see any magazine or newspaper who would pay for the kind of stuff I wanted to write." Since he had just been paid the eighty thousand dollars for film rights to *View from the Fortieth Floor,* Nancy had reasoned "that since I had this Hollywood money, why didn't I do it my own way, for nobody but myself." For her part, his wife predicted that if Kennedy won it would be a terrific book, but "if Nixon won it would be a dog."[13] In an explanation of the project to his former publisher Luce, he wrote, "When you come to think of it, the grand process of choosing an American president is one of the strangest, most complicated, most sophisticated exercises in power and persuasion that politics offer anywhere in the world."[14]

On October 27, 1959, with the election more than a year away, White outlined his first thoughts about the project. The nation's newspapers spoke of the more visible and more immediate issues. "Nothing yet appears on the front page about the election," White wrote. "The pages are covered

12. THW, memorandum to Alfred A. Knopf Jr., June 6, 1961, TWA, Box 17, Folder 9; Arthur M. Schlesinger Jr., personal interview, April 25, 1990.

13. White, *In Search of History,* 454.

14. THW, letter to Henry Luce, February 16, 1960, TWA, Box 17, Folder 1.

with all sorts of news. Soviet pictures of the far side of the moon, juvenile delinquency, the steel strike, [Secretary of Commerce Douglas] Dillon calls for end of trade restrictions on American trade."[15] Yet White knew from his experience as a political reporter that the campaign was already well underway. Behind the scenes, removed from the scrutiny of the press, at least seven men—two Republicans and five Democrats—were developing strategies designed to take them to the White House. His book would trace the steps and missteps of each would-be president and explain how just one of them triumphed. He put each candidate under a magnifying glass and explored the roots of his ambitions, the people who surrounded him, and the strategy each one devised to make the White House his home.

Because his story depended so heavily on dramatic conflicts, again and again as the campaign unfolded, White anticipated disaster for his project. Nelson Rockefeller's announcement late in 1959 that he would not seek the Republican nomination, White fretted, left him without conflict between the conservative and moderate elements of the Republican Party. Similar doubts plagued him right up until the votes were counted on November 8, 1960, when Kennedy's narrow margin robbed White of the sweeping dramatic climax he had envisioned. "This is a hell of a bad gamble," he mused early in the election season. "When I talk the book out it sounds good, yet when I am alone it frightens me."[16]

There is neither a specific day nor a single story that marks the start of the 1960 campaign on the pages of the *New York Times* and the *Washington Post*. Stories about the race slowly accumulated over a period of several years, starting with the speculation about the next presidential race that began immediately after Eisenhower was reelected in 1956. Based on the increased volume and prominence the newspapers gave to 1960 presidential politics, a two-week period between the end of 1959 and mid-January 1960 can be identified as the appropriate beginning of the *Times*'s and *Post*'s election coverage. In the space of a fortnight, Rockefeller, who had been expected to challenge Vice President Richard Nixon for the Republican nomination, abruptly withdrew from the competition, and Nixon announced that he was a "willing" but not a formal candidate for his party's nomination. On the Democratic side, two candidates—Hubert H. Humphrey and John F. Kennedy—announced their intention to seek the nomination, and a movement to draft Adlai E. Stevenson got underway in the Midwest.

15. THW, memorandum dated October 27, 1959, TWA, Box 100, Folder 3.
16. THW, memorandum dated January 14, 1960, TWA, Box 100, Folder 3.

Governor Rockefeller's announcement on the day after Christmas stunned political insiders, according to the *New York Times*. It was, according to the newspaper's page one story, "unforeseen and almost inexplicable to many observers." Following the newspaper's standard approach to political news, the story stuck close to the official announcement and relied heavily on unnamed sources. The article, written by Warren Weaver Jr., reiterated Rockefeller's contention that any bid for the GOP nomination would involve "a massive struggle" because "the great majority of those who will control the Republican convention stand opposed to any contest." Weaver said Rockefeller's reasoning was "a barely veiled method of saying that almost every leading Republican he had met in his tours of fifteen states was formally or informally committed to the Vice President."[17] The article neither identified those leading Republicans nor offered any reasons for their unwillingness to consider Rockefeller.

The *Washington Post* also marked Rockefeller's stunning announcement with a banner headline splashed across its front page on that Sunday after Christmas. The news story characterized the New York governor's move as "a major surprise." A companion front-page story quoted a *New York Herald Tribune* reporter who had recently completed a biography of the vice president as having said that Nixon thought the announcement was a joke when he first heard it and that no one "was more surprised by the news from Albany than Mr. Nixon."[18] The remainder of the story featured reactions ranging from relief to disappointment from prominent Republicans to Rockefeller's move and noted that President Eisenhower had declined comment on the news.

In contrast, White's account of the Rockefeller withdrawal showcased his skills as a reporter, historian, and writer. Rockefeller's sweeping victory in the New York gubernatorial race in 1958 had made him an obvious contender for the GOP nomination. Moreover, according to White, "Nelson Rockefeller made no bones of the fact—he disliked Richard M. Nixon and considered him incapable of the role of President." In his travels around the country, White revealed that Rockefeller was "shabbily mistreated by Nixon zealots in Southern California," but "handsomely received" in the state of Washington. Important bankers and businessmen (many of whom

17. Warren Weaver Jr., "Rockefeller Gives Up '60 Race, Clearing the Path for Nixon," *New York Times*, December 27, 1959.
18. Chalmers Roberts, "Rockefeller Drops Out of GOP Race; Nixon Sees Him in Major Party Role," *Washington Post*, December 27, 1959; John V. Lindsay, "Nixon Surprised by Decision; Praises Governor's Leadership," *Washington Post*, December 27, 1959.

are named) entertained him at their exclusive clubs. But they all considered Rockefeller a political newcomer and a potentially dangerous one at that. What the New York governor discovered, one of his aides told White, was that state chairmen and business leaders shared the same view: "Nelson is too goddamned independent; he was too brilliant and unpredictable; Nelson's money hurt him because he didn't need them." Rockefeller found, according to White, "the bony skeleton of the Party, the hard-core descendants of Thurlow Weed, Hanna, and Taft, would have none of him."[19]

Days later news of U.S. Senator Hubert Humphrey's announcement that he would seek the Democratic presidential nomination made front-page news in both papers. The *Washington Post* observed that although Humphrey was the first Democratic contender to officially enter the race, Kennedy was even then considered the front-runner, a contention echoed in the *New York Times*'s story of Humphrey's entry into the race. A *Times* news analysis by James Reston that accompanied the announcement story added some dimension to the Minnesota senator, explaining that despite his intelligence, industry, and common touch, Humphrey "has never overcome the reputation he acquired in his early days here as a gabby extremist of the Left."[20]

White's personal preoccupation with power led him to question the ways in which other men yearned for power—how and when did those yearnings take shape were the questions he sought to answer in his campaign narrative. Those questions forced him to journey backward from the candidates' official declarations in search of those key moments when the desire for power became tangible. The genesis of Humphrey's political yearnings was in 1958 when "he had begun to permit himself to discuss the long reach for the presidency." Those yearnings were finally transformed into a concrete program, White explained, in the summer of 1959 when Humphrey, his wife, and seven political associates gathered to map strategy in a Duluth hotel room. They realized then that there was only one chance in ten of capturing the nomination, but nonetheless set up the Humphrey for President committee.[21]

Three days after Humphrey had made his formal announcement, Kennedy declared his intention to run for the Democratic nomination at a news

19. Theodore H. White, *The Making of the President 1960*, 74, 80.
20. Robert C. Albright, "Humphrey Will Seek Nomination," *Washington Post*, December 31, 1959; John D. Morris, "Humphrey Enters Presidency Race; Sees Uphill Fight," *New York Times*, December 31, 1959; James Reston, "The Log-Cabin Approach," *New York Times*, December 31, 1959.
21. White, *The Making of the President 1960*, 35.

conference in the Caucus of the Senate Office Building, news that made the front pages of the *New York Times* and the *Washington Post* on Sunday, January 3. The *Times*'s lead story by Russell Baker noted that Kennedy was the first serious Roman Catholic to seek the nomination since Alfred E. Smith ran in 1928 and focused almost entirely on the candidate's official statements. The story—even its headline—made much of Kennedy's emphatic refusal to consider the vice presidential nomination and his insistence that anyone who wanted to be taken seriously as a presidential candidate ought to enter some primary contests. Baker, it seemed, was emphasizing the very points that were critical to a Kennedy candidacy without putting them in any historic or political context. He ignored the fact that primary elections had often meant very little in the process of selecting a nominee. Indeed, Harry Truman had once dismissed them as "a lot of eye wash."[22] Baker suggested somewhat obliquely that part of the Kennedy strategy "is to break out of his political containing wall by showing strength in the Presidential primaries." Thus, Baker's story seemed to legitimize Kennedy's approach but never explained that the Democratic political bosses neither liked nor wanted Kennedy as their nominee and that in entering the primaries Kennedy was making an end run around the party powerhouses who traditionally anointed the presidential candidate. In its frequent references to unnamed "Democratic leaders" and reports of "wide speculation within the party," Baker's story underscores how traditional political reporting often seemed to speak more to insiders than to the average reader.

An accompanying front-page story by James Reston described the controversy Kennedy's candidacy had sparked within the Democratic party and how its leaders viewed the Catholic question. Reston explained that some Democratic leaders viewed Kennedy's unequivocal rejection of the vice presidency as a tactical move, while others considered it a warning to the Democratic leadership—one that suggested they dare not reject his candidacy on religious grounds without alienating his Catholic supporters. Here again in twenty-nine column inches, the "Democratic leaders" were never named.[23]

The *Washington Post*, on the other hand, devoted far less space to the Kennedy announcement and seemed far less concerned with the religious issue than the *Times*. The *Post* paid far more attention to Kennedy's

22. Russell Baker, "Kennedy in Race; Bars Second Spot in Any Situation," *New York Times*, January 3, 1960; David McCullough, *Truman*, 892.

23. James Reston, "Party's Debate on Kennedy Takes Note of Catholic Vote," *New York Times*, January 3, 1960.

"Sherman-style" declaration that he would refuse the vice presidency than to how religion and politics would converge on the issue of his Catholicism. The story, which seemed long on detail but short on insight, noted that the Senator was "tanned and healthy after a Jamaica vacation," that his "famous forelock" had been clipped, and that "his attractive, 30-year-old wife, Jacqueline, sat in the rear of the room as he spoke."[24]

White, in contrast, slowly pulled back the curtain on Kennedy's presidential bid. Readers learned that his run for the office had begun not with his official announcement in the Caucus Room of the U.S. Senate, but rather at his family's summer compound on Cape Cod on October 28, 1959, just one day after White had written himself that earliest memo about this new project. Meeting in the living room of Robert F. Kennedy's home, sixteen family members, aides, and political advisers spent three hours outlining a strategy that would win the presidency. The primaries offered Kennedy his only hope of capturing the nomination. Those victories would leave no maneuvering room for his opponents at the Democratic National Convention, which was to be held in Los Angeles in July. White's explanation of the strategy was straightforward—the Kennedy strategists sought to disenfranchise the Democratic bosses, who were unlikely to choose Kennedy. Quoting Theodore Sorenson, Kennedy's key aide, White explained that "he [Kennedy] had to prove to them that he could win. And to prove that to them, he'd have to fight hard and make them give it [the nomination] to him. If the Convention ever went into the back rooms, he'd never emerge from those back rooms."[25]

Within days of Kennedy's declaration, Nixon announced that he was a "willing" but not a "formal" candidate for the Republican nomination. He would allow his name to be entered in the New Hampshire, Ohio, and Oregon primaries, but would not campaign in any of those races, according to a front-page story in the *New York Times*. Beyond the announced contention that President Eisenhower's planned absences from Washington, D.C., required his presence there, the article by W. H. Lawrence provided no explanation of why Nixon had decided to run a low-profile campaign.

In White's telling, however, the vice president's bid for the presidency had taken shape more than a year before that enigmatic announcement in early January. At a meeting in Key Biscayne, Florida, early in 1959, Nixon

24. Chalmers M. Roberts, "Kennedy Puts Name into Race," *Washington Post*, January 3, 1960.
25. White, *The Making of the President 1960*, 59.

met with five friends and aides who determined that relying on Nixon's posture as "a statesman" would win him the presidency. Polls then showed their man lagging a few points behind Nelson Rockefeller, his only potential Republican rival at the time, but Nixon's role in settling a steelworkers' strike and his 1959 trip to Russia, where he confronted Soviet Premier Nikita Khrushchev in the famous Kitchen Debate, would wipe out that lead in the months to come. Nixon's staff, according to White, had been dismayed at the news of Rockefeller's withdrawal, for they had, in the year since their first meeting in Key Biscayne, decided to square off against Rockefeller in any primary he entered. The campaign they had anticipated would command media attention, invigorate the party, and tune up the GOP machinery for an assault on the Democratic contender in the fall election. But with those hopes disappointed, Nixon would instead continue to play statesman for several more months.

The New Hampshire primary, held on March 8, 1960, traditionally marked the formal opening of a presidential election contest. Kennedy's spillover strength from neighboring Massachusetts gave him an easy victory, but it had little value as an indicator of Kennedy's Democratic strength and therefore offered White little in the way of drama for his narrative. Kennedy's nine-to-one margin over an unknown ballpoint pen manufacturer won him front-page headlines in the *New York Times* and the *Washington Post* on March 9. "Sen. John F. Kennedy of Massachusetts now looks more formidable than ever as a candidate for President," the *Post* declared. Kennedy, however, the story noted, was careful not to read too much into the New Hampshire vote, the impressive turnout notwithstanding.[26] Ever the realist, Kennedy clearly understood he would need far more than New Hampshire's eleven delegates to win the nomination. Kennedy needed 760 delegates to capture the nomination. They would have to come from states that had their own favorite sons and from regions that were decidedly unfriendly to a Catholic contender who had a rich and controversial father. Despite the headlines suggesting Kennedy's New Hampshire victory was a significant triumph because he had amassed the highest total vote ever given any Democratic candidate in a New Hampshire presidential primary, White dismissed that contest in a brief footnote.

The Wisconsin primary, however, marked the real opening of the Democratic competition in White's telling of the story. There, in Kennedy's first

26. Edward T. Folliard, "Kennedy Boost Seen in Big Primary Vote," *Washington Post*, March 10, 1960.

head-on contest, he was matched against Humphrey, the loquacious and highly popular figure in the party's liberal wing. Because neither contender scored a decisive win in that race, their battle continued in the West Virginia primary.

Although White's account of those pivotal Wisconsin and West Virginia primaries would occupy only a fraction of the column inches that the *New York Times* devoted to covering those primary elections in 1960, his account succeeded in introducing readers to a political universe in which the forces of history, politics, contemporary life, and personal ambition interact. Each campaign stop and each campaign speech is definitively tied to the larger purpose of getting to the White House. In White's account, a state's social, ethnic, and political history are interwoven with the central characters in the political drama. The reader meets those characters on a typical campaign day. In settings that newspaper reporters might easily have dismissed as monotonous, White saw politics in the raw and turned it into compelling reading.

White's artistry lay in using a single campaign trip with each contender as the basis for a story that described the dynamics of a day on the road and mixed it with history, sociology, and political science, all linking the immediate question of who would win locally to the longer-term question of who would win nationally. In Wisconsin's Tenth District, for example, with a population of 236,000 in 1960, White found a setting in which to introduce readers to both Candidate John F. Kennedy and the seemingly wearisome grind of campaigning for the presidency. White sketched a preposterous scenario. A lean, energetic young politico stalked voters on a cheerless odyssey through decidedly unfriendly terrain, a district where polls showed the voters were 60 to 40 against him. One pathetic scene followed another as the Catholic candidate made his way across the district on St. Patrick's Day, greeting the overwhelmingly Protestant voters whose responses ranged from indifference to insolence. He reached out to shake hands in village diners and in local factories. "I'm John Kennedy, I'm running for president in the primary," he told the mostly impervious voters he met. The only sizeable audiences his advance man had mustered were in high school civics classes, where the candidate spoke to students too young to vote. For all its apparent absurdity, White cast the day as one that had an important purpose. Viewed in isolation, the candidate's 185-mile journey and his encounter with no more than sixteen hundred people—twelve hundred of whom had yet to reach voting age—seemed devoid of reason. But in the context of the candidate's "master plan," according to White, it represented one of many important steps on the road to the White House.

Victory in the Tenth District had important symbolic value, White explained. It would send an all-vital signal to the big Eastern political bosses. If he could win the votes of farmers and factory workers, of Protestants and Catholics in the Tenth District, he might well win all of Wisconsin. He was counting on all those high school kids to go home and talk to their parents, who could make him a winner on March 8. Win in the Tenth and the Democratic nomination might well be his in Los Angeles. So in his narrative, White drew a clear path that led from the grim, unfriendly, and largely empty streets of the Tenth District across an obstacle-strewn political landscape right to the Oval Office.

The most immediate obstacle in Kennedy's path was his fellow Democrat Humphrey, Minnesota's senator who had distinguished himself as a leading civil rights activist in the late 1940s and early 1950s. Expansive, good natured, thoroughly democratic, and guileless, Humphrey, as described by White, emerged as an admirable but doomed figure, the underdog with a low-budget campaign operation in both Wisconsin and West Virginia. White stood with him at the gate of the Oscar Mayer meat packing plant in Madison, Wisconsin, and followed him to a Jewish Community Center in Milwaukee, to a veteran's hospital, and to a school for deaf-mutes. Alongside that public portrait, White juxtaposed the campaign's unseen moments. Aboard Humphrey's campaign bus as it lurched over snowy, rutted roads, the tired candidate had sipped whiskey from a paper cup and discussed the campaign with the two newsmen who were covering the Wisconsin contest. Humphrey spoke of how he mourned the fate of small merchants who were being squeezed out by giants like Sears Roebuck and Co.; he lamented that young people were leaving family farms; he ruminated about his secret fears of the presidency. "Sometimes I wake up in the middle of the night and I say to myself, 'My God, what if I should be president, what if it should happen to me?' "[27] Such private musings—which fit so well into White's own homespun vision of America—had never before been the stuff of campaign reportage.

William Lawrence of the *New York Times* sat in that small circle listening in as Humphrey philosophized on that frigid night. According to White's notes of the trip, it was, in fact, Lawrence's "fine expense account whiskey" that the threesome had shared. But Lawrence never wrote of Humphrey's

27. White, *The Making of the President 1960*, 95.

monologue about America and his secret fears of the presidency in his reports. What the candidate said in public was all that counted as news back then.

On primary election night in Wisconsin, White had asked John Kennedy to spend the evening with him in the Milwaukee hotel room where he would hear the television returns, promising to be "quiet as Boswell's mouse in a corner." Explaining his purpose on the campaign trail in 1960, White had written to Kennedy, "What I seek is to be an eyewitness to those human episodes in this campaign which mark its turning points." White was, as a result, the only reporter in Room 320 at the Hotel Pfister. The notes he took of the scene on that early April evening hint at his growing enchantment with Kennedy. He noted, for example, "Jack is sprawled with utmost grace on his couch in the corner, in his dark black suit, affecting to read a newspaper, not a single bone or muscle moving and exquisitely handsome and powerful looking."[28]

First in the Wisconsin primary and in the West Virginia contest that followed, the *Times* and *Post* were preoccupied with the political rhetoric and poll predictions that preceded the election. Weeks before the voting in Wisconsin, the *Times* recounted Kennedy's response to Humphrey's charges that he was on a "spending spree" with his family riches. As election day drew closer, stories in the *Times* and the *Post* focused on polls showing that Kennedy held an easy lead. The religious issue became a frequent subject in both contests—could the enthusiasm of Catholics give Kennedy the edge or would the fears and resentments of Protestants derail his candidacy, the newspapers wondered in various articles. Reporters occasionally followed a candidate's campaign swing, and the resulting stories focused exclusively on the public campaign: "Today the Senator rose early to tour the B'Gosh over-all factory in Oshkosh," wrote Austin C. Wehrwein about one Kennedy foray into Wisconsin. "Later he spoke to overflow audiences of students at Oshkosh State College and at St. Norbert's College in DePere. He went on to Appleton, where he was greeted by a crowd in the center of town. At the next stop, Green Bay . . ." Some background stories focused on history, like the one that explained how Wisconsin, "Land of Progressivism," had approved America's first primary election law in 1905, while others raised less-than-burning questions about why the attractive and well-dressed "Kennedy women," who had been active campaigners in other primaries, appeared

28. THW, letter to John F. Kennedy, April 4, 1960, TWA, Box 17, Folder 1; THW, notes dated April 5, 1960, TWA, Box 100, Folder 3.

to have been benched in West Virginia. As the campaign there grew more rancorous, still another article made the inevitable comparison between the contenders and the state's legendary archenemies, the Hatfields and the McCoys. On the eve of both primaries, the *Times* published its own team "surveys" of political trends, which concluded that Kennedy was the easy favorite in Wisconsin and that "every surface political sign point[ed] to a defeat for Senator Hubert Humphrey." Kennedy, however, won only six of Wisconsin's ten Congressional districts and beat Humphrey by two to one in West Virginia. Kennedy's victories were proclaimed in bold headlines in the *Times* and the *Post*, both of which suggested a sense of historic gravity even though both wins had garnered him a total of only twenty and one-half of Wisconsin's thirty delegate votes and not a single firm commitment from any of West Virginia's twenty-five delegates, all of whom ran uncommitted. The newspapers, however, particularly the *Post*, seemed anxious to anoint a winner in the aftermath of Kennedy's Wisconsin victory. Likening Kennedy's style to a high wire act, Chalmers M. Roberts wrote after the Wisconsin results were in, "It takes cool nerves for such an act and there is no doubt that the Massachusetts Senator has just that—iron nerve, strong determination, superb judgment, the characteristics that helped make him an authentic World War II hero in the South Pacific." Clearly smitten with the Massachusetts Democrat, Roberts concluded, "The same qualities pay off in political wars, especially when coupled with intelligence and an attractive personality."[29]

In White's description of the West Virginia campaign—which was essentially a popularity contest—he revealed that the Kennedy team operated according to the guidelines defined in the so-called "O'Brien Manual," a sixty-four-page black bound handbook that detailed, with a kind of military precision, just how the Kennedy forces would be deployed to win this election. Lawrence O'Brien's approach was an artful blend of pragmatic politics and basic psychology built around the idea, according to White, "that every vote counts; that every citizen likes to feel he is somehow wired into the structure of power; that making a man or woman seem useful and important to himself (or herself) in the power system of American life takes advantage of one of the simplest and noblest urges of politics in the most effective way."[30]

29. Austin C. Wehrwein, "Kennedy Offers an Expense Pact," *New York Times*, February 19, 1950; "Team Survey Finds Kennedy Favored over Humphrey in Wisconsin Primary," *New York Times*, December 27, 1959. Chalmers M. Roberts, "Sen. Kennedy's Abilities Are Truly Impressive," *Washington Post*, April 7, 1960.

30. White, *The Making of the President 1960*, 12.

In West Virginia, he knew that Kennedy had commissioned Louis Harris to analyze public opinion in the state two years before the primary election. When the Kennedy caravan moved from Wisconsin to West Virginia, staffers arrived with the expectation that their boss would easily trounce any opponent. But that expectation was based on a Harris poll taken during the previous December, which indicated Kennedy would outpace Humphrey by 70 to 30. In April, however, the numbers were very different, and very ominous. In the intervening months, the voters of West Virginia had discovered one thing they hadn't known when those earlier polls were taken: John F. Kennedy was Catholic.

Although Kennedy resented Humphrey's decision to oppose him in West Virginia, White, with the benefit of hindsight, explained that the Humphrey challenge proved to the Eastern bosses what Kennedy had been hoping to prove in Wisconsin—that he was indeed a winner. White used the religious question that so plagued Kennedy in West Virginia as a way to enlarge his main character in pitting him against a powerful but abstract foe and demonstrating how he triumphed over the forces of intolerance and bigotry. Speaking on a paid campaign telecast just two days before the balloting, Kennedy responded to a question planted by his supporter, Franklin D. Roosevelt Jr. In what White described as "the finest TV broadcast I have ever heard any political candidate make," Kennedy declared,

> when any man stands on the steps of the Capitol and takes the oath of office of President, he is swearing to support the separation of church and state. . . . And if he breaks his oath, he is not only committing a crime against the Constitution, for which the Congress can impeach him— and should impeach him—but he is committing a sin against God.[31]

White's own political loyalties initially had been with Adlai Stevenson, the undeclared candidate who waited out the primary season at his farm in Libertyville, Illinois, giving the appearance of disinterest. Stevenson, however, whose friendship White had "cherished," once sought White's counsel early in 1960 as he wrestled with the question of making a third run for the presidency. "Tell me Teddy, am I in trouble? Is there anything I can do to stop this?" Stevenson asked White on the telephone one morning in April when the Kennedy steamroller began looking unbeatable. According to White's memorandum of the conversation, the man who had lost to Eisenhower in 1952 and 1956 said people kept urging him to run, "but

31. Ibid., 117.

nobody with any delegates. I think they [the Kennedy campaign] have it all buttoned down, don't you, Teddy?" Stevenson asked. "I think its 99 percent buttoned down," White responded, "the only thing not buttoned down is Pennsylvania and California." Stevenson lamented that the Kennedy camp repeatedly put out stories that he [Stevenson] was about to endorse Kennedy. "We talked more about Kennedy," White wrote. "I said they [the Kennedy organization] were so streamlined, so efficient, so ruthless. He [Stevenson] fastened upon that word ruthless and he repeated it."

The memo of that conversation with Stevenson closes with a postscript on the Republicans, one that underscored White's view of Eisenhower as a do-nothing president. "I told him about Nixon-Eisenhower. I said they were almost pathetic."[32]

About two months later, White shifted his spiritual support to Kennedy. White had traveled with Kennedy in June aboard his private plane on a trip from Montana to Massachusetts with just one other reporter, Blair Clark, who had been one of Kennedy's Harvard classmates and was then reporting for CBS News. Together the three men had talked about history and contemporary politics, exchanging casual banter about Theodore Roosevelt and Winston Churchill before moving on to some talk about Kennedy's options for a running mate. Finally, with liquor-induced but nonetheless remarkable candor, White told Kennedy he still resented him for joining in the chorus of criticism of John King Fairbank during Kennedy's first term in Congress. Just as he had berated Chiang when he returned to Chungking after reporting on the Honan famine, White also dressed down Kennedy for his weak-kneed stand against the Communist witch-hunters and for good measure, White added that he didn't like old Joe Kennedy either. "Teddy, you must meet my father someday," Kennedy insisted. "He's not like that at all." It was then, White wrote years later, that he "realized that inside myself I wanted to like this man . . . and gave myself over to the loyalty of friendship." Later, Kennedy swiveled around in his seat and hushed White with the question, "what would you do about Berlin?" Kennedy spoke of how Berlin was a test that could take the next president to the edge of war. It was easy for writers like White to talk tough, Kennedy said, but he wanted to know just how far White would go if the decision were his to make. "It was then I began to realize that he had a sense of the Presidency," White explained in a speech shortly after his book was published. What he had

32. THW, undated memorandum of a telephone conversation with Adlai Stevenson, TWA, Box 100, Folder 3.

seen in Kennedy was an unequivocal desire to be president and a craving for power, two essentials in any man who sought that high office, White told his longtime friend Irving London, a Stevenson admirer who found Kennedy callow and undistinguished by anything but his father's wealth. Stevenson seemed indecisive on the question of grasping for power, but there were no ambiguities about Kennedy's ambition, White told his friend. "So I'm for Kennedy," he declared.[33]

Jack Germond and Jules Witcover both recall White as having had a certain intimacy with the Kennedy forces during the 1960 campaign. Germond, who along with Witcover wrote four of the dozens of campaign chronicles that emerged after the success of White's first book, recalled that a star quality surrounded him. "White was a celebrity. He had been a well-known correspondent for *Time* magazine in China and he'd already written several successful books. He always liked to call himself a reporter, but he was a privileged reporter," Germond said. "He had a different relationship with Kennedy than with Nixon. You just knew they thought of him as one of theirs."[34]

Benjamin Bradlee, White's old friend from the Paris years who was a *Newsweek* correspondent during the 1960 campaign, has similar memories of White on the campaign trail. "Teddy got good service out of the Kennedy campaign," Bradlee recalled. "Jack paid attention to him . . . and so did other people in the campaign. Teddy was a Homer and Kennedy was his favorite." Because Kennedy loved history, Bradlee believed, "He was in love with Teddy's project more than with Teddy."[35]

Access was, of course, the key to White's insider-style journalism, just as it had been in Chungking and Paris. On the campaign trail in 1960, he wanted to be close to the presidential candidates, close enough to capture the sounds and smells and feel of the American political system at work. Ironically, however, in 1960 he seldom had any greater access than the handful of other newsmen who followed candidates. Indeed, sometimes he had even less. The Nixon campaign staff was almost dismissive of him, as it was of most reporters. When he traveled with the GOP contender and his entourage, White's name appeared at the bottom of the roster of press representatives. "Down at the very bottom of the list, like a Pakistani woman

33. White, *In Search of History*, 470; THW, speech to the American Booksellers Association, 1961, TWA, Box 185, Folder 4; Irving London, personal interview, July 14, 1992.

34. Jack Germond, personal interview, March 19, 1990.

35. Benjamin C. Bradlee, personal interview, March 20, 1990.

set off by the wall of purdah, was my name set off from the rest by a wall of asterisks—it read, Theodore H. White, Novelist."[36] He was relegated to the so-called zoo plane, the one that carried the television technicians and other lesser persons. However, most candidates, in those more innocent times, were less guarded than now in what they said in the company of reporters. Far fewer reporters traveled with would-be presidents then. And for the few who did, a campaign trip became a challenge, one that tested the fortitude of both candidate and newsman alike. In reporters, candidates often saw soul mates, people who shared their fascination and love of politics. White, in fact, might well have asked the very question an exuberant Humphrey asked on the night he narrowly lost the Wisconsin primary and decided to challenge Kennedy in the upcoming West Virginia primary. The upbeat also-ran told reporters in Milwaukee that night, "I always told you fellows politics could be fun, didn't I?"

White's hunger for confrontation naturally drew him to the party conventions as obvious settings for political action. In these rituals of democracy, White saw history, spectacle, and a scenario for decisive showdowns. Here again, White juxtaposed the visible events with the less visible maneuverings that collectively helped to decide the nation's future.

Despite Kennedy's crucial victory in West Virginia and subsequent primary victories in Maryland, Indiana, and Oregon, he went to the Democratic convention in Los Angeles with the nomination still in some doubt. He was certain that at least 700 of the delegates would cast their votes for him, but he needed 761 to win the nomination. By convention time, the principal threat to Kennedy's first ballot nomination was Stevenson and the many loyalists who still longed to see him in the White House. Stevenson, the party's nominee in 1952 and 1956, continued to yearn secretly for the nomination, even though he had refused to make a bid for it in the primary elections. He had been a reluctant nominee in 1952, when the Democratic convention delegates nominated him on the third ballot. In 1956, however, he had fought for the nomination in a series of brutal primaries against Estes Kefauver of Tennessee. The memory of those ignoble brawls made him shrink from the prospect of seeking the presidency a third time. In what the Stevenson biographer Porter McKeever called a highly perceptive analysis of Stevenson's conflicting sentiments toward the presidency, White wrote that Stevenson "would not act, or deal or connive or strike a blow to seize the Presidential nomination if his party did not offer it to him. Nor

36. THW, speech to the American Booksellers Association, 1961, TWA, Box 185, Folder 4.

could any man shake him from this simple stand until the last twenty-four hours before the nomination at Los Angeles."[37]

White saw more than a simple confrontation between two would-be presidents in Los Angeles. To his sophisticated reportorial eye, he saw this duel as a moment of transformation, when the older men who had once led the party were being superseded by a new generation that reached out to take control of the machinery. White drew on history, comparing this convention with those of the 1850s when one generation of leaders—Clay-Calhoun-Webster—was forced to relinquish leadership to the generation of younger men who would lead the nation in the Civil War.

White pinpointed the location of this twentieth-century transformation in Room 8315 of the Biltmore Hotel, where the Kennedy team made its headquarters and organized its assault to win the nomination. What White explained was the mechanics of how John Kennedy had taken control of the convention, and he did so by understanding how the Kennedy operation functioned. It is safe to assume that most of the 4,750 reporters assigned to cover the convention could have had access to the very information that made White's account of the Democratic gathering in Los Angeles so compelling. However, none of the dozens of reporters whose articles about the convention appeared in the *New York Times* and the *Washington Post* made mention of Room 8315, or the cottage outside the Los Angeles Sports Arena where the Kennedys had established their communications command post that linked the Kennedy staffers who were roaming the convention floor to the team in Room 8315. Theodore White was the only reporter in that Kennedy communications cottage on the night the convention nominated its presidential candidate.

In his account of the nomination, White deftly juxtaposed the public spectacle unfolding on the convention floor as it erupted in a frenzied last stand for Stevenson with the hard political realities that had transpired behind the noise and chaos. Stevenson's chances of garnering the nomination or even a respectable measure of delegate support had evaporated hours before the boisterous demonstration. His was a hopeless quest, Stevenson realized, after Chicago Mayor Richard Daley, the political powerhouse among Illinois Democrats, told his state's former governor that he could count on only two of his own state's sixty-one delegates.

Once the nominating speeches had concluded, White briefly placed his readers in front of the television set in the same room where Kennedy was watching the tedious state-by-state nominating process. A mood of

37. White, *The Making of the President 1960*, 132.

suspense builds, even though the outcome is clear. Beginning with the Alabama delegation, which casts only three and one-half of its twenty-seven votes for Kennedy, the candidate keeps score on a tally sheet that lists his own breakdown of the 739½ delegates he believes solidly behind him. The evening inches forward as each delegation takes maximum advantage of the opportunity for political pontificating. Plodding alphabetically through its agenda, after six hours, the Wyoming delegation finally anoints the party's new leader, giving him three more than the 760 votes needed for the nomination.

Then White presented the scene that Bradlee would still recall more than three decades after he read the book, one of the principal insights that hit him "like a ton of bricks."[38] Because both self-preservation and the protocols of power dictated that the Democratic political bosses—only a few of whom had been early Kennedy supporters—pay homage to the new leader, they gathered, as if by instinct, at the communications trailer, knowing that was where they could learn whether the candidate would make an appearance that evening. Without waiting for the conclusion of the roll call—which gave Kennedy a total of 806 votes—these men assembled. White, still in the corner of the living room, sat in silence as the party's old war horses filed in: Connecticut's John Bailey, Ohio's Michael DiSalle, Pennsylvania's David Lawrence, and a half-dozen others who once occupied those legendary smoke-filled rooms. There were no cigars here; only Coca Cola and beer were served while these restless party leaders awaited Kennedy's anticipated arrival. White correctly discerned in this a classic scene of power and politics, one that transcended Los Angeles and reached back into history, but one that was flavored with a uniquely American dimension. Kennedy's position now compelled the loyalties of his party's generals, and they would bow to him just as the generals had bowed to Caesar centuries ago. Thus, White used this scene in the communications cottage as an occasion to transform for his readers all the abstract dimensions of power into something tangible.

The *New York Times* and the *Washington Post* dwelt almost exclusively on the official business of the convention in their coverage. Overwhelmingly, the stories in both newspapers recount the public pantomime of statements, speeches, movements, and operations—the rancorous platform debate, Kennedy's symbolic visit with the Texas delegation, the thirteen-minute ovation for Stevenson staged by die-hard supporters when he

38. Benjamin C. Bradlee, personal interview, January 22, 1993.

arrived to join the Illinois delegation on the night before Kennedy won the nomination. These leading newspapers were, in short, engrossed with the veneer of the convention, those often stage-managed events that would be increasingly visible to Americans on their television screens as the country's two networks, which had started covering the party conventions in 1948, discovered a political rite could be packaged and presented on the small screen. In many of the dozens of stories written about those mid-July days in Los Angeles, reporters appeared to round up the usual sources for observations and comments. The result was often journalism that was long on political rhetoric and posturing but short on insight.

"In the incubation of a Convention," White explained in his campaign history, "rumors have the force of fact." Some of those rumors took on the semblance of fact on the pages of the *Washington Post*. "It's Kennedy on the first ballot," declared Edward T. Folliard's lead on a story about the opening day of the convention. "Any doubt about the identity of the man the Democrats will nominate for President—and there wasn't much—vanished today when the big Pennsylvania delegation decided to throw 64½ of its 81 votes to Sen. John F. Kennedy of Massachusetts." Kennedy, the story also claimed, planned to have Stevenson put his name in nomination. Although Kennedy ducked a question about Stevenson's willingness to nominate him, Folliard's story insisted, "the tactic is clearly in the cards."[39] Stevenson, it turned out, still had his own designs on the nomination and had, at last, decided to make a fight for it. Other unexpected reverses slowed the "stampede" the *Post* had described—California Governor Edmund Brown's control over his state's 81 delegates collapsed, leaving their commitment to Kennedy in question; Humphrey announced his support for Stevenson, and the Kansas and Iowa delegations revolted against their respective governors who were then unable to deliver those first-ballot votes for Kennedy.

So by the time Kennedy was nominated in the early morning hours of July 14, what on Monday had been billed as a foregone conclusion had become instead "the most exciting Democratic convention battle since Franklin D. Roosevelt triumphed in 1932." Kennedy had won on the first ballot—"in blitz fashion," according to Folliard, who wrote the *Post*'s lead story.[40]

In an accompanying story inside the paper, Richard L. Lyons provided a moment-by-moment account of the events on the convention floor,

39. Edward T. Folliard, "Kennedy Victory Seen on First Ballot as Pennsylvanians Spark Stampede," *Washington Post*, July 12, 1960.
40. Edward T. Folliard, "Kennedy Wins on First Ballot at a Tumultuous Night Session," *Washington Post*, July 14, 1960.

beginning at 3:15 P.M. when the gavel-pounding Florida governor began making a futile effort to bring the convention's twenty-six hundred rowdy delegates to order. The lengthy story described the very scenes that television cameras had already captured on the convention floor: the delegates chatting while House Speaker Sam Rayburn nominated Senator Lyndon B. Johnson; Gov. James Blair of Missouri nominated Sen. Stuart Symington as "the answer to the Nation's prayer for leadership"; Eleanor Roosevelt entered the convention hall at 10:30 P.M.; a group in the gallery unfurled a twenty-foot banner declaring "Stevenson Won't Panic in a Crisis."[41] But in 1960, television was about to usurp the role of the print journalist. Viewers could see the events on their screens and would soon find little need to read an account of scenes they had viewed the night before. Television, in a sense, by making those print accounts redundant, forced print journalists to become more analytical, to probe for the deeper meaning of events, rather than simply provide a straightforward description of how a political exhibition had unfolded.

And that was the genius of White's journalistic vision. White had looked instead beyond those events that the television cameras had captured on the convention floor, beyond the descriptions of bands striking up another chorus of "Anchors Aweigh" and balloons dropping. He saw in the story of Kennedy's nomination shrewd, calculating middle-aged men who had once carried out the orders of their generals during World War II, and now were using those very same organizational skills not to conquer the German or Japanese enemy but rather to capture the levers of power to run the nation.

The Democratic convention in Los Angeles marked one of the rare occasions when the *New York Times* abandoned its fixation on the public campaign and turned its gaze on the more private and less reported side of the Democratic spectacle. In an account of the bombastic evening on which Kennedy was nominated, Russell Baker exchanged his newspaper's traditionally somber tone for a more irreverent voice and produced a story that bore a remarkable resemblance to White's style. "There is always a threat of Gotterdaemmerung in the air when the Democrats get down to the business of nominating a candidate," Baker told his readers. "Today was no exception." Just as White was to do in his book, Baker established conflict and tension in his opening paragraphs:

41. Richard L. Lyons, "Two Gavels Finally Bring Nominating Session to Order," *Washington Post*, July 14, 1960.

The forces of Senator John F. Kennedy were confidently predicting that their celebrated bandwagon was roaring up the Freeway at full throttle and would smash right through the Arena without even stopping. The forces of Senator Lyndon B. Johnson and Senator Stuart Symington, stiffly upper-lipped to the last, were declaring with equal vehemence that they had fitted the bandwagon with square wheels during the night.[42]

Baker's story described the pomp and the pandemonium of the nominating process while explaining that behind the public spectacle a generational conflict between party loyalists was underway. Many younger Democrats, Baker explained, were fighting to turn the party against the old political ways and set it on the path of the young organization man. The story also disclosed intraparty rivalries—Kennedy's youth "galls the Johnson camp"— and unmasked the absurdity of otherwise serious men behaving like eleven-year-olds. Baker's keen vision and impious voice caught Connecticut's Senator Thomas Dodd unpacking "an assortment of clichés left over from old Senate debates," and Michigan's Governor G. Mennen Williams "looking as hapless as a husband in the lingerie department at Christmastime." Baker also saw the irony in Eleanor Roosevelt seconding Stevenson's nomination while her son, James Roosevelt—a Kennedy supporter—sat glum-faced among the New York delegates. His eye was also on Kennedy aide Theodore Sorenson, who watched those seconding his boss's nomination "like a junior instructor in high-school chemistry keeping an eye on his class."

Curiously, a similar convention analysis piece Baker wrote for the following day described how New Jersey missed the opportunity to participate in the Kennedy triumph. Baker's story contradicted two other *New York Times* articles on that state's misguided nomination maneuvers. Those contradictory articles demonstrate how the newspaper's focus on official statements—the public campaign—made it vulnerable to the machinations of the "spin doctors" long before the phrase entered America's political lexicon. Baker cast New Jersey Governor Robert Meyner as the leading candidate for the convention's "political goat nomination for having stood against the Kennedy blitz and lost." Two articles without bylines that appeared on July 14 and 15, however, portrayed the governor as a would-be kingmaker whose strategy had simply gone awry. Although Kennedy was assured of thirty-seven and one-half of New Jersey's forty-one delegate votes, the governor,

---

42. Russell Baker, "Highlight and Chronology of the Nominating Sessions of the Democratic Convention," *New York Times*, July 14, 1960.

resentful of the pressures the Kennedy organization had put on him for an early commitment, insisted that his delegation first nominate him as a favorite son. In the end, according to Baker, the Kennedy organization gave Meyner "a taste of how Captain Bligh must have felt about Fletcher Christian. . . . The convention hall knew, even while Mr. Meyner was being put in nomination, that the Kennedy rebels would put him out to sea in a rowboat." Apparently members of the New Jersey delegation scrambled to capture the ear of other *New York Times* writers who helped them put a gloss on their embarrassing predicament. The resulting articles claimed that Meyner had merely hoped to take credit for putting Kennedy over the top and thus play a key role in the nomination.[43]

White found the New Jersey wrangle to be worth just a single paragraph— five sentences in which he explained that internal rivalries had split the state's forty-one delegates and resulted in an internal war. Joseph Kennedy, he explained, had quietly enlisted support from the state's northern political leaders several months before the convention, but had, in the process, embittered the governor, "who felt himself bypassed and his machinery of state politics threatened."[44]

Initially, White found much less drama in the Republican camp. Although he enjoyed good relations with Nelson Rockefeller and his staff, once the Republican governor withdrew from the race, White believed he had been robbed of the necessary clash of ego and ambition that he saw at the heart of presidential politics. Rockefeller's withdrawal gave Nixon a smooth ride to the nomination, or so it had first appeared. Rockefeller, however, later hedged on his "definite and final" decision to withdraw. In mid-May, after Soviet fighter pilots downed an American U-2 spy plane over Sverdlovsk, Russia, and after Eisenhower's disastrous Paris summit meeting with Khrushchev, who disparaged Ike as a "hypocrite" and a "liar," Rockefeller announced that the mood of national crisis made him open to a draft by his party.

As a result, White's earlier worries about the absence of drama in the Republican camp would prove to have been premature. Events played out along lines that seemed made for fiction, and White knew how to pump

43. Russell Baker, "Rivals Smashed Trying to Resist," *New York Times,* July 15, 1960; "New Jersey Restores Harmony but Fails in Maneuver to Gain a 'King-Making' Role," *New York Times,* July 14, 1960, and "Tactical Misfire Disturbs New Jersey," *New York Times,* July 15, 1960.
44. White, *The Making of the President 1960,* 174.

all their theatrical potential into his book. With a civil war between the GOP's moderate and conservative factions in the offing, Nixon moved to mend the breach. That he did so in secret—without informing Eisenhower, GOP leaders, or the party's platform committee in advance—gave White an abundance of drama.

On the eve of the Republican convention in Chicago, the vice president of the United States, bowing to the conditions set by the foremost member of America's princely Rockefeller family, flew to New York for a meeting at Governor Rockefeller's Fifth Avenue apartment, where, after hours of wrangling, Nixon agreed to his host's demands in the formulation of their party's platform. The infamous "Compact of Fifth Avenue," as the Nixon-Rockefeller agreement was called, enraged both the president and the party's platform committee. The conditions that Rockefeller had dictated and to which Nixon had agreed were both a repudiation of Eisenhower's national defense policies and an affront to the platform committee. Arizona Senator Barry Goldwater labeled the agreement a "surrender." Eisenhower exploded, according to White, and the 103-member GOP Platform Committee threatened mutiny.

The *New York Times*'s comparatively bland account of that unusual meeting between Nixon and Rockefeller explained that the vice president had sought the meeting "to settle differences over a Republican program." Their agreement, the newspaper cautiously acknowledged, "seemed weighted on the side of Mr. Rockefeller's views." The story did not explain, as White's account did, that the terms of both the meeting and the resulting compact essentially represented a capitulation on Nixon's part. Even in its description of Eisenhower's reaction, the article remained circumspect. "There is some evidence here that the President did not fully share all the sentiments expressed in the Nixon-Rockefeller overnight 'statement of platform principles'—especially in defense and foreign policy," a sidebar story explained.[45]

The *Post* stories on the "surprise agreement" were less cautious and more straightforward in their interpretation of the meeting between the vice president and the New York governor. Members of the GOP platform committee were described as "outraged," particularly over the "blunt criticism" of the Eisenhower administration. Although Rockefeller rejected the notion that

45. William M. Blair, "Secret Nixon–Rockefeller Talks Draft a Basic Platform Accord; Rule Out Governor for 2nd Place," *New York Times*, July 24, 1960.

Nixon had made "concessions," the *Post* said the governor's press secretary said the fourteen-point agreement was "80 to 85 percent a Rockefeller draft."[46]

White, in contrast, described responses to the compact from delegates and the President as "explosions." For members of the Platform Committee, many of whom represented the party's grassroots conservatives, he explained, this agreement signed "in a millionaire's triplex apartment in Babylon-on-the-Hudson" had exposed them as "clowns." The second explosion, a "muted" one, had come from Newport, Rhode Island, where the President was vacationing. The compact, in Eisenhower's eyes, represented "treachery," "personal theft," "credit hogging." The President himself had developed a plan to reorganize the government's executive arm and Rockefeller—at the President's invitation—had served on a small panel that had elaborated on the idea. Now, Rockefeller had imposed the idea on Nixon and made it partisan. "Eisenhower blazed," according to White.[47]

By the end of July, with the minidramas of the primary elections and the spectacle of the conventions concluded, White—using the very techniques he had used in his novels—began to set up his principal characters for their dramatic conflict and showdown. As the Democratic convention drew to a close, White presented Kennedy, haggard and exhausted, accepting the nomination of his party with Richard M. Nixon watching him on television in his Washington, D.C., living room. Sizing up his adversary's flawed presentation, Nixon turned to the two associates who had joined him that evening and told them he thought he could beat this man on television. Having explained how his principal characters vanquished potential rivals in their own parties, White's story became a medieval joust between two proud and powerful egos. In the legendary televised debates of the 1960 campaign, White again found both the drama and detail that made his book so unique. As a reporter, White stretched his professional skills into realms that most political journalists had left unexplored.

White continued to focus his lens beyond the spotlight that captured the attention of his fellow journalists. He looked instead at the unilluminated details of the scene—details that were both monumental and minute. The Andy Griffith Show had been preempted, and Maybelline had advertised its waterproof mascara for fifteen seconds. Then, at 8:30 P.M.

46. Carroll Kilpatrick, "Nixon–Rockefeller Accord Stirs Storm Over GOP Platform," *Washington Post*, July 24, 1960.
47. White, *The Making of the President 1960*, 218.

Chicago time on September 27, 1960, what White called "a revolution in American presidential politics" began to unfold. White understood that this revolution had little to do with what Kennedy and Nixon had to say. It was instead a revolution driven by technology. The television set, which had a place in 54 million American households, was about to become a political common denominator. The first boxy, small-screen television set had been introduced in America at the World's Fair of 1939. The war had slowed down the emergence of this medium, but it quickly developed a growing following in the postwar years. The decade between 1950 and 1960 marked its most explosive growth—by the time Kennedy and Nixon first faced each other on that September evening, 80 percent of America's households had a television set.

Once again, hindsight gave White a clearer view of what had transpired. A transcript of the contenders' statements, White explained, made it clear that while Nixon scored points as a debater, as he had done with much success in high school back in Whittier, California, Kennedy spoke not to some imaginary panel of judges who were scoring each contestant's points, but instead to the 65 to 70 million Americans sitting in front of their television sets. Adding still another estimable quality to the main character of his story, White described Kennedy's triumph as a result not so much in what he said, but rather in his mastery of the medium, which was then a still untested component of the political equation. Nixon, White explained, focused his attention in the studio, on besting his adversary, while Kennedy reached beyond the cameras and addressed his answers to the nation.

White also understood that to those watching the event on television, appearances seemed to matter at least as much, if not more, than substance. No one writing for the *New York Times* explained to readers that the texture of Nixon's skin was a critical disadvantage. Its light, naturally transparent quality, as seen through the television camera, especially in closeups, resulted in magnifying his pores. Thus, the infamous five o'clock shadow that made Nixon look so furtive, so shifty on the small screen.

White identified that first debate as a turning point in Kennedy's campaign. Although he was careful to qualify all his conclusions about the results of those four televised encounters, White related how, following the first debate, the crowds seemed to multiply overnight wherever the Democratic contender campaigned. Poll results that earlier had cast Nixon as the probable winner and showed Kennedy engaged in a difficult battle were reversed by the final debate. Among Republican leaders, a mixture of gloom and anger replaced their earlier buoyant mood.

Ironically, however, despite their enormous potential for helping voters make informed choices, White concluded that the televised debates represented a squandered opportunity, even though they had a considerable impact on the campaign. The format precluded any thoughtful responses and circumscribed any meaningful discussion of the campaign issues, White concluded. The chief accomplishment of those debates, he added, was to give the voters "a tribal sense of participation" and offer them a "living portrait of two men under stress."[48] Those, of course, were the very techniques that White used with such success in his book.

As events moved closer to election day, the newspapers concentrated on the increasingly frenzied public campaign, while White's story abounded with those behind-the-scenes details for which he became so famous. The *New York Times* preoccupied itself with stories about Kennedy's promise to encourage Eastern European countries to break away from the Soviet Union, Nixon's promise to aid student doctors, and ongoing voter surveys that indicated neither candidate had a substantial lead. The debate over Quemoy and Matsu, those much-disputed islands near the shore of mainland China that Nixon insisted had to be defended at all costs and Kennedy claimed were militarily worthless, rated scores of column inches in both the *Times* and the *Post*. The islands were far more than tiny pieces of real estate, Nixon insisted—they represented an American principle, and any thought of abandoning them epitomized the same "wooly thinking that led to disaster in Korea." Kennedy, however, favored a pullback from those islands.[49] In White's history of the 1960 campaign, there is not so much as an index entry on those controversial islands. White's focus was trained instead on the scenes behind those public pronouncements. And what White's readers witnessed behind the rhetoric and bombast were the critical decisions in the campaign.

Near the end of October, festering resentments surfaced among staffers at the Republican National Committee who had been ignored throughout the campaign. White wrote, too, about the frustrations of Nixon's own strategists who never had an opportunity to speak with the candidate. And he described the disaffection Eisenhower felt when the longstanding offer to campaign for his vice president was finally accepted only in the campaign's frantic closing days. White had his readers eavesdrop as Nixon's television advisers groused that they were being ignored and heard a key GOP leader

48. Ibid., 320.
49. Russell Baker, "Nixon and Kennedy Clash on TV over Issue of Quemoy's Defense," *New York Times*, October 8, 1960.

lament, "you could have taken the key to the Republican National Committee, locked the door, thrown the key into the Potomac, shipped all hundred and seventy-five employees off to the Virgin Islands and saved money for all he listened to us."

Similarly, White had his readers listen in as Nixon strategists desperately sought to salvage what, by October, had begun to look like a debacle. At an emergency strategy session, for example, the campaign's high command groped for a way to handle a pledge made by Henry Cabot Lodge, the GOP vice presidential nominee, that a Negro would be named to the president's cabinet. Worried about the effect of that promise on Southern voters, one exasperated strategist declared: "Whoever recommended that Harlem speech should have been thrown out of an airplane at 25,000 feet."[50]

Those private musings among GOP strategists provided White with a neat counterpoint to his description of Kennedy's famous telephone call of sympathy and support to Coretta Scott King, whose husband, civil rights leader Dr. Martin Luther King Jr., had been sentenced to four months at hard labor for a minor traffic violation in October 1960. White characterized the call as a measure of both the compassion and efficiency of the Kennedy campaign. It was, White insisted, a command decision, one that simultaneously underscored the candidate's deep concern for civil rights and his feelings of compassion for a young, pregnant woman whose husband's life was clearly in danger. Later, historians discredited White's interpretation of that famous telephone call and claimed he had created an illusion for the sake of his dramatic narrative.

Taylor Branch, author of the King biography *Parting the Waters*, insisted that expediency rather than compassion shaped Kennedy's stand on civil rights. Kennedy's call to Mrs. King was a spontaneous gesture, done impulsively at the behest of Sargent Shriver, his brother-in-law and campaign aide. It was a move that infuriated Robert Kennedy when he learned of it, according to Branch. Fearing that Shriver had pushed the candidate into a politically explosive situation, an enraged Robert Kennedy told Shriver, "You bomb throwers have lost the whole campaign." Branch assailed White's rhapsodic description of that pivotal telephone call, contending that he had conveniently discarded contrary evidence from both Shriver and Harris Wofford, who directed the civil rights section of the 1960 campaign. That evidence, Branch claims, might have undermined White's celebration of the candidate's power and wisdom.[51]

50. White, *The Making of the President 1960*, 325.
51. Taylor Branch, *Parting the Waters*, 364.

Wofford, who was a Notre Dame law professor in 1960, took issue in his own book with White's descriptions of the Kennedy organization as smooth, tightly run, and hierarchical. Wofford instead recalled the campaign as one characterized by "spontaneity, creative chaos and unbureaucratic responses to conflicting pressures." Long before Wofford's book was published in 1980, James Rowe, the one-time New Deal lawyer who became an adviser to the Kennedy campaign, had told White the same thing. "The Kennedy campaign direction was headless," Rowe wrote to White early in 1961, because Robert Kennedy not only refused to sit still in Washington and make decisions but also refused to delegate authority. Rowe concluded, "The margin could have been different with better planning and better execution."[52]

In developing yet another theme that was ignored in daily coverage of the campaign, White exposed the absurdity of the demands that American presidential politics made on the contenders in the 1960 election. In the frenzied final weeks of the campaign, an exhausted Richard Nixon sometimes replaced his prepared speeches on national issues with a litany of disjointed ramblings. White described how this otherwise intensely private man, in an apparent effort to project himself as "just plain folk," revealed the painful deprivations of his childhood.[53] He told audiences how he had longed for a toy train as a child but never had one; how it had pained him when he did not make the Whittier High School football team, and how he had aspired to be a piano player, but that wish never came true either. His exercise in self-pity peaked in Centralia, Illinois, where he spoke of his sickly older brother's desperate wish for a pony and of how his impoverished parents agonized because they did not have seventy-five dollars to buy it. Like so much of what White witnessed on his campaign travels, the regulars on the press bus did not consider that news. Nor did other members of the press report that in the final days of the campaign, Nixon's own staffers were so certain of defeat that they speculated with reporters about who might be named to the Kennedy cabinet.

Among the most interesting revelations in White's chapter about the closing days of the Kennedy campaign are those he offered about the daily routines of the campaign press during a presidential race. The mainstream media never wrote stories about its role during the 1960 campaign, so once

52. Harris Wofford, *Of Kennedys and Kings,* 19; James Rowe, letter to THW, March 28, 1961, TWA, Box 17, Folder 5.
53. White, *The Making of the President 1960,* 28.

again, the details White provided about how the news reached the readers were both fascinating and entirely new.

White explained how the assignment to a presidential campaign was considered a plum in most newsrooms, one which went most often to the best-seasoned and most senior staffers. Life for the forty- to fifty-member press corps traveling with the two major candidates was a wearisome grind of days that began before dawn and ended well after midnight. For weeks these men and just a few women spent their lives aboard buses and airplanes, in hotel rooms and press centers. They ate sporadically and, as election day approached, many of them drank too much. They were alternately plagued with the demands of deadlines and worries about whether they would find their baggage when the campaign plane landed. It was a system that required these middle-aged reporters to be part roustabouts and part philosophers. As Newark blurred into Pittsburgh and Peoria and Kansas City and Hartford, they were quarantined, isolated from the world beyond the ever-moving conveyor belt of the campaign. Lacking any reference points outside their circumscribed bubble, they came to rely on each other's judgments. It was a variation of the "insider circle" that White had used so successfully in Paris. Having listened to the stump speeches dozens of times, to members of the campaign press corps, the candidates sounded as if their needles were stuck in the etched grooves of a worn-out record. What little solace there was, these reporters found in a sense of brotherhood with one another. Detachment and discomfort were their common bond.

In their conversations about the candidates and the campaign, this corps of correspondents arrived at a consensus, White explained. More than gossip or even casual conversation, he said, those conversations were the foundation of how the traveling press portrayed events. The judgment of the brotherhood, White declared, influenced and colored, "beyond any individual resistance to prejudice or individual devotion to fact, all of what they write. For now they have come to trust only each other."[54] Here again, journalists were making collective decisions, and their stories echoed a shared mind-set and a shared value system.

That Kennedy charmed the press and considered it essential to his victory while Nixon despised reporters and believed they were in a conspiracy to undermine him, White concluded, affected how the contenders were portrayed in daily dispatches featured on the front pages of America's newspapers. Speaking at a Columbia University seminar on public communication soon

54. Ibid., 366.

after the 1960 election, White explained that Kennedy's extraordinary efforts to woo the press had begun four years before the election. Although the candidates' divergent views of the press made it inevitable that Kennedy would invariably get good press and Nixon would generally be cast in the negative, White claimed that journalists nonetheless made some effort to protect him:

> Nixon [went] into a blue funk before the fourth debate. Didn't the newspapers protect him by not writing about this? There is a kind of honor which the press corps has that you don't kick a guy in the belly. Pat Nixon was so sick near the end of the campaign that she was near collapse—you didn't write about that. I can't ever remember sitting in the back of a press plane and discussing whether we would or wouldn't cover something, but there seems to be general agreement that there are certain things you do and certain things you don't do. There was no concerted effort at protection of Nixon. There was the delightful and delirious love of Kennedy on his plane, but you can't fault him for that as he had gone out of his way to cultivate it.[55]

Despite the largely Democratic orientation of the traveling press, concern for professional standards and individual reputations, according to White, compelled its members to set aside their own opinions. Yet the hostility Nixon displayed toward these men and women ultimately generated hostility from them, White explained. For his part, the vice president, as he had with most correspondents covering the campaign, declined White's repeated requests for an interview. Privately, White believed that Nixon had "all the magnetism of a boiled turkey." In his book, however, he obscured those personal feelings with a measure of reserve. "To be transferred from the Nixon campaign tour to the Kennedy campaign tour meant no lightening of exertion or weariness for any newspaperman," White wrote, "but it was as if one were transformed in role from leper and outcast to friend and battle companion." By election eve, the correspondents who had covered Kennedy felt "they, too, were marching like soldiers of the Lord to the New Frontier."[56]

55. THW, speech at Columbia University seminar on public communication, November 18, 1960, TWA, Box 185, Folder 6.
56. THW, memorandum dated October 31, 1960, TWA, Box 100, Folder 4. White, *The Making of the President 1960*, 369.

White, too, became a partisan, just as he had been a partisan in China at the beginning of his career. Later, one *Time* reviewer of *The Making of the President 1960* noted, "There is no question whose campaign button adorned his lapel."[57]

Ironically, however, White didn't cast a vote in the 1960 election because he was unable to get back to New York and had neglected to arrange for an absentee ballot. White had remained instead in Hyannis on election day, searching for the drama of a Kennedy victory to climax his story. Again, he looked beyond the public spectacle and fixed on the movements of the Secret Service. With two teams of agents—one in Hyannisport and the other in Los Angeles—prepared to establish security around America's next president, the agency's top officials had carefully watched the returns on television. Not until one of the contestants had a sure majority of electoral votes would the chief of the Secret Service, Urbanus E. Baughman, give the order to guard and protect the new president. Baughman, who had a telephone link from his Washington, D.C., home to the sixteen-man platoons based on each coast, would make no premature misstep as Eisenhower's press secretary James Hagerty had when he mistakenly sent Kennedy a congratulatory telegram at 1 A.M.—well before the final result was known. With an eye that was ever alert to the tangible manifestations of power, White pinpointed those predawn moments when the Secret Service agents moved in to guard the president-elect as the time when power passed invisibly to John F. Kennedy as the nation's newly anointed leader. From then on White's hero seemed to transcend the commonplace and take on a superhuman dimension as he was walled off "from all other citizens and ordinary mortals."[58]

Here again, White seduced his readers with the titillating details that made his story so effective. Kennedy had gone to bed at 4 A.M. Five and one-half hours later, seated on the edge of the bed in white pajamas, he learned from Theodore Sorenson that he had carried California and thus won the election. He shaved with a straight razor. He had breakfast with his wife and daughter, and then took a walk on the beach with his brother and several aides. At 11 A.M., surrounded by many of the men who had been with him since that crucial meeting late in October 1959, Kennedy had watched Nixon's concession speech, admonishing one of his chattering aides to hush

---

57. "Cliffhanger," *Time*, July 21, 1961, 66.
58. White, *The Making of the President 1960*, 378.

as the vice president began. Finally, riding in a white Lincoln Continental, as president-elect, Kennedy made his way to the Hyannis National Guard Armory, where he spoke to his supporters and to the nation. His voice was even but his hands—out of camera range—shook and trembled beneath the podium as he spoke. After a year of incessant motion, the campaign had finally stopped on election day, White explained, and the tally—like the flash of a high-speed camera—"captured a momentary, yet precise, picture of the moods, the wills, the past and the future of all the communities that made America whole." Moments after he left the podium, the newly elected president paused to shake hands with the man who was about to become his Boswell. Then, as Kennedy left the podium, he told White, "O.K., Teddy, now you can go ahead and write that book of yours."[59]

59. White, *The Making of the President 1960*, 381. White, *In Search of History*, 491.

Chapter Five

. . . .

. . . **The Making of Camelot**

I cannot ever, except in time of supreme

national emergency, see myself inviting

the confidence of men in private and then

using their private confidences to destroy

them in public.—Theodore H. White,

letter to Stewart Alsop, August 13, 1969

Just moments after Theodore H. White walked into the Oval Office for his long-sought interview with the new president, John F. Kennedy, to the astonishment of his visitor, began to undress. White had importuned the White House press secretary for "a talk with the Tiger himself" to gather the material for the final chapter of his book, *The Making of the President 1960*.[1] And now, the "Tiger" was standing there in blue boxer shorts. White had anticipated an encounter with some lofty presence, with a man transformed in the few weeks since his inauguration by the gravity of the American presidency. The plotline White had developed in his nearly

1. THW, letter to Pierre Salinger, February 28, 1961, TWA, Box 17, Folder 3.

completed campaign history required a measure of wisdom and a touch of glory from the newly anointed leader.

White had wanted to spend inauguration day with Kennedy to witness the ritual of how one man relinquished power and another took hold of it. But he had been left to watch those festivities on television at his home in New York, far removed from the principal characters, just as he had been sidelined on election day when Kennedy had declined White's request to spend the day at his side. "I've been with the campaign for so long and my chips are so heavily committed to Jack," White had written to Salinger a few weeks before the campaign ended, "that I feel I must be as close to him as possible in order to finish the book with its natural triumphant climax."[2] White, nevertheless, was nowhere near Kennedy when the outcome of the election was clear. So now, in the early days of March, White had come as an author in search of a final grace note with which to ornament his narrative.

White had first seen the Oval Office in the summer of 1960 when, in anticipation of his book, he requested an opportunity to inspect the famous room during one of President Dwight D. Eisenhower's vacations. He had found it, as he later wrote, "almost too peaceful and luminous a place to echo the ominous concerns that weigh on the man who occupies it."[3] The new president, he noticed, had added the curving cream-white sofas along with the aging naval prints on the walls. Kennedy was, however, using the same oaken shipboard desk fashioned from timbers of the old *HMS Resolute*, which Queen Victoria had given to Rutherford B. Hayes in 1880 as a token of Great Britain's friendship with America.

White had expected to find a towering leader holding court in "his purple toga, sitting in majesty." Instead, the president he encountered was half-dressed and surrounded by three New York tailors who had come to measure him for a new suit. And in place of the sage, philosophical pronouncements about the glories and burdens of his new office that White had awaited, Kennedy instead began interviewing him. How much money did he expect to make on the book? What were the chances that the Readers' Digest Book Club would buy it? The president also wanted to know whether White had read the newly published transcripts of the Kennedy and Nixon speeches at outdoor campaign rallies. Commenting on his opponent's rhetoric, the president asked, "Did you ever read such shit?"[4]

2. THW, letter to Pierre Salinger, October 1, 1960, TWA, Box 17, Folder 2.
3. White, *The Making of the President 1960*, 404.
4. White, *In Search of History*, 498.

Reflecting back on that afternoon more than a decade and a half later in the pages of *In Search of History*, White recalled that when their conversation turned to the business of the presidency, Kennedy seemed uncertain that day, less confident than he had been during the campaign. He was struggling for a direction, as so many presidents had, in his interaction with Congress. An ending for White's nearly completed book, however, required the Leader of the Free World to be preoccupied with something more grand than the mundane intricacies of the feed-grain bill that had squeaked through Congress that day with a spare margin of only seven votes. White's epic tale of political ambition and ego required those purple togas and a few trumpet fanfares as well. A half-dressed president uttering profanities about his rival and musing over his petty feuds with those lesser mortals in Congress would hardly give White appropriate material for the triumphal conclusion he had hoped to write.

"Am I saying what you want?" the president asked, perhaps sensing White's chagrin. "Was there any particular kind of question you wanted to ask?" White steered him into the foreign policy arena where the larger questions of war and peace and history converged. Kennedy's thoughts meandered around the globe—from Africa to South America to Russia and Southeast Asia. Kennedy asked White, should he attempt to resolve the deteriorating situation in Laos by writing directly to Mao and Chou? White flinched at the prospect of giving instant advice but promised to think about the question and respond later. (When he did advise the president, White took the same position as the State Department had and said the time was not right for personal contact with China's leaders—advice that White later conceded had been wrong.)[5] Kennedy's monologue soon veered back to his vexing problems with Congress and the inertia that had cemented itself into that institution during Eisenhower's presidency. White, aware that Vice President Lyndon Johnson was waiting to see the President, kept rising to leave "like a jack-in-the-box," but Kennedy kept insisting that he stay.

White had gone to the Oval Office in search of an epiphany. He came away enormously disappointed, fearful that the material was inappropriate for his narrative line. A letter he wrote to his publisher, Simon Michael Bessie, underscored his disappointment with the White House meeting:

> The sad fact of the matter is that when I went to call on him he treated
> me not as a working philosopher but as an old friend. There I was, all

5. Ibid., 500.

prepared to describe him in the first chapter in his purple toga, sitting
in majesty. . . . So I came out with this which strikes me as flat.[6]

The presidential portrait that eventually emerged in White's final chapter,
however, was that of a man in control—no doubts, no anger, no four-
letter words to mar the image of America's leader as both erudite and
forceful. It was a picture of power. Indeed, White is credited as the first
writer to affix capital letters to the name of the presidential office—which
had earlier been referred to as the "oval room" in books about the White
House. "White's inventive use of capital letters for the Oval Office swept
into standard usage in many languages, becoming a symbol of the modern
United States,"[7] Taylor Branch observed in *Parting the Waters*. White focused
on the "hush" that surrounded the Oval Office—where the President "must
sit alone"—as one manifestation of power. The trio of chalk-wielding New
York tailors had been banished from the canvas. In the eighteen-button
telephone console atop the president's desk, White saw still more evidence
of power, an equivalent symbol of "the sword and the mace in the politics
of the middle ages." That telephone, with its maximum security line and red
buttons, could mean "life and death for the human race," according to his
grandiloquent prose. Clearly, Kennedy's fascination with how much money
White's book might earn had no place in this narrative either. That his hero
had asked White for advice about writing to Mao and left his vice president
to suffer the indignity of cooling his heels in an outer office were similarly
inappropriate to the story line.

White instead rearranged the conversation so that Kennedy's comments
on foreign affairs preceded those about Congressional inertia. The president called his election victory "a miracle," in White's telling. Kennedy's
observations about his opponent were reduced and softened so that White's
readers find the president gently wondering why Nixon, whom Kennedy
had otherwise known as a "forthright" and "cogent" speaker in private,
had "talked down to the people" in his public appearances during the
presidential campaign just passed. In the transformation from contender
to president, White saw that Kennedy's eyes had changed—they were "very
dark now, very grave, markedly more sunken and lined at the corners than
those of the candidate."

6. THW, letter to Simon Michael Bessie, March 21, 1961, TWA, Box 17, Folder 9.
7. Branch, *Parting the Waters*, 377.

In the process of glorifying the American presidency, White also glorified the president. By wrapping him in an aura of power, White's words helped to suffuse Kennedy with the qualities of an all-American Superman—missing only the blue Spandex body suit and red cape. White was, of course, expanding on a characterization—albeit far more subtly—that Norman Mailer had made in his November 1960 *Esquire* profile of the Democratic contender. In "Superman Comes to the Supermarket," Mailer concluded that while Kennedy's mind was "too conventional," a certain mysterious and heroic presence made him "a great box office actor." The famous Kennedy "charisma" was taking shape in the media.

Portraits of the president swaddled in grandeur helped to develop in Americans the expectation that their president would indeed have some regal presence of a king and even a touch of a deity's omnipotence. Presidential powers had begun to expand in the early days of Franklin D. Roosevelt and the New Deal when what Theodore J. Lowi called the "president-centered national government" began to evolve. Paralleling those administrative changes that enlarged the presidency at the expense of Congress was an ever larger focus by the media on the president as personality. The convergence of power in the executive branch at the expense of the legislative and judiciary branches of government resulted, according to Arthur M. Schlesinger Jr., in "the imperial presidency." The unprecedented centralization of power, according to Schlesinger, was largely a product of the same forces that created the postwar consensus on foreign policy: "the belief in permanent and universal crisis, fear of communism, faith in the duty and the right of the United States to intervene swiftly in every part of the world,"[8] all conspired to undermine the constitutional system of checks and balances. In addition, the decline of the political parties and the electronic revolution, Schlesinger explained, all served to endow the presidency with additional powers. Media portrayals of a majestic, larger-than-life figure in the Oval Office helped to fix in the public consciousness an image of America as a benevolent and infallible force. Those efforts by White and his fellow journalists to ennoble the president had two far-reaching consequences. Americans later found it difficult to accept revelations that a variety of human frailties afflicted their nation's leaders. And America's leaders were unaccustomed to the kind of scrutiny and criticism that a succeeding generation of journalists considered

8. Theodore J. Lowi, *The Personal President*, 56; Arthur M. Schlesinger Jr., *The Imperial Presidency*, 208.

an appropriate function of their profession. Those leaders, in fact, had been more conditioned to accommodation and cooperation from journalists than to criticism.

From election day in 1960 until November 22, 1963, White was a booster of the Kennedy administration. His relationship with the president and a number of his appointees underscores the accuracy of an observation made by *New York Times* reporter Howell Raines: "Kennedy was alarmingly successful at turning journalists into cheerleaders." Journalism critics in the late 1980s and early 1990s would look back on this journalism of the postwar years with disdain. In *Feeding Frenzy*, Larry Sabato traces the evolution of journalistic practices in the latter decades of the twentieth century from what he called the "lapdog" style that evolved from the self-imposed censorship of the war years and was carried to an unconscionable extreme during the Kennedy presidency. During the Johnson and Nixon presidencies, a "watchdog" approach developed as a consequence of the "institutionalized hypocrisy" that had made the media "part and parcel of the Kennedy public relations team." Later, the disclosures about Kennedy's flagrant personal behavior provided embarrassing evidence of just how protective the press had been of Kennedy's private life. In their zeal to prove they would never again be co-opted by their political subjects, journalists emerged as what Sabato calls "junkyard dogs," and modern political reporting became a blood sport that not only lacks civility but also has potentially dangerous consequences for democracy.

Because White's work appeared at least to have "served and reinforced the political establishment," just as it had during World War II, in the framework established by Sabato, White would have been ranked among the "lapdog" journalists. "Sure Teddy sucked up to the Kennedys," acknowledged his old friend Ben Bradlee. "We all did."[9] White nonetheless demonstrates how journalists worked to empower government by not only voicing approval of its policy decisions but also becoming participants in those decisions. In empowering government, they of course empowered themselves. Journalists were simultaneously kingmakers and powerful servants of the "king" they had crowned. Kennedy clearly was charmed with how White had burnished the presidential image for history and, as a consequence, he took special pains to charm White.

Power fascinated Theodore White. He enjoyed his proximity to power in the way that a former poor boy who spent an anguished childhood on the

9. Raines is quoted in Larry J. Sabato, *Feeding Frenzy*, 39. Bradlee's quote is from a personal interview with the author, March 20, 1990.

outside looking in might. As a teenager during the Great Depression, White was left at the mercy of powerful forces over which he had no control. All his life he would recall the primitive power of a local news wholesaler at whose sufferance he was allowed to peddle newspapers on Boston's streetcars. The coveted nickel-plated medallions which that wholesaler dispensed were a crude yet unmistakable manifestation of power. White also found power in its abstract form an enduring source of intellectual fascination. Ancient Rome and its leaders absorbed him at an early age. When he was just sixteen, White read all six volumes of Gibbon's *Decline and Fall of the Roman Empire.* Later at Harvard, in Professor Roger Merriman's History I classes, the bespectacled old scholar pounded on the lectern to underscore his point about the enduring imprint ancient Rome had left on Europe's collective psyche: "Unity, gentlemen, Unity," he told them; the only lasting, binding heritage of the Roman Empire was the afterglow in the European mind that unity would again someday be achieved. The life and reign of Julius Caesar intrigued White, so much so that for years he worked on a play about the Roman leader's pivotal moment of decision at the Rubicon in 49 B.C. when he marched against Pompey. "I feel the modern world can neither understand Jesus Christ nor Democratic politics unless we understand Caesar first," he once told Robert Kennedy. In China, France, Israel, and finally in America, White watched men grasp at power, and he observed with considerable sadness how some were intoxicated by it, others corrupted by it. "Something happens to people when they come to power," White once said. "You lose some sort of sensitivity."[10] To wield words, White first discovered early in his career, was to wield power. And the power he acquired through his achievements as a writer was a psychological balm that soothed the wounds he had carried from a disenfranchised childhood into his adult life.

Even late in his long and successful career, there remained in White a mild disbelief that he had come so far. Yet he, too, came to enjoy his proximity to power and his first-name acquaintance with the men who were shaping history. White wrote of—and sometimes it seemed for— the administration he greatly admired. There was a parallel between his reporting of the brief Kennedy presidency and his early work in China when he had so candidly confessed his "pro-Chinese bias" to his editor.

10. For White's comment about Professor Roger Merriman see THW, speech at 25th Reunion—Harvard University, Class of 1938, June 1953, TWA, Box 185, Folder 9; for White's comment to RFK about Caesar see THW, letter to Robert Kennedy, December 27, 1963, Box 49, Folder 9. White's comment on the effects of power is from the author's personal interview with White, May 5, 1982.

Back then, youth and inexperience were the cause. More than two decades later, however, one could no longer claim, as John Hersey had done in an observation about White's early career, that he had not "had much chance to come to understand, or even wonder about, professional standards of journalism." In the late 1930s in China, he had worked simultaneously as a propagandist for Chiang's Nationalist government and as a correspondent for Time Inc.—a conflict in which Time acquiesced, to be sure. In the early 1960s in America, White's work, like that of other members of the elite press who were "on the team," brings to life the results of Kennedy's much-touted ability to charm the press and underscores concepts of media theorists about the interaction of those who govern and those who report on the governed. White's interaction with President Kennedy and his appointees demonstrates how the press and government functioned within a closed system that served to reinforce the tight consensus that framed America's domestic and foreign policy.

Long before *The Making of the President 1960* reached the hands of book reviewers, its chapters had already been reviewed by some of its key characters. Letters in White's archive indicate that Robert F. Kennedy and Pierre Salinger read and approved the entire manuscript prior to publication. President Kennedy also read a chapter or two. In addition, several chapters were also sent to some of White's Republican sources, principally to members of Nelson Rockefeller's staff and key figures at the Republican National Committee. The move provided White with a system of fact checking—something he understandably worried about, given the pace at which he was writing the book. It was, however, clearly a step that some contemporary journalists would regard as inappropriate.

Early in December 1960, White sent a rough draft of his first chapter to William Walton, a *Time* war correspondent who left journalism to become an artist. Walton, long a close friend of Kennedy's and a veteran of the Wisconsin, West Virginia, and New York campaigns, had spent election day with the candidate and his wife at their home in Hyannisport. Walton provided the details that so enriched White's first chapter: the candidate had had a Daiquiri—his first drink of the day—and discussed art with his wife in their antique-filled sitting room. Dinner was served later in the elegant, red-carpeted dining room. Finally, the Kennedys and their guest sat in front of the television as tallies from the industrial states rolled in and it appeared that Kennedy would win in a landslide. It was then that Walton overheard Jacqueline Kennedy tell her husband, "Oh, bunny, you're President now!" Aware that this early margin was certain to narrow,

Jack Kennedy quietly responded, "No . . . no . . . it's too early yet." And it was Walton who had watched the Secret Service detail secure the Kennedy compound just before dawn on the day after the election. In a letter that accompanied his manuscript, White asked Walton to check his opening chapter for "bloopers and indiscretions" before he showed the manuscript to Pierre Salinger.[11]

In February, White sent the 350 pages of his manuscript to Emmet J. Hughes, a Rockefeller campaign aide. The accompanying letter asked Hughes to "treat the information in this manuscript as confidential. Since I have received so many confidences I must determine whether others will insist on withdrawing what they told me from the record." Finally, in March, White sent his manuscript to Kennedy's people. The first two-thirds of the book went to Robert F. Kennedy early in the month and a week later White sent on the final third accompanied by a letter that echoed one he had sent David Bruce a decade earlier in France: "Could you pay particular attention to the beginning of Chapter Nine where I do a thumbnail sketch of the present Attorney General of whom I am so fond and whom I do not want to hurt. Don't be shy if you object to my remarks."[12]

White also sent portions of the book to Pierre Salinger on the same day and in an accompanying letter he asked for his comments on the section based on his Oval Office interview with Kennedy. Did Salinger think the passage about Kennedy in the Oval Office should be eliminated? White had asked in his letter. The author thought his talk with the president had come off badly—Kennedy had seemed so tired and apparently under such pressure, White explained, that it "seemed unfair to ask him those stupidly profound questions whose answers," White had imagined, would give him a closing for the book. "I know the president said that he wanted to see this last third, but I don't know whether he said it out of intent or out of courtesy. However, I hope you will offer it to him."[13] Others who saw the manuscript in advance of its publication were the Kennedy pollster Louis Harris, White House aide Kenneth O'Donnell, and James Rowe, a Washington attorney long active in Democratic politics.

Correspondence indicates that the Kennedy aides assumed their assignment went beyond simple fact checking. Robert Kennedy, for example,

11. White, *The Making of the President 1960*, 20; THW, letter to William Walton, December 8, 1960, TWA, Box 17, Folder 2.
12. THW, letter to Emmet Hughes, February 3, 1961, TWA, Box 17, Folder 3; letter to Robert F. Kennedy, March 17, 1961, Box 17, Folder 3.
13. THW, letter to Pierre Salinger, March 17, 1961, TWA, Box 17, Folder 3.

wanted to be sure that his younger brother, Edward M. Kennedy, was acknowledged as mastermind of the election campaign in the Western states. The newly appointed attorney general's five-page memorandum also pointed out that White overlooked some of the major contributions that Sargent Shriver had made to the campaign. White had failed to give sufficient credit to Stephen Smith, another brother-in-law, who had worked on the campaign, Kennedy observed. "I think, if possible, it would be nice to mention this in a phrase or a sentence," Robert Kennedy wrote. "This will be the best book, without question, on this campaign and that kind of tribute would be nice for one's children and grandchildren," he added, as if White were writing some official family history. The attorney general also took issue with White's conclusion that Nixon was victorious in California because of the "atrocious mismanagement" of the Kennedy campaign and because of the violent disputes within the state's Democratic organization. White based those conclusions on the insights of Paul Ziffern, a California attorney long active in Democratic politics. Kennedy lost, Ziffern told White, because he apparently had been ill-advised about where he might best make personal appearances, and because the campaign was poorly organized. Moreover, because Kennedy had paid some but by no means all of his volunteers, he had created a serious morale problem within the ranks of that vital component of any presidential campaign. Robert Kennedy, however, argued that anti-Catholic sentiment in districts adjoining Los Angeles accounted for their loss in California. Although White disagreed with Kennedy's analysis in a subsequent letter, he nonetheless retreated: "I acknowledge that my statement 'atrocious mismanagement' is extravagant and I am withdrawing it."[14]

The president's only quarrel with White's manuscript was a remark he was said to have made on election night as he walked across the lawn in the Kennedy compound from his brother's house to his own. The outcome of the election was still in doubt since such key states as Illinois, Michigan, and California had yet to complete the vote count. Thus, Kennedy was about to go to bed at 4 A.M. without knowing whether or not he had won. Mary McGrory, one of three pool reporters stationed just outside the family compound that night, had told White that as Kennedy walked across the lawn with Cornelius Ryan at 3:40 A.M., when asked how he felt, had responded, "I'm angry." White cast the remark as an uncommon crack in the candidate's composure in his manuscript. The president, however, told

14. Robert F. Kennedy, memorandum to THW, March 23, 1961, TWA, Box 49, Folder 9; Paul Ziffern, memorandum to THW, February 2, 1961, TWA, Box 17, Folder 2; THW, letter to Robert F. Kennedy, April 5, 1961, TWA, Box 49, Folder 9.

White, "that wasn't what I said in the dark. What I said was, 'I'm hungry.' "[15] Neither quote appeared in the book.

Although his March 1961 deadline for the book had left White almost wholly absorbed in writing after election day, he nevertheless took some time off to became an unofficial adviser to the president-elect. White eased himself into that role just two days after Kennedy won his narrow victory with a letter to Theodore Sorenson, Kennedy's speech writer and alter ego, in which he recommended that Edward R. Murrow, White's friend and fellow journalist, be appointed as America's ambassador to England, a post that the president-elect's father had held just before World War II. Kennedy instead appointed White's old friend David Bruce as ambassador to the Court of St. James's.

White nonetheless continued to recommend potential appointees to members of the administration both before and after the inauguration. On November 20, 1960, for example, he wrote to Adam Yarmolinsky at the Democratic National Committee in an apparent response to a request for the names of prospective appointees. White suggested to Yarmolinsky— who later worked with Defense Secretary Robert McNamara at the Pentagon —that Donald Straus be appointed to a position in the Department of Health, Education and Welfare, and that his longtime acquaintance, Brigadier General Edward G. Lansdale, be named to administer American policy in Southeast Asia. White's letter also noted that, like so many Kennedy staffers, he was being swamped with requests from all manner of acquaintances to put in a good word for them with the president-elect:

> This letter will be brief because you said you wanted whatever names I could suggest fast. I am, of course overwhelmed (as you must be to a far greater extent) by the cascade of letters and requests from people who think that I have some particular access to the Kennedy clan because of this year's work. Most of the suggestions that come to me are junk.[16]

Later, as he raced to complete his book, White wrote to the presidential aide Kenneth O'Donnell recommending that Stanley Cleveland, an acquaintance from his Paris days whom he described as "one of the most brilliant young men in our State Department," be considered for an appointment to the White House staff. In that same letter White raised the more delicate subject of John S. Service, who had been badly burned during the

---

15. Mary McGrory, letter to THW, November 10, 1960, TWA, Box 100, Folder 6; and Arthur M. Schlesinger, Jr., *Robert Kennedy and His Times*, 219.

16. THW, letter to Adam Yarmolinsky, November 22, 1960, TWA, Box 49, Folder 4.

McCarthy era for his role in "losing" China and had since been banished to insignificant State Department assignments, such as consul general in Liverpool, England, where he was stationed early in 1961. "There are great political hazards in bringing him back to Washington," White acknowledged, "but the hazards are probably outweighed by the benefit we might have in establishing close at hand to American policy the man who knows best the men who menace that policy most."[17] Despite White's suggestions, the old China hands were neither given positions of any significance in the Kennedy State Department nor absolved of their purported transgressions in the fall of China.

A year later, White wrote to Ralph Dungan, a special assistant to the president, recommending "a few civilian names of governmental quality from New York City." The letter apparently resulted from a conversation White had had with Dungan during a party at Robert Kennedy's home. Emmet Hughes, a former war correspondent, Eisenhower speech writer, and political strategist for Nelson Rockefeller, topped White's list of potential appointees. Because Hughes was becoming "restless" in his job with the Rockefellers, White explained, he would most certainly consider an appointment to the State Department. White's list also included the names of John J. B. Shea, an attorney who might be appropriate for the Securities and Exchange Commission, and Donald B. Straus, whom he again described as "a major talent."[18]

White also wrote to John F. Kennedy himself following the election. In his first letter, White wrote that he approved of all the appointments Kennedy had made and offered his services for whatever assistance the new president might need of him. He was, just as he had been in China, a patriot first—devoted both to his country and especially to its new president—and a journalist second. The text of that letter reflects not only his esteem for the newly elected president but also the measure of loyalty and responsibility citizens felt they owed both their country and their president during those troubled and tense cold war years. "If you need my help in any way," White wrote, "I could interrupt even [this book]; you need only call on me. I say that to you as a citizen to his President—but I hope also as one friend to another."[19] In that same letter, White told the president of his disappointment in the election results and observed that in the absence

17. THW, letter to Kenneth P. O'Donnell, March 21, 1961, TWA, Box 49, Folder 4.
18. THW, letter to Ralph Dungan, June 19, 1962, TWA, Box 49, Folder 4.
19. THW, letter to John F. Kennedy, December 9, 1960, TWA, Box 49, Folder 2.

of an undeniable victory, he would "have to create the policies and the movements with your own gut and skill, so that in 1964 the battle is fought on your terrain, not theirs."

White's book became, as Robert F. Kennedy had predicted, the best campaign history of the 1960 election. It made the *New York Times* Best Seller List in the fall of 1961 and won a Pulitzer prize for general nonfiction in 1962. That success along with his admiration for the Kennedys helped to put White's name on some of Washington's most-sought-after guest lists. White's diary records one occasion when the attorney general dispatched the family airplane to fly White and other New York guests to boisterous, star-studded parties at Hickory Hill. "Mad night at Bobby's. Great fun. He sent the Caroline up from Washington, we got aboard at 5:00, followed by Harry Belafonte and his wife Julie . . ." one entry revealed, "Finally Bobby makes a toast to me; to which I respond with Thucydides; then respond again with comparison of Lenin-Trotsky-Stalin; . . . then Ethel says grace, concluding 'God bless Teddy White for voting for Kennedy,' to which I interrupted, 'I didn't vote, I was stuck in Hyannisport.' " On yet another occasion, White wrote Ethel Kennedy an effusive thank-you, forewarning her he planned to steal a memory of the recent party he had attended for a political novel he planned to write someday: "I've rarely seen a guest list so perfectly put together, the old and the new, the beautiful and the glamorous, the prestigious and the friendly."[20]

Once *The Making of the President 1960* was published in July 1961 and White had completed his book promotion tour, he took off on a six-week trip around the world. Apparently at the behest of Arthur Schlesinger Jr., his Harvard classmate who had become a member of Kennedy's White House staff, White wrote an assessment of the situation in Southeast Asia for the president.

> Any investment of troops in the paddies of the delta will, I believe, be useless—or worse. The presence of white American troops will feed the race hate of the Vietnamese. It will force us into a guerrilla war which cannot be won except by a military exertion of the same order as the British in Malaya from 1949–1954.
>
> May I say (I hope not presumptuously) that you have handled the Berlin crisis superbly; as your official chronicler I am unutterably proud

20. THW, diary entry January 26, 1962, TWA, Box 193; THW, letter to Ethel Kennedy, June 18, 1962, TWA, Box 20, Folder 15.

of your calmness, firmness, and grace in that area. I think also that
the Laos situation has been handled beautifully—this is a diplomatic
Dunkirk for which credit will be given only in history books, not in
current politics. But this South Vietnam thing is a real bastard to solve—
either we have to let the younger military officers knock off Diem in a
coup and take our chances on a military regime (as in Pakistan and
South Korea) or else we have to give it up. To commit troops there is
unwise—for the problem is political and doctrinal (in the long-range
intellectual sense); until a government in South Vietnam comes about
that inspires its people to die against Communism, as Communism
inspires men to die against others, our troops can do no good.[21]

By far the most effusive letter White wrote to the president followed the
invitation White and his wife received to a small dinner party in the family
quarters of the White House on Lincoln's birthday in 1963. That day marked
an important milestone in White House history, one that was mentioned in
White's notes of the evening only in the context of the "noise and babble"
he and his wife heard as they waited for the elevator to take them to the
mansion's family quarters. What White referred to as the Emancipation
Day celebration was the largest group of black Americans ever to assemble
in the White House. At a time when only token numbers of blacks had
been received in the president's home, the reception for hundreds of the
nation's Black elites was a historic occasion indeed. Presidential aides—
Arthur Schlesinger among them—had hit on the idea as an alternative to
the Second Emancipation Proclamation, for which black civil rights leaders
had unsuccessfully sought Kennedy's blessing. Unlike their predecessors,
this president and first lady were "completely relaxed at social gatherings of
Negroes."[22] Some black leaders, however, perceived the Lincoln's Birthday
event as an empty symbolic gesture undertaken by a president who was
too fainthearted to endorse any bold legislative steps to end segregation.
Instead of signing a proclamation that would echo Abraham Lincoln's daring, century-old manifesto aimed at achieving racial justice, this president
invited unprecedented numbers of blacks for canapés and small talk. As
a result, Dr. Martin Luther King Jr. sent the president his regrets. A. Philip
Randolph, head of the Brotherhood of Sleeping Car Porters, and Clarence
Mitchell, the NAACP's chief Washington lobbyist, also joined King's White
House boycott.

21. THW, letter to John F. Kennedy, October 11, 1961, TWA, Box 49, Folder 3.
22. Branch, *Parting the Waters*, 687.

Neither the extraordinary reception nor the boycott appears to have pre-occupied the president or his guests upstairs later in the evening. Joining the Kennedys and the Whites at dinner were Benjamin and Antoinette Bradlee and Harry Labouisse, America's ambassador to Greece, and his wife, Eve. While they sipped cocktails, White and the president chatted not about racial issues but about the Cuban missile crisis. They speculated about what might have happened if Khrushchev had not backed down in that confronta-tion. Kennedy also griped about how Republicans were second-guessing the outcome of that crisis and how much coverage those critics were getting in the press. During the meal, "a mediocre rack of lamb," the conversation turned to politics, and Kennedy wanted to know whether White thought Nelson Rockefeller would get the GOP presidential nomination in 1964. "I said he owned it if he wanted it," White wrote the following day, and also told the president, "but he likes you." Ever the pragmatist, Kennedy responded, "That's unimportant. I like him, too. But he'll get to hate me. That's inevitable." In praising *The Making of the President 1960*, Kennedy turned to Nancy White and said, "It's not that he said anything so new, but that he said it so beautifully."[23]

A thank-you letter White wrote the following day is noteworthy both in the way it flatters the president and criticizes members of his own profession:

> I bounced all the way back to New York after Tuesday night. The evening was so much fun that every now and then I had to slam on my emotional brakes and say "Whoa! You're Dining With The President of the United States." The President of the United States should be a remote figure of respect, trust and majesty—he should not be so completely enjoyable. The wine was great, the conversation better.
>
> This thought remains with me about the few moments of seriousness we had before dinner: that perhaps public pressure about Cuba weighs on you more than it should. The situation there is a rotten one. But it has to be handled in its own terms, by what reality dictates, not by consideration of what will best satisfy an ignorant Congress, press or commentators. So far, I think you have withstood this kind of wolf-pack pressure magnificently. You are doing what the situation calls for, not what politics calls for.
>
> I am provoked to write to you as flat-footedly as this because I had the impression early in the evening, that some of the wood-peckers,

23. THW, memorandum "At the President's," February 13, 1963, TWA, Box 49, Folder 3.

like Keating, were getting under your skin. In politics (as you know so
much better than I) once they feel they can reach a sensitive nerve (like
Cuba), once they feel they can get a live response, an exasperated twitch,
they will never let up. You are doing what you must do in the eyes of
history and you are doing it beautifully. . . . Don't let yourself be jostled
from your own sequence of decisions on the matter in order to please
Congress or the press.[24]

   With that abundant admiration for the president and a commitment to
his mission as cheerleader to the New Frontier, White produced two important profiles of Kennedy Cabinet members for *Life* and *Look* magazines in
1962 and 1963. (In a renewed association with Time Inc., White had signed
on as a contract writer in the early 1960s.) Both profiles illustrate the convergence of insider journalism and the journalism of illusion. White's approach
to the two stories, one about Secretary of State Dean Rusk and the other
about Secretary of Defense Robert McNamara, are evidence of the latitude
that the conventions of objective journalism afforded journalists. White's
profile of Rusk, which appeared in *Life* in June 1962, obscured President
Kennedy's ambiguous comments about the secretary in the very way that
White's dispatches from Chungking had overlooked the distasteful aspects
of Chiang's government. When he wrote about McNamara the following
year, White again demonstrated to what degree the canons of objectivity
could be compromised, just as he had done with his David Bruce profile
written in Paris in the early 1950s.
   Rusk was an oddity in the Kennedy administration, a man who didn't
quite fit in with the youthful, action-oriented swingers who came to power
in the early days of 1961. He had neither the forceful, high-profile style that
characterized the New Frontiersmen nor the Establishment pedigree that
so many of them possessed. Kennedy had wanted to be his own secretary
of state. Powerful men in the tradition of Dean Acheson and George C.
Marshall, the secretaries of state on whom President Harry Truman had
depended so heavily to guide America through the postwar years, would
have no place in the Kennedy cabinet. Foreign affairs, the new president believed, should be run from the White House, and that dictated the selection
of a complacent appointee. Kennedy had initially sought out Robert Lovett,
hoping the luster of his Establishment credentials and his far-reaching experience in the Roosevelt and Truman administrations would add some sorely

24. THW, letter to John F. Kennedy, February 15, 1963, TWA, Box 49, Folder 3.

needed gravity to his fledgling government. Lovett declined but advised, as so many other knowledgeable people did whenever Kennedy asked for suggestions, that Dean Rusk was among those worthy of his consideration. An article Rusk had written for *Foreign Affairs* in the spring of 1960 suggested that he shared Kennedy's belief that only a president could shape foreign policy. So Rusk, "everybody's Number Two," according to David Halberstam, was appointed almost by default—not so much for what he was, but rather for what he was not.[25] As head of the Rockefeller Foundation he had the appropriate Establishment imprimatur. He would, however, remain an anomaly; an older, blander presence on a New Frontier populated with aggressive men, and an outsider to the glittering Georgetown social circles of which White had become a part. Rusk's name was not on Bobby and Ethel Kennedy's guest list, but his name was occasionally a subject of derision among some of the people who regularly attended the Kennedy parties at Hickory Hill.

White detailed the story behind his Rusk profile in the opening pages of the unfinished sequel to his autobiography, where it stands as a reminder of that ageless journalistic struggle to reconcile the issues surrounding on- and off-the-record comments. Kennedy was one of the last presidents who could trust in favored journalists and rely on their discretion. When he nonchalantly confided in White the details of his immense dissatisfaction with Dean Rusk's performance as secretary of state, it is doubtful that he had first proscribed those remarks as "off the record." Presidents were routinely afforded the privilege of choosing which of their remarks could be quoted, even when it required a journalist to forsake a sensational story.

White had known Rusk since the early 1940s when he was a young colonel in the China-Burma-India theater during World War II who served, for a time, as Stilwell's deputy chief of staff. Rusk returned to Washington, D.C., after the war, and took jobs first in the Pentagon and later in the State Department as assistant secretary of state for Far Eastern affairs.

White's story in *Life* analyzed the unexpected controversy that had grown up around America's fifty-fourth secretary of state in the year and a half since Kennedy had taken office. "Does He Drive or Is He Driven?" the headline asked. The problem, White's story explained, was one of personalities— the president was an "action" man while his secretary was an "issues" man. Kennedy's privileged background had bred in him a taste for risk and impetuosity, while Rusk, the son of a Georgia preacher and a Rhodes scholar,

25. David Halberstam, *The Best and the Brightest*, 32.

was a man given to "wary deliberation." The story carefully balanced the criticism with the praise—almost all of it from unnamed sources—that White had heard about Rusk. Admirers applauded him as a superb negotiator and a masterful problem solver; detractors sneered that he was a man of limited capacities and one who spent too much time away from Washington, D.C. The president's assessment was simple and straightforward: "He's got guts," Kennedy said of Rusk. "And his judgment is good. And in final analysis those are the qualities a Secretary of State needs. I wouldn't want to make a final decision on a vital matter involving our security until I'd heard his view. He sits on my right."[26] The secretary of state, White's story concluded, "pleases this President."

But according to notes White made following his interview with Kennedy in April 1962, the president was anything but pleased with Rusk. White had opened his interview with the president by offering him an opportunity to sculpt the Rusk profile. "I told him I could prove Dean Rusk either a great secretary or a poor secretary, that the essential thing was his opinion, what did he want and find in a secretary of state." The president dissembled briefly, but his anger and exasperation soon surfaced. "Kennedy began obliquely, as politicians do, with the kind of gossip we both enjoyed. . . . But Kennedy was in one of those finger-snapping moods of his, and he went on. He wanted action from the State Department, action." Kennedy, White found, was clearly irritated and impatient on the subject of his secretary of state. Rusk was too slow, too methodical, the president had complained. "When Rusk talks he never gets it out on the table, there's nothing to chew on," Kennedy fumed. Besides, there was too little follow-through from Rusk, who for example had taken three weeks to provide a response to the president's questions about aid to Yugoslavia. Rusk had returned from a conference of foreign ministers in Geneva the day before White's interview, but the president was still awaiting a report from him. Kennedy also criticized some of Rusk's ambassadorial appointees: Julius Holmes was too old for the post in Iran, John Emerson (once a part of the State Department's China crowd) wasn't up to the post in Tanganyika to which he was appointed. However, despite his obvious dissatisfaction with what he called an excess of deadwood in the department, Kennedy urged White "not to make an attack on the Foreign Service, these people have these hardship posts, they have all these problems." The State Department has no political savvy, Kennedy

26. Edward T. Thompson, ed., *Theodore H. White at Large,* 53.

complained, returning to his list of grievances. Bobby could whip the State Department into shape, the president added; his brother would be of more use to him there than as attorney general.[27]

Stunned, White sought out Pierre Salinger immediately after the interview and asked, "Did the president expect me to publish in *Life* what he had just said. If so, was I the one supposed to force Dean Rusk's resignation?" White asked the White House press secretary. Salinger, who appeared equally startled, asked White to hold his story. The telephone rang in White's New York brownstone soon after he had arrived home. It was Pierre Salinger. The president was afraid he'd given White the wrong impression of Dean Rusk. Would White find it convenient to return to Washington for a further chat, Salinger wanted to know. So, the following week White and the president met again in the Oval Office and worked out an acceptably innocuous quote for the article. The president, however, began a new diatribe about the secretary's shortcomings. Finally, Kennedy asked White, "How do you get rid of a secretary of state?"[28] Neither the president's question nor extensive criticisms he had voiced in two interviews with White were ever made public.

About a month before the Rusk story appeared in *Life*, White wrote to Theodore Sorenson asking for comments on what he called the "much tortured script" that accompanied his letter. "The president has approved his quote as it stands," White explained, "and Rusk has meticulously edited the last five pages of his own statement. But neither has seen any more than their [*sic*] own quotes."[29] The master White served was not his readers, but rather his president. In White's system of journalistic values, disclosing the president's dissatisfaction with Rusk would have been considered irresponsible. Ironically, by contemporary standards, the journalist who kept those remarks secret would be considered irresponsible.

White's profile of Secretary of Defense McNamara is an equally revealing episode, one that demonstrates the lengths to which he and other journalists went to please their subjects, perhaps as a way of ensuring professional access. Once again, the story behind the story presents further evidence of a willingness to compromise that apparently had become an acceptable part of the way journalism was practiced in the early 1960s. The McNamara

27. THW, notes of interview with John F. Kennedy, March 28, 1962, TWA, Box 49, Folder 3; White, first draft, Chapter 1, "In Search of History, Vol. II," TWA, Box 187, Folder 2.

28. White, "In Search of History, Vol. II."

29. THW, letter to Theodore Sorenson, May 8, 1962, TWA, Box 21, Folder 4.

article, which appeared in *Look* in April 1963, was as glowing as the Rusk profile had been circumspect. White was a social acquaintance of the man who became America's eighth secretary of defense when John Kennedy took office. Unlike the Rusks, the McNamaras were regulars at Bobby and Ethel Kennedy's fabled parties—as were the Whites.

In his rather breathless prose, White traced McNamara's brilliant career from his low-paying job as a statistician with the War Department to the presidency of the Ford Motor Co., a position to which he was named just one day after John Kennedy won the election. When he left Detroit for the Pentagon, McNamara gave up his $420,000 salary and stock options worth several million dollars. Of McNamara, White wrote, "Power becomes him—gravely and easily." White paused to dwell on the secretary's day and evening personas, observing that the rigidity and self-discipline that were so in evidence at his office gave way to a charm and wit that made him "one of the most completely engaging dinner companions on Washington's inner social circuit."[30]

White's description of the Pentagon's inner workings appears to have been constructed to enlarge McNamara and present him as a genius. With an incisive mind and a no-nonsense managerial style, according to White's story, McNamara had taken on the muscle-bound bureaucracy at the Pentagon, applied his uncommon gift for data analysis and statistical calculation, and had brought America's military establishment under his control. "A stupefying task," White called it, one whose success meant that "if America's leaders invite Americans to die in battle or under bombardment in the next few years, it will be by reasonable decision, rather than by accident or spastic reaction." Was it any wonder Americans came to think of these Kennedy appointees as the best and the brightest? Was it any wonder Americans came to believe, in that guileless pre-Vietnam era, that these men could do no wrong?

The McNamara profile focused first on the East Coast Ivy League crowd that the new secretary had placed in the Pentagon's key civilian jobs. They were, White insisted, "almost all the kind of men, from the kind of families, who would have gone charging up San Juan Hill with Teddy Roosevelt."[31] He extolled their prep school educations, distinguished marriages, and

30. Theodore H. White, "Revolution in the Pentagon—Robert McNamara," *Look,* April 23, 1963, 31.
31. Ibid.

Establishment family roots, explaining that they "have enough wealth and devotion to make America's welfare their primary concern in life." In a description of the Pentagon's so-called Think Staff—those analysts trained in science and technology whose roots were largely in California—White explained they were interested in war as a system of intellectual propositions and were most at home with a piece of chalk and a blackboard.

The files in White's archive reveal the author not only allowed McNamara to read the story in advance of publication to ensure that he had not inadvertently breached U.S. security but also permitted him to make a wide assortment of changes, few of which appear to have been based on factual errors. The carbon of the story that McNamara edited reveals both a measure of hubris in the secretary's character and the questionable professional standards in White's approach to his work. The copy bearing McNamara's "tiny cramped handwriting," which, according to White's story, had become famous in the Pentagon, demonstrates the liberties that the author offered his subject. McNamara not only deleted descriptive passages such as "slick black hair," and "a Midwestern innocent"—which White left in the story— but the defense secretary also rewrote his own quotations, a privilege White granted him. McNamara, for example, elevated himself from a "good talker" to a "great talker," and scratched a quote from an unnamed source who remembered that during the Bay of Pigs invasion, the defense secretary had behaved "as if it were someone else's party." McNamara also deleted the names of three individuals who had recommended him to Kennedy for the Pentagon post—Dillon Read, a Wall Street lawyer; Neal Staebler, a Michigan congressman, and Jack Conway, AFL-CIO chairman. More remarkably still, McNamara also deleted a harmless but telling anecdote about his youth, one that White had gleaned from Annalee Jacoby, his former China colleague. Jacoby, who had an occasional date with McNamara when they attended the same California high school, told White that when McNamara was a teenager, his father had given him a Ford roadster. "Bob had promised to drive no more than 20 miles per hour and while others whizzed by him to and from dates, Bob always pushed his green-wheeled Ford at exactly the speed promised."[32]

McNamara's sterling reputation in Washington was hardly happenstance, according to David Halberstam, who wrote after McNamara had left

32. THW, second draft of "Revolution in the Pentagon," with corrections by McNamara, TWA, Box 81, Folder 4.

government, "He knew about the importance of public relations, and played that game with surprising skill." When McNamara discovered that Arthur Sylvester, his top public relations aide in the defense department,

> was a man of limited sophistication and ability, McNamara quickly learned how to use him to stand as a lightning rod and filter between the Secretary and the average working reporter, essential to fend the press off and deflect the heat (leaving many reporters to wonder why a man as able as McNamara had a press aide as inept as Sylvester; the answer was that it was deliberate). At the same time he used Adam Yarmolinsky, a former Harvard Law School professor and a man with unusually good connections with the liberal establishment, to do the more serious job of protecting the secretary's image with major writers and columnists.[33]

Ironically, Sylvester had sought White's advice about staffing in the Pentagon's public affairs division soon after White had sent him a draft of the McNamara story. In a letter marked "confidential," White responded that, "unequivocally, yes," the Defense Department did need a major new personality, specifically a journalist with both magazine and book experience, but he did not suggest any particular individual for that position.[34]

President Kennedy had asked White about the progress of his McNamara profile during that small White House dinner party in February 1963, and White's response seems to corroborate Halberstam's assessment of the defense secretary's public relations savvy. "I said what a wonderful guy he [McNamara] was," wrote White in his notes about the evening he dined with the Kennedys. The president asked White why he "hadn't been around to talk to him on this one; I said I didn't need help on this one, he [McNamara] was so obviously good."[35] The story, no doubt, further cemented White in the Kennedy circle's good graces.

Frederick Palmer, a foreign correspondent who had covered World War I for the *New York Herald*, long ago explained the price newsmen paid when they subjected themselves to censorship in exchange for access on the European battlefronts:

33. Halberstam, *The Best and the Brightest*, 217.
34. THW, letter to Arthur Sylvester, February 5, 1963, TWA, Box 22, Folder 7.
35. THW, memorandum, "At the President's," February 13, 1963, TWA, Box 49, Folder 3.

> Day after day we sallied forth from our chateau to different headquarters
> and billets for our grist, and having written our dispatches, turned them
> over to the officers for censorship. We rarely had our copy cut. We
> had learned too well where the line was drawn on military secrecy.
> The important items were those we left out; and these made us pub-
> lic liars.[36]

In the semipermanent state of siege that the Cold War created, journalists
of the 1950s and 1960s, it seems, had also learned only too well where
the line was drawn. Hollywood had it backwards in the opening scene of
The Green Berets, when a gung-ho soldier sets out to convince a cynical
American reporter about the importance of America's presence in Vietnam.
For the most part, many members of the American press landed in Vietnam equipped with the same convictions American soldiers carried—they
believed their cause was right and their motives were just. "I didn't come
to think of it [the war] as immoral until the very end," explained Charles
Mohr, who reported the war for *Time* and later for the *New York Times*. In
fact, armed with an M-16, Mohr joined the U.S. Marines in retaking the
Hue Citadel after the Tet offensive in 1968. White, however, even in the late
1960s, stubbornly resisted the idea that America's presence in Southeast
Asia was improper or immoral. "I do not want America to surrender in
humiliation in Vietnam either. To surrender abjectly will not advance the
cause of peace; it will destroy it. I want out of there. But nothing infuriates
me more than the charge that this is an immoral war," he wrote to his friend
Stewart Alsop in 1969.[37]

No censor had to draw a line for journalists in the 1950s and early
1960s; the journalists had already drawn it for themselves, and in doing
so they joined an alliance in which they were the acquiescent partners
in their relationship with political authority. With "the national security"
as their overarching concern, the nation's leaders and the journalists who
reported on their activities took up arms against the perils of communism.
They never publicly questioned the validity of those perils or what our
constant preoccupation with military preparedness did to us as a society.
As an unexpected bonus, the bond that emerged from the alliance between
the press and government officials enhanced the stature of journalists by

36. Hallin, *The Uncensored War*, 127.
37. Knightley, *The First Casualty*, 381; THW, letter to Stewart Alsop, August 13,
1969, TWA, Box 29, Folder 13.

making the men who wielded power dependent upon them. Thus, the image-makers were granted entree into the citadels of power as government officials sought to ensure themselves of an appropriately positive image. To preserve that hard-won stature, journalists were loath to offend those who had provided them access to those coveted inner circles. The relationship had seductive qualities for both parties—the McNamaras could fashion their own splendid images on the pages of America's best-read magazines, while the Whites were embraced socially and their egos were massaged when the nation's leaders sought their advice.

Clearly, with the sorts of compromises White and his colleagues in the mainstream media willingly made, government officials had become conditioned to a posture of accommodation. They had been confiding in journalists for years, and journalists had willingly kept their secrets. Journalists and government officials had joined forces, and together they worked to create illusions. On what basis, therefore, would government have anticipated anything but complicity from the press? With journalists so willing to back down on statements such as "atrocious mismanagement" and so eager to cater to requests that siblings and in-laws be properly acknowledged for their campaign contributions, as Robert Kennedy had done with White, reporters had cast themselves in a submissive role. Why would government officials have expected anything but cooperation from the press? Hadn't some of America's leading journalists unapologetically reported to the Central Intelligence Agency throughout the cold war, a practice that some of them still stoutly defended as proper even in the late 1970s? "The notion that a newspaperman doesn't have a duty to his country is perfect balls," proclaimed a defiant Joseph Alsop, who was the dean of Washington's conservative columnists. "I call it doing my duty as a citizen."[38]

And many journalists apparently felt it was also a duty to keep secrets on behalf of their government—even when the so-called secrets were hardly well kept. For example, America's U-2 spy flights were, by the late 1950s, known to a number of journalists. Hanson Baldwin, the *New York Times* military correspondent, had seen one of the planes at a West German airport in the summer of 1958 and told a CIA official he planned to write a story. "Jesus, Hanson, no," the CIA man responded, claiming that it would undermine one of America's critical intelligence operations. Baldwin protested, and finally CIA Director Allen Dulles talked to the *Times* publisher, Arthur H. Sulzberger, who agreed to hold the story. Top people in Washington

38. Carl Bernstein, "The CIA and the Media," *Rolling Stone*, October 22, 1977.

journalism circles learned about the U-2, according to David Halberstam—including Arthur Krock, James Reston, and Chalmers Roberts—but none of them wrote a story.[39]

Hadn't newspaper publishers—of the *New York Times* and the *Louisville Courier-Journal*, among others—agreed to provide cover for CIA operatives? American newspapers had declined an invitation from the Communist Chinese government in 1956 to send correspondents to China for the first time in seven years. "We did not want to embarrass our government," *Times* editor Clifton Daniel said, explaining why the Chinese offer was refused. The *Times* had agreed to tone down its Cuban invasion story early in 1961 on the eve of the Bay of Pigs debacle after President Kennedy argued that it was in the national interest to do so.[40] Having so easily commanded such ample measures of deference and loyalty, it is hardly any wonder that government officials expected—indeed even took as their due—that same type of treatment in Vietnam.

When Homer Bigart of the *New York Times*, the first reporter representing a major American daily to be assigned to Vietnam, returned from his assignment in 1962, there seemed to be an undertone of surprise in his observation about the treatment correspondents in Saigon were receiving from American military officials. "[We] seem to be regarded by the American mission as tools of our foreign policy," he wrote in the company's house magazine. "Those who balk are apt to find it a bit lonely, for they are likely to be distrusted and shunned by American and Vietnam officials."[41] But based on what had become standard postwar journalistic practice, it would appear the press had little basis for the surprise it demonstrated at the government's propaganda and concealment efforts during the Vietnam war. The wonder is not that President Kennedy had suggested to Sulzberger in 1963 that David Halberstam (Bigart's successor in Vietnam) be removed from the newspaper's Saigon bureau and transferred to Paris or Rome. The wonder is instead that the newspaper refused that request. Sulzberger's decision ran counter to many of the other signals the press had sent public officials during the postwar decades.

Michael Schudson suggests in his book *Discovering the News* that the moment when the none-too-gifted Arthur Sylvester decreed that the government had a right to lie to the press was an important turning point in the

39. David Halberstam, *The Fifties*, 708.
40. Michael Schudson, *Discovering the News*, 172; Gay Talese, *The Kingdom and the Power*, 5.
41. As quoted in Knightley, *The First Casualty*, 375.

relationship between the press and government. Speaking at a news briefing on October 30, 1962, Sylvester contended: "In the kind of world we live in, the generation of news by actions taken by the government becomes one weapon in a strained situation. The results justify the methods we used." Four weeks later he presented that same idea more forcefully in a speech to the New York chapter of Sigma Delta Chi. "I think the inherent right of the government to lie—to lie to save itself when faced with nuclear disaster—is basic, basic."[42] Eisenhower had, of course, lied in 1960 on the eve of his Geneva summit meeting with Khrushchev when he claimed that the U-2 spy plane piloted by Francis Gary Powers and shot down over the Soviet Union was a weather research flight.

Kennedy continued that same tradition when he was questioned about Vietnam by Tom Wicker of the *New York Times*. "Mr. President, are American troops now in combat in Vietnam?" asked Wicker at a press conference on January 15, 1962, sternly posing a question that he and his editors had "honed to what we thought was a fine point."[43] The president looked at Wicker "as if he thought I might be crazy," and answered with a single word. "No." There were nearly one thousand military "advisers" in Vietnam on the day that Wicker asked his question. Less than three weeks before that January press conference America had suffered its first combat casualty when U.S. Army Spec. 4 James T. David was killed in a jungle ambush outside Saigon. Because the twenty-four-year-old Tennessee soldier's death had attracted little media attention, Kennedy easily dismissed Wicker's question.

In yet another step to maintain secrecy, late in 1962 the State Department issued the infamous Cable 1006, a directive designed to keep information on the widening conflict in Vietnam from the American people. "Correspondents should not be taken on missions whose nature [is] such that undesirable dispatches would be highly probable," the cable ordered. "It is not—repeat not—in our interest to have stories indicating that Americans are leading and directing combat missions against the Vietcong." Neil Sheehan, the United Press International correspondent in Saigon who later, as a *New York Times* reporter, broke the story of the Pentagon Papers, recalled that American correspondents "believed in what our government said it was trying to accomplish in Vietnam, and we wanted our country to win this war." Even Halberstam, whose reports had so angered President Kennedy,

42. Schudson, *Discovering the News*, 171–72.
43. Tom Wicker, *On Press*, 92.

agreed: "I believe that Vietnam is a legitimate part of that [our] global commitment," he said.[44]

Schudson reasoned that the crudity of Sylvester's comments about the right of government to lie disrupted the fragile balance of interests that had evolved between the press and public officials. "For the press to cooperate with government in keeping news from the public was one thing; for the government to keep information from the press was something else."[45] But Sylvester's comments called the very value of "news" into question. If the government had given itself authority to lie, then how much of the news was believable? The presumption of truth was the bedrock of journalism— truth gave news its urgency, its importance. If what appeared in the columns of newspapers across the country was fiction, lies fabricated to advance the government's secret agenda, then whatever value news held was severely diminished. Journalists had clearly failed in their jobs as guardians. What need was there for a so-called fourth estate? Sylvester had jabbed at the press when he proclaimed the government's right to lie. He forced the press to consider the responsibilities that its First Amendment privileges obliged it to fulfill. So the press, like some hulking bear, awoke from hibernation and struck back—or at least some of its members did. Others—White among them—were unable to relinquish their tenacious embrace on the rules of the game in which they had enjoyed such success. Indeed, the Sigma Delta Chi audience in New York gave Sylvester a standing ovation after his declaration of the government's right to lie.

While the notion of adversarial journalism began to take root as an apparent outgrowth of the government's increasing efforts to manage and, when it wished, to distort the news, White and others became ardent defenders of journalism's traditional conventions. Long after Joseph McCarthy's excesses had provided abundant proof of the inherent flaws in "objective" journalism, White claimed to practice it and continued to defend it. As a way of maintaining his code of neutrality, White was registered as an Independent and he declined to discuss the personal choices he made on the top ballot in presidential elections.[46]

Although White's own work during the Kennedy years shows how the system of objective journalism could sometimes be distorted, he remained

44. William McGaffin and Erwin Knoll, *Anything but the Truth,* 79; Neil Sheehan, *A Bright Shining Lie,* 271; David Halberstam, *The Making of a Quagmire,* 319.
45. Schudson, *Discovering the News,* 173.
46. Theodore H. White, personal interview, May 5, 1982.

its advocate throughout his career. His passionate defense of objectivity appears in a letter he wrote to Stewart Alsop in 1969, after, as he explained to Alsop, the New York book critics blasted *The Making of the President 1968* as "the hoarse croaking of a starved buzzard":

> My concept of political reporting: you try to describe the great social forces that press for resolution; you try to understand and report the men who must make decisions under such pressure; you try to give some sense of the agony and torment and chicanery and compromise in which great decisions are necessarily made. In other words, to be old fashioned about it, you try to be fair—to give both sides (hopefully [*sic*] writing well as you go) while giving the reader enough information to make up his own mind. . . . The very difficulty of understanding the issues of the day makes it seem all the more imperative to me to cling to the hard virtues of stubborn, objective reporting and balancing of fact. This old faith of mine seems to be going out of fashion these days.[47]

What he called that "old tradition" of journalism was by far the preferable approach, White told Alsop. "Opposed to this is another tradition—which I refuse to call the 'new reporting.'" The "journalist engagee," or the European tradition of committed journalism, White explained, was as old as Karl Marx, Emile Zola, and Upton Sinclair. "The reporter and his friends assume that they, and they alone, know the whole truth—and facts are relevant only as they demonstrate the truths that their emotions or politics or intuitions or prejudices have already a priori established." Disparaging the likes of Norman Mailer and Jimmy Breslin, White wrote, "The easy way out for the reporter is to display a spurious clarity of style—by writing of the whole world, all of its events, as if he were Richard the Rover, as if his own personality and his reflections and his artistic sense of fitness were the essence of what he reports." White conjectured that while "journalism engagee" might work in France where, during the early 1950s, there were nineteen daily newspapers, it was inappropriate for America. White predicted trouble for American journalism if it pursued the French example. New York City, he explained, was dominated by a single newspaper, the *New York Times*, whose influence reached not only the other national media that operated out of New York but also an "almost indefinable nationwide spectrum of executive and intellectual policymakers." Its influence, White said, was not only greater than any other single newspaper in America, but also—with the exception

47. THW, letter to Stewart Alsop, August 13, 1969, TWA, Box 29, Folder 13.

of Pravda—greater than any single newspaper abroad. "If the *Times* turns its critical columns over to the journalists of commitment, à la Francaise, we have a unique and dangerous situation."[48] White was apparently blind to the reality that in his professional love affair with the New Frontier, he too was no less committed than those whose work he scorned. White practiced in the style of the journalist engagé—his commitment had been to the aggrandizement of an ideology and a personality named John F. Kennedy.

Presidential politics became White's business for the rest of his life. He wrote subsequent chronicles of the presidential campaigns of 1964, 1968, 1972, and 1980. But in each of those elections he faced growing competition from imitators determined to capitalize on and expand his invention. Increasing numbers of journalists were all prying for the inside details, searching for the emblematic anecdotes, and pumping sources for the quotes that had made White's 1960 book so revolutionary. In future elections, the Associated Press editors gave their political reporters unequivocal marching orders: "When Teddy White's book comes out, there shouldn't be one single story in that book that we haven't reported ourselves." At the *New York Times*, Managing Editor A. M. Rosenthal made a similar declaration to reporters and editors: "We aren't going to wait until a year after the election to read in Teddy White's book what we should have reported ourselves."[49]

From the perspective of more than three decades, the flaws in White's first book on America's presidential elections are clear. He was, above all, enchanted with John F. Kennedy, the wealthy and sometimes ruthless politico whom White transformed into the clever and dashing hero of his book. His close alliances with that "band of brothers" who served the New Frontier would be considered inappropriate by his colleagues who covered subsequent elections. Clearly, White had crossed that invisible and ill-defined line that should separate journalists from the men and women about whom they write. Earlier in his career he traversed the line to thwart the designs of a fascist invader or to protect America from the perceived evils of communism. This time, however, those larger—and perhaps justifiable—purposes were missing. This time, it appeared, White crossed the line on behalf of the powerful men who had invited him into their orbit. Those transgressions, however, should be judged in the context of White's intellect and social conscience. The man who enjoyed his proximity to power was also driven by his sense of justice to defend the defenseless Chinese peasants, and to

48. Ibid.
49. Crouse, *The Boys on the Bus*, 36.

stand up for those friends in government who had been falsely accused of undermining American interests in China.

When White did cross the line, he was following a path already well defined by others, even the éminence grise of twentieth-century American journalism, Walter Lippmann. Although he had never been invited to the White House during Eisenhower's presidency, Lippmann became a counselor to the Kennedy administration. Members of the New Frontier, according to Lippmann's biographer, viewed him as "a prime asset." Several days before Kennedy's inauguration, the president-elect's speech writer, Theodore Sorenson, sought Lippmann's approval of the inaugural address. Arthur Schlesinger once proposed that Lippmann, who was his old friend, be named ambassador to France. In his memorandum to the president, however, Schlesinger acknowledged that Lippmann might be more useful to the administration as a friendly columnist than as ambassador. He soon became a familiar lunch guest at the White House, was frequently invited to state dinners, and enjoyed, in the words of his biographer, "a participation and an influence he had not known since his World War I days." While Lippmann continued on occasion to be critical of the administration in his "Today and Tomorrow" column, he was more frequently a defender and occasionally even a spokesman for administration policies. Indeed, in some Washington circles he was perceived to be the president's messenger. During the Cuban missile crisis, when journalist John Scali became an intermediary between the State Department and the Soviet embassy, he once felt compelled to explain to the Russians, "Everything Mr. Lippmann writes does not come from the White House." Not long after the missile crisis was settled, Lippmann assumed the role of administration spokesman when he insisted in a major speech to European journalists in Paris that an American monopoly on the control of nuclear weapons was essential and that any strategy that required nuclear sharing, as General DeGaulle was then demanding, would be not only ineffective but also perhaps disastrous.[50]

White was, to be sure, an instrument in creating not only a Kennedy myth, but also an American myth. The America of his 1960 book was a pure and virtuous nation led by a president with superhuman abilities. He tried, with less and less success, to perpetuate that illusion in succeeding campaign books.

But for all his flaws, Theodore H. White deservedly remains an icon of American journalism, although he himself later questioned the direction

50. Ronald Steel, *Walter Lippmann and the American Century,* 524, 535.

his invention had taken in the hands of other reporters. White would have found it unthinkable to ask Gary Hart, as *Washington Post* reporter Paul Taylor did in 1987, "Have you ever committed adultery?" Yet White was the pioneer who opened the journalistic terrain that led directly to Taylor's surprising question. Three campaigns after Kennedy's victory, White wondered whether his focus on personality and preoccupation with strategy had given birth to a monster. Ruefully acknowledging that he had helped to create the atmosphere of ceaseless scrutiny under which presidential candidates would later find themselves, White, during the 1972 campaign, declared, "It's appalling what we've done." Speaking of how legions of reporters had been paraded in and out of George McGovern's hotel room after he won the Democratic presidential nomination in 1972, White said, "All of us are observing him, taking notes like mad, getting all the little details. Which I think I invented as a method of reporting and which I now sincerely regret. If you write about this, say that I sincerely regret it. Who gives a fuck if the guy had milk and Total for breakfast?"[51]

51. Crouse, *The Boys on the Bus,* 37.

· · · · · · · · · ·

· · · **Conclusion**

This is my story," Theodore White yelled to George Hunt, the managing editor of *Life*, moments after he learned that President John F. Kennedy had been shot. "O.K. Get going now—to Dallas," Hunt responded, sounding like the Marine commander he had once been. White had first learned of the shooting from a waiter during lunch. Driven by what he called his "journalistic instinct," he had dashed back to Time Inc.'s New York offices where he watched as a grim bulletin announcing the president's death clattered off a wire service news ticker.[1]

As they did each Friday afternoon, *Life*'s presses in a Chicago printing plant were already rolling off copies of the new edition—dated November 29, 1963. Roger Staubach, star quarterback of the Navy football team, was on the cover, and the second installment of White's study of Black life in the nation's cities filled ten inside pages. *Life*'s editors stopped the presses. The Staubach cover was scrapped; so was a frothy spread on the season's crop of debutantes.[2] When the presses began rolling again, President Kennedy was on the cover and the assassination news—including an essay by White— covered more than three dozen pages. That hastily remade edition of *Life* was destined to be carefully saved by its readers as a memory of the tragedy in Dallas, as if the mere possession of it might provide some measure of understanding.

1. White, *In Search of History*, 513.
2. Curtis Prendergast, *The World of Time Inc.: The Intimate History of a Changing Enterprise, 1960–1980*, 121.

Washington, D.C., rather than Dallas became White's destination once he learned from the car radio that Kennedy's body would be flown home from Dallas to the capital. That evening at Andrews Air Force base he waited on the tarmac in silence, surrounded by men who had been the subjects and sources of his stories, men with whom he had partied, Cabinet members, Congressmen. White watched in shock and grief as the last of his heroes returned home in a dark bronze coffin. "It was moist and chilly and the twilight bars of pink had just given way to a quarter moon hung with mists when Air Force No. 1, the presidential jet, silently rolled up the runway from the south. . . . One wished for a cry, a sob, a wail, any human sound,"[3] White wrote, describing the dead president's arrival. Years later White said, "I was crying as I wrote."

White followed the motorcade from Andrews Air Force base to Bethesda Naval Hospital, where he caught a glimpse of Mrs. Kennedy, still blood-stained and looking numb. "I could not bring myself to speak to her."[4] Later White made his way to Pennsylvania Avenue where he watched people walking in silent mourning. Around midnight he entered the White House; inside he found "none but weeping people." Finally, he sought refuge at Averill Harriman's Georgetown home, where he spent that seemingly end-less weekend alternating what he called his "reportorial duties" around the capital with long sessions glued to the television set in the Harriman parlor.

Television, he discovered, had a disquieting allure; it offered its viewers a sense of emotional participation in the funeral rituals underway. His own work at interviewing began to seem like a chore. Although he had paid his respects in the East Room on Saturday morning and, in the company of Averill Harriman, attended both the services at St. Matthew's Cathedral and at the graveside in Arlington National Cemetery, years later it was difficult for White to discern which of his notes were taken from events he had personally witnessed and which ones were taken in front of the television set. Television on that assassination weekend, White concluded, "made John F. Kennedy's burial a tribal ceremony and made the man into a myth." In arriving at that conclusion, however, White obviously ignored how *The Making of the President 1960* had helped to give birth to the myth. And just days after the president's funeral, White was to make his most lasting contribution to the myth.

3. Theodore H. White, "One Wished for a Cry, a Sob, Any Human Sound," *Life,* November 29, 1963, 78.

4. White, *In Search of History,* 516.

One week, almost to the hour, after he had seen Mrs. Kennedy outside Bethesda Naval Hospital, White arrived at the Kennedy compound in Hyannisport for his memorable talk with the president's widow, the conversation from which the "Camelot" elegy in *Life* originated. Looking back on that night a decade and a half later, White concluded in his autobiography that Mrs. Kennedy's fundamental message was that one man, by trying, may change it all. "Whether this is myth or truth I still debate," he wrote, apparently still wishing to believe in her idyllic and simplistic world of heroes and noble deeds.

Gay Talese has claimed in *The Kingdom and the Power* that the Kennedy family had initially approached White to write the definitive history of the assassination weekend. Family members turned next to Walter Lord and finally to William Manchester after White declined.[5] Correspondence in White's archive, however, indicates that while Robert Kennedy had proposed that White write about his late brother's administration, there is no indication that they discussed the project as an official history of the assassination. White expressed considerable interest in the proposal but had a number of reservations. "You know how completely I gave my heart to John Kennedy; you know my loyalty and affection," White wrote to Robert Kennedy. Nonetheless, he explained that he had no interest in writing an "authorized" history. Unless he had final authority over the manuscript and freedom to write of the dead president's missteps and blunders as well as his greatness, White said he would not undertake the project. "You would have to trust in my love for him and my good sense," White wrote to the attorney general.[6]

Remarkably, however, even a decade and a half after the assassination, after all the revelations and revisionist histories of the New Frontier, White still stubbornly ignored the late president's less admirable qualities. White, for example, never found fault with Kennedy's efforts to muzzle the press, most notably following the Bay of Pigs fiasco when the president had berated members of the American Society of Newspaper Editors to impose on themselves a measure of self-censorship. "If the press is awaiting a declaration of war before it imposes the self-discipline of combat conditions, then I can only say that no war ever posed a greater threat to our security," the president had insisted. Nor did White perceive Kennedy's unwillingness to expend any political capital on civil rights issues or his appointment

5. Talese, *The Kingdom and the Power,* 388.
6. THW, letter to Robert Kennedy, December 27, 1963, TWA, Box 49, Folder 9.

of segregationist federal judges in the South as the affront Black leaders considered them to be. And while others saw in Kennedy's handling of the Cuban missile crisis a dangerous predisposition for brinkmanship, White believed that the showdown between the United States and the Soviet Union in October 1962 represented "a parable in the wise use of power."[7] Finally, while the disclosures of the late president's notorious infidelities with Mafia molls and movie stars could hardly have surprised him since he had heard whispers about Kennedy's extramarital affairs during the 1960 campaign, White, like so many of his colleagues in the press, dismissed them as unimportant.

Out of a commitment to the ideology of the cold war and a fondness for Kennedy in particular and powerful people in general, mainstream journalists seldom probed beneath the surface of presidential pronouncements. In short, journalists provided America's leaders with sufficient license to lie. And in doing so White—and the many others who shared his perspective—undermined the profession to which he had committed both his loyalty and his life.

Journalists had doubtless helped to create the unprecedented level of citizen trust in their society—which social scientists say reached its height in the late 1950s and early 1960s. Later, it became apparent that the men who led the nation hardly deserved that widespread trust. In the early 1960s, Americans lived on the slope of a volcano. In China, where White had also lived on the slope of a volcano in the mid–1940s, he had known "the landscape was heaving." But in the early 1960s, White and too many of his colleagues had little sense of the social unrest simmering around them that their own children would spurn the society their elders created. Tom Hayden's "Port Huron Statement" of 1962, which advocated participatory democracy and denounced Kennedy's relentlessly pragmatist approach to governance, might as well have been written in a foreign tongue. "To be idealistic is to be considered apocalyptic, deluded," his statement read. "To have no serious aspirations, on the contrary, is to be tough-minded."[8] But like so many ideas that reached beyond the boundaries of the consensus ideology, Hayden's words were largely ignored by the mainstream media. Many Americans, as a consequence, had as little inkling in the early 1960s

7. John Tebbell and Sarah M. Watts, *The Press and the Presidency*, 487; Theodore H. White, *The Making of the President 1968*, 155.
8. Norman Isaacs, *Untended Gates: The Mismanaged Press*, 206; E. J. Dionne, *Why Americans Hate Politics*, 35.

of the approaching social upheavals in their own country as they had had about the impending political upheavals in China a quarter of a century earlier.

As the Vietnam war expanded and as Watergate demonstrated the fragility of democracy's institutions—theoretically grounded in the assumptions of honesty, trust, and goodwill—some journalists grew increasingly skeptical of government pronouncements, a skepticism that soon developed into antagonism when the government's duplicity became increasingly obvious. White, however, even at the end of his life, could not or would not acknowledge that the democracy he cherished had been ill-served by both its leaders and its journalists. He had thrived in the meritocracy that the American system offered its brightest citizens. In spite of or perhaps because of his impoverished beginnings, he came to believe in a nation led by an elite ruling class, one whose membership represented a combination of class privilege and noteworthy intelligence. The success and fame White had achieved by the early 1960s earned him a place in America's "Establishment." And once he had taken his place inside that circle, he ardently defended its bastions, with as much or perhaps even more energy than one whose birthright had placed him in that realm. Although he had generally insisted on maintaining his independence and final authority in any book arrangement with the Kennedy family, White, as they well knew, viewed the world from their angle of vision. He remained, for the rest of his career, the privileged person whom Jack Germond had first seen during his presidential campaign travels in 1960.

Unable though he was to acknowledge it, White was the journalist engagé, the man committed to a cause. White's cause by the 1960s had become the status quo. For the rest of his life, he wept for Camelot, that mythic kingdom where he had been a minor player in the vast tableau of government. With Kennedy in the White House his voice was heard, his ideas were considered, his work was admired. Although he achieved a measure of esteem from succeeding presidents—Richard Nixon and Ronald Reagan invited him to state dinners and private briefings—he would never again enjoy the intimacy he had with the New Frontier.

Rather than write about the Kennedy administration, as Robert Kennedy had proposed, White resolved instead to write about American presidential elections and planned to spend two years out of every four producing a "making of the president" opus until 1980. Indeed, he had already begun his research on the 1964 book when Kennedy was shot in Dallas. A symbiosis evolved between White and his political subjects. The prestige of the presidency heightened his own stature, and presidential aspirants used

White's prestige to enhance their images. His 1964 book was measurably less successful than his first, in part because Lyndon B. Johnson was so offended by White's characterization of him in the 1960 book that he refused repeated requests for an interview. Johnson was portrayed, nonetheless, as the white knight who carried the torch of Camelot. I. F. Stone, who had praised the 1960 book as a "minor masterpiece of political reporting," found its sequel mawkish and gushy. Commenting on White's ability to put the kindest interpretation on all manner of questionable political behavior, Stone tweaked at White after the 1964 book was published: "A writer who can be so universally admiring need never lunch alone."[9]

By 1968, Richard Nixon was no longer the "boiled turkey" that White had perceived him to be during the 1960 campaign. White, in fact, thought there was a new Nixon, someone who had been "transformed from the impulsive, wrathful man of the 1950s." Soon after his 1968 campaign book was published, White sent President Nixon one of the first copies, accompanied by a letter in which White pronounced him "a hero." The book, White's accompanying letter declared, "tries to describe . . . the campaign of a man of courage and of conscience; and the respect it wrung from me."[10]

In the 1972 campaign history, which went to press as the Watergate cover-up began to crack, White continued to admire Nixon, offering praise for the president's "astonishing mind," applauding him as a peacemaker and a foreign policy genius. On March 17, 1973, White had lunch at Sans Souci and sat down at the table of his old friend Art Buchwald for a cup of coffee before going to the White House for the last of his interviews with Nixon. "It was at the height of the Watergate scandal and Teddy was more pro-Nixon than I cared about," recalled Buchwald. "He told us he was going across the street to the White House to find out the truth about Watergate. We all just laughed and said, 'Sure you are, Teddy.' "[11]

Indeed, there was not so much as a whisper about Watergate during White's two-and-a-half-hour conversation with the president. Those many unasked questions, White later confessed, "did not, at that moment, seem relevant." Ultimately, Anthony Lewis took aim at White's illusions and scolded him on the op-ed page of the *New York Times*. It was time, Lewis declared, for someone to say, "the emperor has no clothes."[12]

9. I. F. Stone, *In a Time of Torment*, 63.
10. Christopher Hitchens, "Minority Report," *Nation*, June 5, 1989, 788.
11. Art Buchwald, personal interview, February 1985.
12. Theodore H. White, *The Making of the President 1972*, 353; Anthony Lewis, "The Making of Myths," *New York Times*, August 30, 1973.

White was guilty, indeed, of more than a few grave misreadings of history. He persisted, it seems, in reaching for Henry Luce's skewed concept of enlightened journalism—to present not what was, but rather what ought to be. The illusions he created ennobled scoundrels and romanticized presidential politics. White, however, had considerable company in the business of mythmaking. He was exceptional only for the depth and persistence of the illusions he created. Although White's behavior was sometimes astounding in the context of contemporary professional standards, it is important to remember that his "making of the president" books, for all their hyperbole, made an original and important contribution to American journalism. Beyond the pure, larger-than-life characters he placed in the Oval Office, White's style helped to educate a generation of voters to the political process. His work became a beacon, and, although he could not follow his own light, its rays succeeded in opening the political system to scrutiny and influenced the way newspapers and later television covered presidential campaigns. Although Taylor Branch criticized White's rhapsodic celebration of Kennedy's civil rights campaign strategy, he also observed that White's vision of an election campaign "caused fundamental changes in campaign reporting, if not in the conception of the American presidency itself."[13]

Like so many of his contemporaries in journalism, Theodore White was an unabashed patriot, in an age when it was still possible for patriotism to have a quality of innocence. Like his mother, he too rejoiced that he had been "born in the good old U.S. of A." World War II solidified his commitment to his country. The postwar years reassured White and his generation of America's benevolence and invincibility. For White, whom a friend once described as "impatiently Jewish," democracy became the substitute for the religion he was born into, but could never quite embrace. An election was one of the sacraments of his faith and, White believed, "its verdict is to be defended as one defends civilization itself."[14]

13. Branch, *Parting the Waters,* 378.
14. William Walton, personal interview, April 25, 1990; THW, memorandum to Penn Kimball, January 20, 1960, TWA, Box 100, Folder 3.

Bibliography

. . . .

Aronson, James. *The Press and the Cold War.* New York: Monthly Review Press, 1970.

Baughman, James L. *Henry R. Luce and the Rise of the American News Media.* Boston: Twayne Publishers, 1987.

Bird, Kai. *The Chairman John J. McCloy: The Making of the American Establishment.* New York: Simon and Schuster, 1992.

Branch, Taylor. *Parting the Waters.* New York: Simon and Schuster, 1988.

Bryce, James. *The American Commonwealth.* New York: MacMillan, 1919.

Carpenter, Humphrey. *Geniuses Together: American Writers in Paris in the 1920s.* Boston: Houghton Mifflin Company, 1988.

Chambers, Whittaker. *Witness.* Chicago: Regnery Gateway, 1952.

Crouse, Timothy. *The Boys on the Bus.* New York: Ballantine Books, 1974.

Dallek, Robert. *The American Style of Foreign Policy.* New York: Alfred A. Knopf, 1983.

Davies, Joseph E. *Mission to Moscow.* New York: Simon and Schuster, 1941.

Dionne, E. J. *Why Americans Hate Politics.* New York: Simon and Schuster, 1991.

Downey, Fairfax. *Richard Harding Davis, His Day.* New York: Charles Scribner's Sons, 1933.

Elson, Robert T. *The World of Time, Inc.* New York: Atheneum, 1968.

Fairbank, John K., ed. *The Missionary Enterprise in China and America.* Cambridge: Harvard University Press, 1974.

Galbraith, John K. *A Life in Our Times.* Boston: Houghton Mifflin Company, 1981.

The Gallup Poll: Public Opinion 1935–1971. New York: Random House, 1972.

Goodwin, Richard. *Remembering America.* Boston: Little, Brown and Company, 1988.

Hahn, Emily. *China to Me.* Boston: Beacon Press, 1988.

Halberstam, David. *The Best and the Brightest.* New York: Random House, 1969.

———. *The Fifties.* New York: Villard Books, 1993.

———. *The Making of a Quagmire.* New York: Random House, 1964.

———. *The Powers That Be.* New York: Alfred A. Knopf, 1979.

Hallin, Daniel. *The Uncensored War.* New York: Oxford University Press, 1986.

Hodgson, Godfrey. *America in Our Time.* New York: Vintage Books, 1978.

Isaacs, Harold. *Scratches on Our Minds.* New York: J. Day Company, 1958.

Isaacs, Norman. *Untended Gates: The Mismanaged Press.* New York: Columbia University Press, 1986.

Isaacson, Walter, and Evan Thomas. *The Wise Men.* New York: Simon and Schuster, 1986.

Knightley, Phillip. *The First Casualty.* New York: Harcourt Brace Jovanovich, 1975.

Levine, Hillel, and Lawrence Harmon. *The Death of an American Jewish Community.* New York: The Free Press, 1992.

Linsky, Martin. *Impact: How the Press Affects Federal Policymaking.* New York: W. W. Norton Co., 1986.

Lowi, Theodore J. *The Personal President.* Ithaca: Cornell University Press, 1985.

Manchester, William. *The Death of a President.* New York: Harper and Row, 1967.

McCullough, David. *Truman.* New York: Simon and Schuster, 1992.

McGaffin, William, and Erwin Knoll. *Anything but the Truth.* New York: G. P. Putnam's Sons, 1968.

Mellow, James R. *Charmed Circle.* Boston: Houghton Mifflin Company, 1974.

Miller, Nathan. *F.D.R.: An Intimate History.* New York: Doubleday and Co., Inc., 1983.

Mills, C. Wright. *The Causes of World War III.* Armonk, N.Y.: M. E. Sharp, Inc., 1958.

Morton, Marian J. *The Terrors of Ideological Politics.* Cleveland: The Press of Case Western Reserve University, 1972.

Navasky, Victor. *Kennedy Justice.* New York: Atheneum, 1971.

Neustadt, Richard. *Presidential Power.* New York: Wiley, 1960.

North, Robert C. *Moscow and the Chinese Communists.* Stanford: Stanford University Press, 1953.

Patner, Andrew. *I. F. Stone: A Portrait.* New York: Pantheon Books, 1988.

Pells, Richard H. *The Liberal Mind in a Conservative Age: American Intellectuals in the 1940s and 1950s.* New York: Harper and Row Publishers, 1985.

Peterson, Theodore. *Magazines in the Twentieth Century.* Urbana: University of Illinois Press, 1956.

Prendergast, Curtis. *The World of Time Inc.: The Intimate History of a Changing Enterprise, 1960–1980.* New York: Atheneum, 1986.

Rossiter, Clinton. *The American Presidency.* New York: Harcourt Brace and World, Inc., 1960.

Rosten, Leo C. *The Washington Correspondents.* New York: Harcourt Brace and Company, 1937.

Sabato, Larry J. *Feeding Frenzy.* New York: The Free Press, 1991.

Schlesinger, Arthur M., Jr. *The Imperial Presidency*. Boston: Houghton Mifflin Company, 1973.

———. *Robert Kennedy and His Times*. Boston: Houghton Mifflin Company, 1978.

———. *A Thousand Days*. Boston: Houghton Mifflin Company, 1965.

———. *The Vital Center*. Boston: Houghton Mifflin Company, 1949.

Schudson, Michael. *Discovering the News*. New York: Basic Books, Inc., 1978.

Service, John S. *The Amerasia Papers*. Berkeley: University of California Press, 1971.

Sheehan, Neil. *A Bright Shining Lie*. New York: Random House, 1988.

Sorenson, Theodore. *Kennedy*. New York: Harper and Row, 1965.

———. *The Kennedy Legacy*. New York: Harper and Row, 1969.

Spence, Jonathan. *The Search for Modern China*. New York: W. W. Norton Co., 1990.

Steel, Ronald. *Walter Lippmann and the American Century*. Boston: Atlantic Monthly Press, 1980.

Stone, I. F. *The Haunted Fifties*. New York: Vintage Books, 1969.

———. *The Hidden History of the Korean War 1950–1951*. Boston: Little, Brown and Company, 1988.

———. *In a Time of Torment*. Boston: Little, Brown and Company, 1967.

———. *The Truman Era 1945–1952*. Boston: Little, Brown and Company, 1953.

Strober, Gerald S., and Deborah Hart, eds. *Let Us Begin Anew: An Oral History of the Presidency of John F. Kennedy*. New York: HarperCollins Publishers, 1993.

Swanberg, W. A. *Luce and His Empire*. New York: Charles Scribner's Sons, 1972.

Talese, Gay. *The Kingdom and the Power*. New York: World Publishing Co., 1966.

Teachout, Terry, ed. *Ghosts on the Roof*. Washington, D.C.: Regnery Gateway, 1989.

Tebbell, John, and Sarah W. Watts. *The Press and the Presidency*. New York: Oxford University Press, 1985.

Thompson, Edward T., ed. *Theodore H. White At Large*. New York: Pantheon Books, 1992.

Tocqueville, Alexis de. *Democracy in America*. New York: Alfred A. Knopf, 1945.

Tuchman, Barbara. *Stilwell and the American Experience in China, 1911–1945*. New York: MacMillan, 1970.

White, Theodore H. *America in Search of Itself*. New York: Harper and Row, 1982.

———. *Fire in the Ashes*. New York: William Sloane Associates, 1953.

———. *In Search of History*. New York: Harper and Row, 1978.

———. *The Making of the President 1960*. New York: Atheneum Books, 1961.

———. *The Making of the President 1964*. New York: Atheneum Books, 1965.

———. *The Making of the President 1968.* New York: Atheneum Books, 1969.

———. *The Making of the President 1972.* New York: Atheneum Books, 1973.

White, Theodore H., ed. *The Stilwell Papers.* New York: William Sloane Associates, 1948.

White, Theodore H., and Annalee Jacoby. *Thunder Out of China.* New York: William Sloane Associates, Inc., 1946.

Wicker, Tom. *On Press.* New York: Viking Press, 1978.

Williams, William Appleman. *The Tragedy of American Diplomacy.* Cleveland: World Publishing, 1959.

Wofford, Harris. *Of Kennedys and Kings.* New York: Farrar, Straus and Giroux, 1980.

Index

• • • • • • • • • • •